A HISTORY OF DIGITAL MED

From the punch card calculating machine to the personal computer to the iPhone and more, this in-depth text offers a comprehensive introduction to digital media history for students and scholars across media and communication studies, providing an overview of the main turning points in digital media and highlighting the interactions between political, business, technical, social, and cultural elements throughout history. With a global scope and an intermedia focus, this book enables students and scholars alike to deepen their critical understanding of digital communication, adding an understudied historical layer to the examination of digital media and societies. Discussion questions, a timeline, and previously unpublished tables and maps are included to guide readers as they learn to contextualize and critically analyze the digital technologies we use every day.

Gabriele Balbi is Assistant Professor in Media Studies at USI Università della Svizzera Italiana (Switzerland), where he is Director of the China Media Observatory and teaches media history and sociology at the Faculty of Communication Sciences. His main areas of interest are media history and historiography of communication.

Paolo Magaudda is Senior Post-Doctoral Research Fellow in Sociology at the University of Padova (Italy), where his research is in technology, culture, and society with particular reference to media and consumption processes. Since 2013, he has been Secretary of STS Italia, the Italian Society for the Study of Science and Technology.

A HISTORY OF DIGITAL MEDIA

An Intermedia and Global Perspective

Gabriele Balbi and
Paolo Magaudda

Routledge
Taylor & Francis Group

NEW YORK AND LONDON

First published 2018
by Routledge
711 Third Avenue, New York, NY 10017

and by Routledge
2 Park Square, Milton Park, Abingdon, Oxon OX14 4RN

Routledge is an imprint of the Taylor & Francis Group, an informa business

© 2018 Taylor & Francis

The right of Gabriele Balbi and Paolo Magaudda to be identified as the authors of this work has been asserted by them in accordance with sections 77 and 78 of the Copyright, Designs and Patents Act 1988.

Library of Congress Cataloging in Publication Data
Names: Balbi, Gabriele, 1979- author. | Magaudda, Paolo, author.
Title: A history of digital media: an intermedia and global perspective / Gabriele Balbi and Paolo Magaudda.
Other titles: Storia dei media digitali. English
Description: New York: Taylor & Francis Group, 2018. | Includes bibliographical references and index. | "In several sections the text is an elaboration of the Italian book Storia dei media digitali. Rivoluzioni e continuità, published in 2014 by Laterza, Roma-Bari."–Back of title page.
Identifiers: LCCN 2017050517| ISBN 9781138630215 (hardback) | ISBN 9781138630222 (pbk.)
Subjects: LCSH: Digital communications–History. | Digital media–History.
Classification: LCC TK5103.7 .B358413 2018 | DDC 384.3/309–dc23
LC record available at https://lccn.loc.gov/2017050517

ISBN: 978-1-138-63021-5 (hbk)
ISBN: 978-1-138-63022-2 (pbk)
ISBN: 978-1-315-20963-0 (ebk)

Typeset in Interstate
by Florence Production Ltd, Stoodleigh, Devon, UK

Translated by Isabelle Johnson. Translation funded by Fondazione Hilda e Felice Vitali.

In several sections, the text is an elaboration of the Italian book *Storia dei media digitali. Rivoluzioni e continuità*, published in 2014 by Laterza, Roma-Bari. We acknowledge that Gabriele Balbi wrote Chapters 3 and 4, Paolo Magaudda wrote Chapters 2 and 5, while the remaining sections have been written jointly.

CONTENTS

FIGURES

TABLES

BOXES

ACKNOWLEDGMENTS

When we started to plan an English adaptation of our previous book, originally published in Italian in 2014 (*Storia dei media digitali. Rivoluzioni e continuità*, Roma-Bari, Laterza), we thought it would have been an easy task. The book we published in Italian, well-received in the Italian academic community and appeared in syllabi of several courses, would just require minor updates, we believed. As it commonly happens, things have been much more complicated and what we imagined as a "translation" turned out to be a substantial re-writing, with an entire new chapter and substantial changes in all the other chapters—now all with learning materials, images, figures and especially much more global and intermedia than before. This work has not been done by the two authors in isolation, but many (new and old) ideas emerged during several discussions with friends and colleagues in many of the conferences and Italian book presentations we attended and were invited to between 2014 and 2017. Among the dozens of people that have directly or indirectly contributed to our work, we would like to thank a few colleagues specifically, while being well aware that we are going to forget many others: Raffaele Barberio, Luca Barra, Eleonora Benecchi, Tiziano Bonini, Paolo Bory, Davide Borrelli, Attila Bruni, Stefano Crabu, Alessandro Delfanti, Philip di Salvo, Andreas Fickers, Matthew Hibberd, Richard R. John, Juraj Kittler, Katharina Lobinger, Paolo Mancini, Alberto Marinelli, Massimo Mazzotti, Manuel Menke, Andrea Miconi, Sergio Minniti, Francesca Musiani, Simone Natale, Federico Neresini, Gianluigi Negro, Peppino Ortoleva, David Park, Benjamin Peters, John Durhman Peters, Benedetta Prario, Nelson Ribeiro, Giuseppe Richeri, Maria Rikitianskaia, Valérie Schafer, Christian Schwarzenegger, Daya Thussu, Assunta Viteritti and Guobin Yang. Massimo Scaglioni in Milan and Daniel Boccacci in Parma have provided logistical support in delicate phases of our work, when we were delivering the manuscript. Special gratitude goes to Isabelle Johnson, who has been in charge of the translation and was able to cope with all our requests and delays. Our thanks go also to our Italian publisher, Laterza, who allowed us to adapt the original Italian version for an English edition. We are also grateful to the team at Routledge and especially Erica Wetter, who helped us to sharpen our initial idea, and Mia Moran, who assisted us along the process.

Finding images is not easy for copyright issues and because they are not often considered relevant in academic works (we think exactly the opposite). So, we would like to thank all the people that made our image search easier: Beth Bernstein of RAND Corporations, Dave Walden, Nicholas Roche of NATO Archives, Pierre Philippi of Orange Archives, Timothy H. Horning of the Archives of University of Pennsylvania and Elisabeth Schares of Stiftung Deutsches Technikmuseum–Berlin. As mentioned, images are not always easy to get, so we decided to explore Instagram and search for private pictures, then asked permission from authors. Consequently, we thank Gary Hunt, Andy Leonard, Jack-Benny Persson, Matthew Ratzloff, and Marcin Wichary for allowing us to use their photos in the text (even though some of them didn't find place in the final version of the book). The Biblioteca universitaria di Lugano has assisted us particularly with the data appendix and we would like to thank especially Alessio Tutino; data are mainly taken from ITU Library and Archives Services, magnificently managed by Heather Heywood and Kristine Clara.

Gabriele Balbi would also like to thank an annoying friend called jet lag, who was always extremely helpful in this phase, because he allowed him to work during the night (I am writing this sentence at 3.04 am). We especially want to thank Betty and Ilenia because, in one way or another, they have been our great support during the long journey to complete this book. Finally, this book is also a welcome to Demetra, part of the next generation that will see the future of digital media.

Gabriele Balbi and Paolo Magaudda
Lugano and Bologna, September 30, 2017

Introduction

A History of Digital Media is an introduction to the study of the multifaceted phenomenon of digitization from a historical, intermedia, and globally-sensitive perspective. The book is primarily designed to be used as a textbook in media and communications studies or for those interested in familiarizing themselves with a historical approach to the understanding of technologies in everyday life, digital economy, and innovation processes. This does not mean that the book is of no interest to other readers. The book was, in fact, conceived on various levels to make it *of use* to students and teachers intending to adopt a historical dimension to digital media studies; to be *relevant* to scholars and researchers interested in digital media history and digital media as a whole; and finally, *accessible* to a wider readership interested in some of the technological and cultural changes that have influenced our everyday lives both now and in the past.

The book's historical perspective is its primary and genuine original feature. The history of computers, the internet, mobile phones, and analog media digitization is mainly narrated with a mixed combination of secondary sources (mainly books and papers) and some primary sources (including reports, newspaper articles, visual materials, and other documents). The main aim is to provide a broad picture and an extensive literature review on digital media history, combining a theoretically-driven perspective with a series of approaches (especially from Media studies, Science & technology studies, and Cultural studies) that only very recently have begun to talk to each other in a more systematic way.

As a result, this volume is a tale of interwoven phenomena, which date right back to the late nineteenth century and intensified from the second half of the twentieth century onwards. This is what we will call a *long term*, or *longue durée*, approach applied to digital society, although we are aware that, seen from the original perspective of French historian Fernand Braudel (see Chapter 1), this period of time would actually look rather short. Nevertheless, given that digital media studies generally focuses on the present or, at least, on the last two decades of digitization evolution, the decision to widen the time span of our analysis at least to the nineteenth century is a meaningful choice designed to provide a broad and consistent picture of the ways in which digital media became so relevant to contemporary societies. We also believe that this periodization brings out all of digital media's unpredictability, continual muta-tion, and the inextricable interweaving of digital *change* and forms of *continuity* with the analog media system. The dialectic between the two extremes of this continuum—change and continuity—is one of this book's cornerstones and a historically well-founded and pondered response to one of contemporary society's most fashionable, and at the same time misleading, *mythologies*: the idea of a permanent *digital revolution*.

But what digital media history are we talking about? Like all histories, the story that unfolds in this book is necessarily partial and selective. We have focused on three major digital media and on the consequences digitization had for the main analog media, inevitably leaving to one side a number of digital and analog media contexts, whose stories would perhaps be equally interesting. Our reasons for this were primarily space-related and we hope that the book will succeed all the same in offering a wide-ranging and variegated overview and suggest further avenues of in-depth study, which individual readers may decide to undertake.

Furthermore, as Chapter 1 makes clear, we did not want to limit ourselves to an *event-based* history approach (the so-called *histoire évènementielle* that the French Annales School, and Fernand Braudel specifically, attempted to avoid), in which the main aim is to set out events and dates in chronological order. Rather, the volume aims to identify crossroads, successful turning points and dead ends, and to throw light on the composite and heterogeneous set of processes and influences that contributed to the emergence of digital media: from the political and economic decisions made by governments and inter-national bodies to the role of small, local startups and powerful global com-panies, to the unpredictable and unexpected forms of appropriation of digital technologies by end-users in different regions across the globe. The history of digital media in this book will thus be told from a range of points of view and by means of multiple interpretative tools with the aim of throwing light on the relationship between media technologies and the most profound political, economic, cultural, material, and symbolic structures that sustain the production and consumption of media in contemporary societies. And all this to gain an understanding of the way in which digital technologies have shaped diverse human cultures in various ways, but also of the ways in which they themselves have been influenced by social arrangements in a process that scholars in Science & Technology Studies often define as *co-construction* and *mutual shaping* occurring between society and digital media technologies.

In addition to the diachronic dimension, this book also brings in and adopts two other fundamental guidelines and perspectives: an *intermedia* approach and a distinctive sensitiveness to the *global range* of digital media development.

As far as the notion of intermediality is concerned, while readers will find separate chapters on computers, internet, and mobile phones (we decided to look at these three media separately and not all together for reasons of analytical simplicity and because scholarly work has traditionally separated them out), this book frequently underlines the need to consider digital media in its mutual and recursive interaction. The interaction and mutual influence of different media in the same historical period was also a feature of analog media. For some decades, therefore, media historians have been underlining the importance of studying every medium in relation to others. TV history cannot, for example, be understood without considering its institutional continuity with radio broadcasting, audio-visual contents, and practices originating with the movie industry, the role of new technologies such as satellites, VCRs, and remote controls, as well as social networks like YouTube or streaming platforms such as Netflix (where many cult TV series are produced and released nowadays). Nevertheless, there is no doubt that digitization has intensified and driven this phenomenon further and this change has been identified using a range of concepts and definitions specifically addressed at the beginning of Chapter 5 (see Box 5.1). Not only are contemporary digital media increasingly interconnected but digitization's progress has also brought together and interwoven different and previously distinct devices, markets, aesthetics, and user practices. The result of this increasing digital media interdependence and intermediality is what we will define *digital media pattern* in the book's last and longest chapter, devoted to the consequences of digitization on analog media taking into account mutual influences between *old* and *new* and the fact that the analog media are often the working foundations on which "digital native" media have been developed and appropriated.

Finally, the book has adopted a perspective that is distinctively sensitive to the global changes that digital media are subject to. *Global* here does not imply that mention will be made of *every* country in the world but rather that the book will constantly swing between innovation centers and technological peripheries, thus analyzing specific case studies that are capable of bringing out all the geopolitical and cultural tensions and contradictions that digitization generates. As we will see, while production and appropriation of digital media are dominated by specific countries and areas of the globe (the Western world and the United States, at length, joined by Asia over the last decade), digital technologies are also making their way into other parts of the world with various degrees of complexity and some evident ambiguities.

The book is divided into five chapters—each with teaching material and exercises to be used by students to test themselves—and a conclusion. Chapter 1 defines digital media, identifies fundamental tendencies in digitization and revises the theoretical fields, which can be considered a "tool box" for students looking for a well-founded historical interpretation of the digital media phenomenon. The two basic questions we attempt to answer in this chapter are: why and how write a history of apparently constantly changing and present-orientated technologies (such as digital media) generally interpreted as disruptive innovations and radical breaks with the past? And, which theories and concepts can we mobilize to build a more effective interpretation of the multiple tensions surrounding the role of digital media in our everyday lives?

Chapters 2, 3, and 4 develop the specific histories of three main digital media: computers, internet, and mobile phones. These communication media are emblematic of the so-called "digital revolution" but grew out of analog ideas and precedents. Their history interweaves with technological developments and political-economic and cultural dimensions just as both successful developments and dead ends, which turned out to be useful for the understanding of specific characteristics. The book will be as unhurried as possible and attempt to identify clear and perhaps overly simplistic periodization with the intention of supplying readers and students with reference time frames to facilitate study.

Chapter 5 is entirely devoted to intermedia logic, looking at how digitization has influenced analog media and paving the way to what we define in the chapter as a *digital media pattern*: a set of interlaced devices, markets, aesthetics, and practices in which the original media entities are still recognizable but have already metamorphosed into different and distinctive media environments. More specifically this chapter will analyze the emergence of the digitization process in relation to six specific sectors: music, books and newsmaking, cinema and video, photography, TV and radio, tracing the main tendencies through which the digitization developed in each.

In our conclusion, we will tie up the loose ends on certain processes and tendencies, focusing on the major *mythologies* that characterized the cultural emergence of this digital media environment and some *counter-hegemonic narratives*, underlining the constant dialectic between change and continuity in the shaping of digital media technologies in their recent or more distant past.

The book is then completed by two other resources: a series of boxes that are easily identifiable in each chapter and an appendix with statistical and quantitative data. More precisely, there are two types of boxes: one named *Documents* made up of short and relevant texts that are able to shed light on some specific episodes or technology in the long process of digitization; the second typology is named *In-depth Theory* because these boxes aim at deepening specific theoretical notions and at giving relevance to specific case studies emerged in the various chapters. Finally, the data appendix focuses on historical series able to show the main trends in the development of digital media at a global level. Recombining data from institutions such as the International Tele-communication Union, the World Bank, Internet World Stats, market research firms, and many others, the reader will find together—maybe for the first time—comprehensive data and maps on computer, internet, and mobile phone's penetration in major world countries and in world macro-regions from the 1990s to today.

All this considered, there are many digital media history-linked topics that this book will either not touch on at all or will receive just a cursory mention. On one hand, this is understandable when such a broad and comprehensive overview is attempted: stories have to be cut out and emblematic case studies selected to achieve a synthesis. On the other hand, as we will point out in the conclusion, this book is designed to act as the main entrance to a vast and still unfinished building an introductory starting point from which other paths and follows-ups will branch out in the future. A lot of work still remains to be done in digital media history and our main hope is that this book may stimulate, inspire, and motivate (including in its weaknesses and gaps) a next generation of media studies scholars and of media industry professionals to think about digital media in different and less taken-for-granted ways.

1 Why Study the History of Digital Media and How?

1.1 Contextualizing *Digital* in Contemporary Societies

From the 1990s onwards digitization has increasingly shaped the collective imagination of contemporary societies. Digital media have become one of the main *obsessions* of our time: getting online (or more frequently being constantly online), sharing "likes" on social network pages, downloading apps, updating virtual profiles, exchanging e-mails, text messages and WhatsApp or WeChat messages are just some of the infinite array of routine activities that have become part of the daily lives of billions of people. Digital has contributed to the formation of new "communities", which were previously unable to interact with one another and also to new barriers and inequalities. Digital has been interpreted variously in different cultures taking on positive or negative connotations that are in any case deeply rooted in these communities. Digital has, above all, impacted on the daily lives of billions of people. Just think of our compulsive use of mobile phones, our constant access to knowledge as a result of the World Wide Web and the ease with which we access media contents, often free of charge, which were previously either difficult to source or expensive (think of films and songs). In recent years, the controversial presence of digital media in social relationships has found its way into the popular imagination through TV series such as *Black Mirror* (first season in 2011), created by a well-known British satirist and columnist, which gives an overview of the many dystopic and disturbing consequences ubiquitous media technologies may have on people's lives in the present or near future. And this is not all. Digital media and our use of them has also become the defining metaphor of late twentieth and early twenty-first-century society. French philosopher Stéphane Vial (2013) has spoken of *digital ontophany*, using an expression drawn from religious semantics (from the Greek *on* meaning "being" and *faneia* "appearing") to illustrate the totalizing effect of the digital universe and the extent to which it is affecting our experiences and perceptions of the world itself.

Digital media, with their transformative power and metaphorical force, require explaining and defining because the more we go in depth, the more we discover that the meaning of *digital* is a medley of somewhat ephemeral and constantly evolving ideas. The adjective "digital" comes from the Latin *digitus* (finger, toe) and, as Ben Peters (2016a) has argued, we can say that human beings are "naturally" digital, because they have to always count, point, and manipulate with their fingers—exactly what digital media are.

As a starting point, digital is often defined in contrast to *analog* almost as if they were two extremes on a scale, even if they are not. A concrete example of a common definition of digital vs. analog comes from the music field—comparing and contrasting vinyl records and CDs. Vinyl record lovers know that the sound they like is a product of contact between the player's needle and the grooves scored into the vinyl. These grooves are continuous in the sense that there are no interruptions in the spiral of frequencies containing the music and words. There is thus a physical *analogy*, a similarity between the sound and the grooves: a different groove depth produces a different sound. With CDs, on the other hand, sound is broken up (or sampled) into a multitude of points and thus into discrete and non-continuous units whose values are registered on support surfaces in binary format as 0s and 1s. Sound is generated by laser reading of the values of these discrete points, which, translated into sound frequencies, can be listened to in sequence, recreating listening continuity.

This definition assumes that analog is everything not digital and vice-versa, but as Jonathan Sterne (2016, p. 32) claimed, the distinction between analog and digital is far more intricate, first because "the idea of analog as *everything not-digital* is in fact *newer* than the *idea of digital*". What we mean today by the word "analog" is more an historical outcome of cultural distinctions and shifting symbolic boundaries, than an objective technical feature of some kind of technology: in the 1950s "analog" was indicating anything *related* to computers, in the 1970s the term's use started to signal something *in contrast* with electronic devices and, finally, only in the 1990s it began to be used with the connotation of "old-fashioned" and even "vintage". In short, we can see how the definitions of analog and digital have evolved together and changed across time in dialectic and reciprocal relationship.

That said, the CD/vinyl record example helps us to introduce the two basic elements in digital media technologies: digitization and binary language (Lister, Dovey, Giddings, Grant & Kelly, 2009). Digitization is, above all, a process converting contents, which were previously expressed in different forms, into numbers (to the extent that in languages such as French the term *numérisation* is used). In the analog model, video, audio and text are transmitted as continual signals and each of these three content forms differs from the others. With digitization, video, audio and text are, on the other hand, all codified in the same "material", i.e. numerical data that allows information to be transferred and stored independently of the original content type.

It is often mistakenly believed that digitization means converting physical data into binary information. In actual fact digitization—as the name itself (from the English word "digit" i.e. number) suggests—is simply a matter of assigning numerical values. On the other hand, the fact that contents are numerized in strings of 0s and 1s (called bits) has hugely simplified this process and made it much cheaper because it reduces each component to two states: *on* or *off*, electrical *flowing* or *not-flowing*, *0* or *1*. For example, the programs we see on our digital TVs are simply sequences of 0s and 1s, which break down the continuous waves generated by sounds and images into value strings that are no longer *analogous* with the original in any way. It is thus our TVs or decoders that translate and reconstitute these sequences of 0s and 1s into understandable sounds and images for human ears and eyes.

If this can work as a technical description of the differences between analog and digital media, there are far more relevant elements to be addressed if we are to understand the wide range of features involved in the media digitization process. For example, treating all forms of communication in the same way *apparently* enables digital media contents to be *dematerialized*, it enables us to compress them and thus transfer them more quickly, store them on supports that take up little space (think of the difference between the few hours of video that can be contained on a VHS tape and the gigabytes stored in an external hard disc or in a *cloud*) and manipulate or modify them simply. One of the often pointed out differences between analog and digital media is that, with analog media, all these processes were more complex and costly, if only because cutting and copying physical material supports and transferring them concretely from one place to another was often required. Again, this assumption can be contested if considered from an historical perspective: for example, at the origins of computer, large and "heavy" supports were needed to store memory (see Chapter 2), while non-digital small photographic film on the other side recorded plenty of information in a short space. Furthermore, and contrary to the argument of dematerialization, digitization has encompassed an explosion of new hardware dedicated to reproducing and storing these contents: from computers to telephones, DVDs to USB sticks, MP3 readers to cameras, to cite just a few. So, a side effect of this aspect is the fact that, rather than translating into a dematerializing of culture as we said before, the digitization process has actually stimulated the dissemination of material devices.

In order to get to the bottom of digitization's deeper meaning, however, we also need to consider the ways in which representations and images of the digital world in contemporary culture have evolved. Let's start from certain theoretical categories that were especially visible after World War Two. In the 1950s, theories linked to cybernetics (Wiener, 1948) and, in the 1970s, those linked to the postindustrial society (Bell, 1973) contributed to popularizing the central importance of computers in society. Even the *information society* definition—a locution that highlights the relevance of IT and information itself as an irresistible force capable of revolutionizing the world of work, the economy and politics (Dordick & Wang, 1993)—contributed to placing digital center-stage in the debate on the transformation of contemporary cultures well before the internet was invented. A notion of how an information society might evolve was already taking shape in the 1960s and 1970s and one of the earliest documents to place the information concept at the heart of political and economic processes was a report by the Japan Computer Usage Development Institute (1972), which illustrated a government plan for the achievement of a "new national goal" consisting precisely of the computerization of Japanese society.

Full consideration of the advantages of digitization from the economic and political points of view, however, emerged explicitly only in the 1980s and early 1990s, when governments in a number of countries simultaneously got to grips with the need for radical modernization of their telecommunications infra-structure. As the 1990s wore on, the American and Japanese governments and the European Union (see the 1990 *Bangemann Report* or the 1994 white paper *Growth, Competitiveness, Employment*) started to construct a *digital myth* narrative, advocating measures favoring the digitization of their communication infrastructures in the somewhat deterministic belief that this constituted not simply a transit channel for data flow but also a crucial resource ensuring economic, social and cultural progress (Richeri, 1995; Mosco, 1998). The most famous and frequently cited of these various governmental plans was, unsurprisingly, American: the well-known Clinton government document *The National Information Infrastructure: Agenda for Action* published in September 1993. This report placed the *information networks* (or what Clinton's adminis-tration called for promotional purposes *information superhighways*), at the center of US economic and industrial policy, which was to guarantee American citizens and especially American companies universal access to the services and contents, which would circulate on this infrastructure (Kozak, 2015; see also Box 3.3 for an excerpt). From this moment onwards, in many countries, digital infrastructure and the circulation of digital contents on the networks was one of the main focuses of interest in national communications policies. The belief that citizens' wellbeing, business potential and nations' very future prosperity depended on their digital information infrastructures was a constant feature of the political economy debate in the years to come.

There is effectively no doubt that digital media are now a crucial sector in contemporary society. Also in a sense of their economic, productive and thus political weight. In 2015, the global digital communications market accounted for 3,829 billion Euros, the greatest revenues coming from telecom services (29%), IT services and software (25.9%), devices (18.9%), TV and video services (10.7%) and internet services (just 8.5% but the fastest growing segment in recent years) (IDATE, 2017, p. 34). Despite growing more slowly than global GDP (in 2015, global GDP grew by 4.8% in nominal value while the digital global market grew only 3.9%, and this trend emerged in the early years of the second decade of this millennium), digital media have contributed to transforming global communication flows and geographies and, on occasions, digitization has played a part in widening the existing inequality gap between the various parts of the globe (a phenomenon generally defined as the *digital divide*; see Box 3.4 for more on this concept). Proportionally to their populations, moreover, certain world regions are producing and consuming far more digital goods and services than others. In 2015, 31.9% of the digital media market was concentrated in North America, 29.7% in Asia/Pacific and 25.5% in Europe, while the remaining regions were playing a much smaller part: 7.2% in Latin America, 5.7% in Africa and the Middle East (see IDATE, 2017, p. 37). On the other hand, it is precisely thanks to digital, and above all mobile phones—as we will see in Chapter 4—that many regions of Africa, Latin America and Asia are currently accessing communications that were once mainly the exclusive preserve of the richer continents and, moreover, it is precisely in these parts of the world that some of the more interesting and unexpected uses of digital media have emerged.

Thus far we have attempted to define digital and sketch an outline of the political, economic and cultural motives, which have made it a modern obsession. Now is the time to look at how this subject of study can be analyzed: what are the useful research trajectories that give us a better grasp of digital media evolutions; and what, primarily, are the advantages to approaching digital from a long-term perspective. In other words, why study the *history* of digital media?

1.2 Theoretical Paths

The front-rank role played by the digital media referred to above has attracted ever increasing scholarly attention from a range of social studies and humanities disciplines in recent decades. Sociology, for example, has looked at the consequences of what was initially defined as "new media" on identity and community bonds concentrating on issues such as privacy, social networks, inequalities, celebrity and many others. Psychology, on the other hand, has concentrated greater attention on digital's impact on interpersonal relationships and on the minds and brains of users (often with discordant results ranging from its reinforcement of intelligence to incentivizing collective stupidity). Economics have examined digitization, and more generally digital IT, as a powerful force for change in productive practices and in the traditional relationship between supply and demand (there is nothing accidental about the fact that the so-called *new economy* has essentially become a synonym for the digital economy). Political science, lastly, has seen the internet and social media as places of aggregation and debate on shared political values oscillating between an enthusiasm for new forms of political participation (for example, direct digital democracy) and concern for the totalitarian style control facilitated by digital technologies.

This book's approach to digital media history is a generally neglected one. The history of digital media has received limited attention because *new media* are an apparently recent phenomenon—even if this term has been used since the 1960s and 1970s in reference to satellites, video cameras and other, at the time, new communication technologies. New media seem to change so quickly and are considered so radically "revolutionary" (thus provoking a drastic break with the past) that historical analysis has often been difficult to apply and, ultimately, useless for a vision concentrated on the present and future (not by chance named "presentism").

This book—following the research agenda of media historians as Lisa Gitelman (2006), Jonathan Sterne (2012), Benjamin Peters (2009), Dave Park, Nick Jankowski and Steve Jones (2011) and many others—will argue against this idea, showing that new or digital media *have to* be analyzed from a broader and more questioning perspective, keen to better understand what is "truly new" about them and what the profound and long-lasting consequences of digitization are.

Obviously, a historical analysis cannot limit itself to a chronological or events-based (*évènementielle*) framework made up of a sequence of relevant dates and inventions. Quite the contrary, historical analysis also and above all implies adopting interpretative concepts and perspectives aimed at gaining an in-depth understanding of the main long-term implications of digital media. It is for this reason that we have taken insights and inspirations from diverse fields of study, which have adopted specific concepts and theories to understand the role such media play in society. Hence, before embarking on the history of digital media *per se*, it would be useful to spend a little time looking at the main research currents in media and communication studies dealing with digital technology. This will be our basic "toolbox", which we will then draw on over the next few chapters to retrace the evolution of digital media and give our analysis conceptual depth.

Media, Communication and History

Media history is naturally this book's primary reference discipline. Communication and history have long been considered different branches of knowledge that only began to overlap at the end of the twentieth century. For a great deal of time, in fact, the study of communication and many of its foundation disciplines such as sociology, psychology, semiotics and linguistics have analyzed the media as if they were, in some sense, timeless (Butsch, 2007, p. 86). By contrast, history focuses on past sources and places (museums, archives, private collections) and, more generally, makes the past a formative element. For this reason, the historical mainstream has often regarded the media with some suspicion if not with downright snobbery. Media have long been ignored as historical research sources (Dahl, 1994), as an autonomous academic subject to be inquired into with traditional methodologies and professional practices (Allan, 2008) or even as agents for political, economic and social change (O'Malley, 2002, p. 164). For historians, then, the media have not existed or have remained marginal subjects of long-term research.

History and media and communication studies have long been distinct sectors and this has been true of their research goals too. While history rebuilds micro-stories brick-by-brick on the basis of the available sources, communication scholars have often read media history through "great narratives" (Nerone, 2006, p. 255) such as the fascinating visions of history structured according to the dominant media put forward by Harold Innis (1951) and Marshall McLuhan (1962). These great narratives have often been criticized by mainstream historians suspicious of their simplicity, as well as the difficulty involved in proving them. However, it was precisely the Toronto school of communication, and specifically Marshall McLuhan's work, which led to a progressive closing of the gap between history and media studies from the 1960s onwards. McLuhan's work is still, today, the clearest expression of a vaster and more heterogeneous media and cultural technologies study approach, which encompasses the work of a great many scholars: some examining oral and writing evolutions such as Elizabeth Eisenstein (1979), Walter Ong (1982) and Jack Goody (1986), some the consequences of such media for changes in cultural flow, as in the case of James Carey (1989), Joshua Meyrowitz (1985) and Henry Jenkins (2006) and, finally, some focusing on digital media forms and languages such as the work of Jay David Bolter and Richard Gruisin (1999) and Lev Manovich (2001).

While this scholarly work is very varied it has two main features in common: first, it sees media's technological forms as a decisive factor in the development of modern and contemporary society; and, second, as much of this work embraces a historical perspective, it has thus contributed to "blazing the trail" for a new generation of media scholars who have explicitly made history *the* main perspective from which to analyze the role of media in the contemporary context. The historical approach to communication studies has never been as vibrant as it is today as the recent success of the history of communication research shows with its rereading of texts, theories, founding authors and "classic" schools of thought on communication studies (as, for example, in the work of Park & Pooley, 2008 and Simonson & Park, 2016).

Alongside media history, there are a number of disciplines, methodologies and fields of study which, while not primarily historical in approach, can contribute to a long-term perspective analysis of digital media, further expanding our "toolbox".

The Political Economy of Communication. States, Politics and Markets

Throwing light on the history of digital media requires taking a close look at the role played by politics, national and international institutions and private companies in the public arena and the market: these are the central themes of the political economy of communication. This school of thought focuses on studying the relationships, which make possible and impact on communication production, distribution and consumption and pays special attention to the functioning of the economic and political system and to government, industry and citizen power dynamics (Mosco, 2009; Winsek, 2016). Media political economists assume that media systems and *cultural industries* (Miège, 1989) are a fundamental factor in understanding how society, and the contents transmitted by it, function.

The fundamental contribution brought to digital media history by the political economy of communication is at least twofold. On one hand, this approach identifies media's roots in a market capitalist system, which tends to generate inequality and power imbalances at the heart of the debate. From this perspective, digital media history cannot be uncoupled from an understanding of the way these new media emerge, grow and evolve in conjunction with specific economic and political power dynamics in a globalized economy. This means, for example, that the history of digital media is influenced by evolutions in dynamics between large corporations, governments and citizen-consumers and thus also by the clear differences that exist between the North American model (based principally on market logics) and the European model (in which public intervention has played a preponderant role in both traditional and digital media contexts). With its global vision, the political economy of communication is especially attentive to the way in which media evolutions are accompanied by forms of cultural imperialism and American dominance in the media sphere (Herman & McChesney, 1997; Mirrlees, 2013). This domination has gone beyond cultural contents and models with digital media to encompass the platforms, software and media devices themselves (Chakravartty & Zhao, 2008). In critical approaches influenced by Marxist tradition, digital media are essentially the new terrain on which updated Marxist theories on capital, markets and free labor find their place (Terranova, 2000; Fuchs, 2014).

On the other hand, the political economy of communication encompasses a clear historical component with a sense of the role of timeframe processes in an understanding of media-power dynamics. As Murdoch and Golding (2005, pp. 63-64) noted, in fact, the political economy of the media has used and endorsed a historical dimension in at least five ways—which can easily be applied to digital media too: 1) the development of media as an economic, social and cultural system; 2) large corporation *power* evolution and intensification both in terms of direct influence on culture and the indirect effect of their growing political weight (there is nothing accidental about the fact that the CEOs of large companies such as Google, Apple or Alibaba deal directly with heads of state and their visits to various nations have something of the air of official state visits); 3) the intensification of the *commodification* of culture and communications, which increasingly invade the private and family sphere (think of the fact that social media increasingly draw on their user experiences data for profit); 4) the evolution of the citizenship context into the media sphere and its global scale universalization, for example in relation to access identification as the characteristic feature of digital citizenship; finally, 5) evolutions in the state-market dynamic in relation to the decreasing weight accorded to public services and ownership—this has led, in particular, to digital media's most recent evolutions moving hand-in-hand with a neo-liberal and neo-capitalist economics model.

Digital media history—like that of analog media—is punctuated with many examples of the way in which the classic directives of political economy, decided by governments and large corporations, for example, have impacted on digital developments. To cite just three of the many possible instances examined in this book: the political guidelines, which have shaped the form and meanings given to internet networks in a range of contexts (see Chapter 3); the GSM standard applied to mobile telecommunications in Europe and then gradually adopted in a great many other countries (see Chapter 4); and, finally, the most popular formats in the digital universe such as MP3 as a product of political and economic negotiations (see Chapter 5). This book will also devote a great deal of space to the role that some digital companies have played over the last few decades: Amazon, Google, Facebook, Alibaba, Tencent and Apple, for example, will be examined in their historical and *mythological* relevance, paying special attention to their symbolic status in the so-called digital revolution. It is the political economy of communication that enables all these elements to be brought out precisely because it is a discipline at the crossroads between politics and economics, the state, the market and the corporate world.

Science & Technology Studies. Flexibility, Users and Materiality

Science & technology studies (STS) approach is a research field that has been focusing on understanding how scientific innovations and new technologies–including media technologies–are not external to social processes but rather an integral part of an *engineering of the heterogeneous* in which material, symbolic and political aspects converge to shape social realities (Law, 1987; Latour, 1991/1993). STS has often focused on large technical systems as rail or electric networks, on the scientific work in laboratories, on artifacts such as keys or bicycles, but in recent years has turned its attention to media directly and in particular to digital media (Boczkowski & Lievrouw, 2007; Balbi, Delfanti & Magaudda, 2016). This new attention to the world of media as technologies is principally to be explained by the fact that, while the social importance of the media was for many years powerfully associated with the entertainment, leisure time and cultural industries, the ubiquity and popularity of digital media such as the internet, smartphones and social networks has now made these technologies important to contemporary citizenship experiences, turning them into a *infrastructure of modernity* (Wajcman & Jones, 2012).

One of the issues on which STS focuses, and one that is especially relevant to an understanding of digital media history, relates to questioning the widely-held belief that the dissemination of technologies occurs as a *linear* and one-way process. Innovation (and digital innovation especially) is not a matter of a linear trajectory triggered by an idea, which then takes concrete form in a product and is only subsequently disseminated in social contexts. By contrast STS has highlighted the fact that technology and society are recursively related, i.e. technologies take shape in the societies in which they are imagined and created and, at the same time, social activities change or are reaffirmed on the basis of the presence of technology in a process of ongoing *mutual shaping* and *co-production* (McKenzie & Wajcman, 1986; Jasanoff, 2004).

From a theoretical point of view, one of the initial models adopted to aid an understanding of technological evolutions in the STS sphere was the Social construction of technology (SCOT), an approach propounded in the mid-1980s by Trevor Pinch and Wiebe Bijker (1987). First, the aim of the SCOT approach is to demonstrate that technological artefacts, above all in their early stages, are subject to a high degree of *interpretative flexibility*, i.e. they can be imagined, built and used in different ways by the various players, or better, relevant social groups involved in designing and using them (see Box 2.3). New technologies are also subject to *closure* and *stabilization* processes in which they take on their definitive forms from both the technical perspective and from the point of view of the shared social uses they are put to.

Digital communication technologies have certainly not escaped this process and have been radically and repeatedly modified over their history. Computers have evolved from military to personal tools (Chapter 2), the internet has been viewed differently by its various players (Chapter 3), mobile telecommunications have been interpreted as wireless telegraphs, telephones, cameras, digital agendas, recorders, clocks and even wallets (Chapter 4). Thus, it is the history of digital media's *interpretative flexibility* that will enable us to gain an understanding of the *alternative pasts* and potential futures of these media, some of which have never come to fruition while others have crystallized into widely-used and socially-shared practices. This work implied a sort of *symmetric* sensibility, aimed at considering not only the "winning" trajectories of those media technologies that found a stable place in social life, but also those innovation paths that have been later abandoned or discarded.

The aim of SCOT is to link this process of closure add stabilization to the wider social context highlighting that technologies, and thus also media, are the fruit of a socio-technical process in which devices and users, manufacturers and the wider social context are in constant, mutual co-evolution. It is also from the starting point of the SCOT approach that STS has developed as an area of study centered on the role of end users (Oudshoorn & Pinch, 2003; Hyysalo, Jensen & Oudshoorn, 2016). Thus STS reminds us that technologies do not depend solely on the work and ideas of those manufacturing them but are also the fruit of impulses and bonds linked to the world of use and consumption with feedback taking on a fundamentally important role in the process of technological evolution: the birth of text messaging, alternative uses of e-mail, photographic practices on the cusp between digital innovation and analog nostalgia– these are just a few examples of the fundamental role played by users in shaping digital media development cited in subsequent chapters.

Another issue that comes through powerfully in the STS approach is the role played by materiality in digital communication. This has, in particular, been the Actor-Network Theory (ANT) approach advanced in the mid-1980s by a number of scholars close to the STS school including Bruno Latour, Michel Callon and John Law (Latour, 2005). This approach recognizes the active role played by technologies as material artefacts within socio-technical processes, defining them precisely as *non-human actors* capable of actively influencing innovation and social appropriation processes. For ANT, technologies are significant not simply in so far as they are vehicles for meanings and ideas but also because their technical and material dimension comprises *scripts*, i.e. *action plans* embodied in technologies that interact with and influence human behavior

(Akrich & Latour, 1992). Media materiality is a central theme today in studies on digital media manufacturing, conservation, distribution and consumption: from servers hosting cloud data in well-defined centers and locations (Hu,2015), to undersea cables through which more than 90% of international internet traffic passes (Parks & Starosielski, 2015), from the obsolescence of digital items that rapidly go out of fashion and are replaced or recycled (Tischleder & Wasserman, 2015) to the pollution generated by the apparently eco-friendly digital technologies in contemporary cultures (Gabrys, 2011; Cubitt, 2017). The role played by digital media's material dimension is a recurring theme in the various chapters of this book focusing attention on large infrastructures as the hubs that host data gathering and network cables or consumer items such as personal computers, smartphones, MP3 readers and many others.

Cultural Studies. Power, Identity and Globalization

A last research perspective adopted in this book revolves around the cultural studies tradition, a highly variegated inter-disciplinary field, which was founded in the United Kingdom in the 1960s. In cultural studies, humanities and textual studies have, over time, interacted with social and political studies to explore issues on identity, culture and communication and, for this reason too, have overlapped significantly with other fields of study such as media studies and political economy of communication (Hesmondhalgh, 2007). Cultural studies has highlighted: a) the power of negotiations of the audience such as TV viewers (considered mainly "passive" prior to cultural studies), young people, ethnic minorities and women; b) the changing role of media in a culturally differen-tiated and increasingly globalized world and countries on the margins of the global economy; c) and finally, from a methodological point of view, the import-ance of qualitative and, in particular, ethnographic research, bringing them into the media studies debate in a stable way.

While the role of TV in society has been a major departure point of cultural studies at large (Williams, 1974), the first ethnographic research project was probably David Morley's *Nationwide* (1980/1999), which analyzed how different types of viewers interpreted and "decoded"–the *encoding/decoding model* was introduced by another well-known exponent in this field, Stuart Hall (1973/1980)–a popular BBC TV program called *Nationwide*. In developing an empirical approach to the use of media not only have cultural studies contributed to supplying a picture of the role played by such media in the private and family context but they have also definitively enriched the theoretical tradi-tion based on McLuhan's work to empirical studies of media technologies as material objects (Moores, 1993). This, for example, was the contribution of Roger Silverstone and Eric Hirsh's (1992) *media domestication* approach, which described the household media integration process, understanding technology as concrete objects within the private and family sphere and focusing in particular on the role and space occupied by TVs at home. This approach also blazed the way for digital media consumption studies and this book will look at the vicissitudes and successes that have punctuated the slow absorption and domestication of computers, mobile phones and the internet, the ongoing dialectic between companies and users (and non-users) and the attempts of the latter to adapt these media to their own cultural and symbolic culture of reference.

An alternative trajectory of cultural studies is the so-called post-colonial perspective. Returning to the work of scholars who cast doubt on the Western approach to the colonialism phenomenon—such as Franz Fanon (1961/1963), Edward Said (1978) and Gayatri Spivak (1990)—in the cultural studies tradition, the Western ethnocentric approach to cultural flow and identity has been challenged. Scholars such as Paul Gilroy (1993) and again Stuart Hall (1990) thus opened up debates on various issues such as identity, modernity and ethnocentricity, offering a more transnational reading of cultural processes, more attentive to local interpretations of globalization. Post-colonial theory's transformational drive thus melded around the emergence of an alternative interest in the consequences of globalization for media studies. David Morley (2006), for example, has challenged the simplistic idea according to which contemporary media simply enhanced globalization of spaces and flows, underlining the fact that the very notion of globalization is a largely Western cultural and political invention and a long way from being an inevitable historical process. As Shome and Hegde (2002) have argued, many of the concepts that emerged in the context of post-colonial theory—such as *hegemony, subalternity, marginality* and *hybridity*—have become increasingly important in media and communication studies. There is an increasingly powerful need to pay attention to local and apparently marginal points of view in media and digital technology studies, too, if we are to grasp the meaning of media processes which are, by contrast, increasingly global and transnational. Alternative macro and micro narratives illustrating the appropriation of the diverse digital media, which has taken place in regions of the world considered marginal to the US or European models will punctuate the various chapters of this book. The rise of the multilateral model supported by China and Russia against the American driven multistakeholder model in the global governance of the internet (Chapter 3) or the use of mobile telecommunications in a number of African countries (Chapter 4) or micro-histories as globalization of Korean-pop via YouTube (Box 5.2) or the dominance of Japanese firms in digital camera market (Chapter 5): these are just a few examples of new research trends capable of identifying and locating tensions and differences in approaching digital media in various world regions. More generally this approach has prompted a consideration of the history of digital media from a truly global perspective, in which *global* does not mean that we will examine digitization histories in *every* region of the world but rather help to de-Westernize it and to locate the currently dominant interpretation of the impact of digital media in the social sphere.

1.3 A Few of the Benefits of a Digital Media History

A fundamentally important question justifying the relevance of this book remains to be answered: why adopt a historical perspective to digital media analysis? We have already noted that historical approaches to digitization are less popular than other fields of study but this is not in itself sufficient justif-ication. We would argue, moreover, that an overview of past processes is useful and perhaps indispensable to better grasp the underlying features of what communication scholars consider constantly changing objects—digital media. The greater usefulness of historicizing digital media very probably consists in its potential to counter, or at least mitigate, three recurring and interrelated fallacies faced by social sciences and the humanities as applied to media: the *newness ideology*, the *alienation inherent in constant change or constant continuity* and the *winning technologies narrative*.

The Newness Ideology

By the newness ideology we mean a frequently predominant approach in media studies that tends to see every new means of communication as inno-vative and a breakthrough as compared to anything that came before it. Historians call this *teleology*, meaning that in the field of communication the newest media are often considered the most evolved and best outcome of a historically linear process, in which, quoting Martin Lister: "the nature of the past is explained as a preparation for the present. The present is understood as being prefigured in the past and is the culmination of it" (Lister, Dovey, Giddings, Grant & Kelly, 2009, p. 54). Take for example the narrative that argues that smartphones are the end point, or better, the culmination of a process that began with Marconi's wireless telephony and, inevitably, linearly, unproblematic-ally ended with iPhones.

The newness ideology does not contribute to a better understanding of the digital media for at least two reasons. First, the newest medium is just a tem-porary (and historical) concept, which in all likelihood will be old tomorrow. Second, there is no linear poor to rich forms of communications process. As Lisa

Gitelman and Geoffrey B. Pingree (2003) have underlined, the most recent medium is not always the best one and media histories are often a process of trial and error, forms of *metabolization* and rejection by potential users.

How can a historical approach help to counteract the so-called newness ideology? First and foremost, media as we know them today are the fruit of a process of "historical selection" (Stöber, 2004, p. 503). For example, the internet–as Chapter 3 will show–has changed many times in the course of its history: from a network designed for military use to a tool for the sharing of academic research; from a counter-culture concept of free and unlimited communication to repository of world knowledge as WWW is; and finally from immense virtual retail market to social network, which has changed the daily habits of billions of people. All these phases of internet history have left *formative influences* on it in the sense that certain network logics designed in the 1950s or 1960s have disappeared, while others are still part of this medium's cultural dimension. In other words, anyone attempting to study digital media in their current and *newest* form alone would find it impossible to avoid historic stratification.

History also helps us to counter the newness ideology by throwing light on the strong bond between old and new means of communication: it is almost impossible to distinguish between old and new media because the latter often imitate or are, at least, inspired by older forms and these are then in turn subjected to a process of remediation and meaning transfer prompted by new technologies (Bolter & Grusin, 1999; Balbi, 2015; Natale, 2016). In any specific historical period, in other words, the various media are all interrelated and reciprocal according to an intermedia logic (on intermediality, see Box 5.1), one of the dominant themes of this book. If we consider the history of mobile telecommunications, for example, it is clear that it cannot be fully understood without considering the history of landline telephones, wireless telegraphs, computers and the web, photography and even phonography or rather the history of sound recording (see Chapters 4 and 5). Thus, communication media– and this is even more true of digital media in which convergence processes have brought down the barriers between a number of technical and cultural characteristics that were once separate–cannot be studied in isolation and their economic, technical, socio-cultural and even anthropological dimensions can only emerge in the context of the media ecologies they are an integral part of. As mentioned in the introduction, this is one of the book's most original features: it studies the various digital media in relation to other media both past and present and also to other non-communication technologies. Consequently, opposing rigidly old and new media and looking at the latter as the best, most evolved and "naturally winning" ideas risks concealing many relevant features of digitization.

The Alienation Inherent in Constant Change or Constant Continuity

The second objective of this historical volume follows on from the first: balancing two alternative visions which, on the one hand, see digital media as continuously changing because of their high degree of technological innovation and, on the other, the opposite vision of stasis and continuity (change and continuity are widely discussed throughout the book but see, specifically, Chapter 5). The first, typical of media sociology, emphasizes the radical and perpetual instability of media and the permanent revolution they are subject to. The second can be summarized by the motto "nothing really changes" (Cavanagh, 2007, p. 6) and, embraced mainly by historians, aims to underline the fact that continuities have been more important than breaks in the field of digital media, too. These are two forms of determinism that can both be considered dangerous (Balbi, 2016).

The alienation inherent in constant change comes from the fact that some scholars (and journalists) have attempted to interpret or, in the worst cases merely to describe, a never-ending process: digital communication's technological (r)evolution. The digitization idea itself has thus assumed legendary and *mythological* status as if it were a sort of radically innovative phenomenon capable of ushering in a brave new world of economic prosperity, new knowledge and access potential. This emphasis on the revolutionary character of digital media comes out in a range of contexts. First, the revolutionary theme is very popular in the world of academic research as the dozens of books and academic articles in a range of languages containing in their titles the words *digital revolution* or similar expressions shows (for a historical critique of the concept of "communication revolutions" see Behringer, 2006; Fickers, 2012; John, 1994). Moreover, this expression has been used rhetorically by politicians to justify their decisions, by media moguls to promote their products and by experts and technicians to justify investments in the digital sector. It is also as a consequence of this economic and political pressure for digitization from the 1990s onwards that the term *digital revolution* has become such common currency and feature of public debate. A "digital revolution" frequency search in the Factiva database (containing thousands of newspapers, magazines, political and corporate documents and archive images from almost every country and in 28 languages) is a clear indication of the way this definition has increased in popularity over recent years (see Figure 1.1).

History does not reject the idea of change; on the contrary, change is perhaps the "central dimension of media history" (Poster, 2007, p. 46). History indeed is, perhaps, the discipline in communication studies best suited to a dynamic perspective, i.e. getting us used to the idea that media are changing

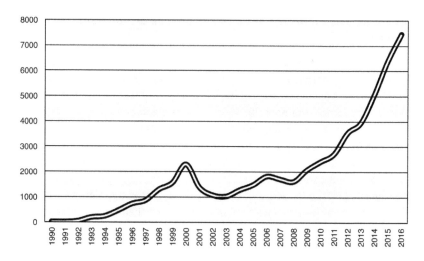

Figure 1.1 Frequency of the term "Digital Revolution" in Factiva Database, 1990-2016

Source: Authors' elaboration on Factiva data, accessed on May 2017

over by long- and short-term time frames (Brügger & Kolstrup, 2002). Consequently, change is a crucial dimension of media history and especially of digital media history because it helps scholars to conceive such technologies as unstable, transitional, part-old-part-new objects (Thorburn & Jenkins, 2003; Uricchio, 2004; Peters, 2009).

Nevertheless, what change, what degree of revolution and what instability are we talking about? As an effective metaphor by the French historian Fernand Braudel (1958/1960) exemplifies, seas are characterized by three degrees of movement: quasi-static deep abysses; undersea currents, which are constantly moving and deep down; and constant surface ridges. Historical research, particularly that introduced by the French Annales school, suggests examining all three dimensions together but especially focusing on the first and the second because it is only over the long term (*longue durée* in French) that the most profound and meaningful social changes take place. Even if the *longue durée* of digital media could look quite short, this is another of the benefits that history can bring to digital media studies: it can help in an understanding of the fact that the frenetic daily rhythm of digital innovation does not correspond to the slow and uncertain pace with which these same technologies are absorbed into our socio-cultural fabric.

Understanding that digital media do not change human beings on daily basis but that their relevance has to be understood in a long-term perspective does not mean looking at them statically: this is the second form of alienation we referred to at the beginning of this section. Indeed, a conflicting and equally risky trend exists: looking at digital media exactly as if they were analog media, as if digitization had not contributed to change contemporary societies or changed the ways humans communicate. This is what we refer to as the alienation inherent in constant continuity and it is a form of determinism concealing two crucial risks for media historians: anachronism (or placing historical events, in this case digital media, in a mistaken chronological order as if they belonged to past societies) and forced genealogies (or the need to find ancestors of modern communication technologies and underline that nothing has really changed). This determinism often affects media historians attempting to compare past and present media and underline similarities to a much greater extent than discontinuities. The political, economic and cultural realities in which digital media have emerged are completely different from those of the nineteenth or twentieth century and, similarly, digital media are different from the classic analog media: think about the scale of our access to communication, the potential for continuous and perpetual contact, the quantity of free and accessible information, the individual dimension of digital media and related worries about the "filter bubble" effect.

The aim of this book is to consider continuity and change adopting a perspective in which they are not alternative and mutually exclusive concepts. Tension between them obviously does exist, between the breakthroughs and leaps forward, which the dissemination of new digital technologies are frequently associated with and the profound and frequently long-term bonds between these very media and their own pasts. The idea that there is an analog *past* and a digital *future* is replaced in this book by an acknowledgement of the reciprocal consolidation and influence taking place between the analog and digital media universes: as Chapter 5 will show, the infinite buying opportunities provided by sites such as Amazon stimulate sales of paper books, platforms such as Flickr are an opportunity to play with the analog past of photography and the renewed popularity of vinyl indicates the resistance and reinvention of apparently antiquated consumer habits.

The Winning Technologies Narrative

The third and last common misconception in digital media studies that history can help to counter is the notion of one-way direction of technological change, which is generally, in the case of digital media, seen as unstoppable and incontrovertible. As STS scholars have emphasized, it is important to adopt a *symmetrical* approach, which devotes parallel attention to "winning" media and those that lost out or have not been fully integrated. This approach has been recently reinforced by the so-called *media archaeology* (Huhtamo & Parikka, 2011; Parikka, 2012), a heterogeneous framework embracing a range of methods and theories and focusing on past media through an attention to media's alternative roots, forgotten trajectories and neglected ideas. A consideration that scholars identifying with media archaeology have in common can be summed up in a phrase attributed to cinema historian Noël Burch: "it could have been otherwise" (quoted in Parikka, 2012, p. 13). This means that media evolutions could have taken different trajectories from those we are familiar with today and for this very reason communication technology forms and ideas crystallized in a given moment of the past should also be studied. This *archaeological* sensitivity gives us a better insight into the role played by forms of technology, which are now extinct but embodied specific visions of digital's role in relationships and social contexts at the moment of their initial popularity.

For digital media, this means adopting a long-term, diachronic perspective capable of understanding how mobile phones, for example–an idea that dates to the early twentieth century and then re-surfaced at the end of the century like a Karstic undercurrent–went from forgotten niche technology to the greatest success story in the history of communication technologies. The history of digital is replete with "losing" choices and policies and this leads us to an axiom, which was also true for analog media: new media death rates are high and errors of judgment by governments and companies have often been more the rule than the exception (see the DAB–Digital Audio Broadcasting for radio in Chapter 5); in other cases certain "technologies of the future" have been rapidly forgotten or left behind (think of CD-ROMs); other digital media created for a specific purpose have been subsequently adapted to specific political, economic and cultural requirements (the history of the internet shows all this very clearly). This brings us, then, to our final consideration on the importance of the historical approach to an understanding of digitization: throwing light on the fragility and reversibility of "digital innovation"–often seen as a one-way and linear process–can contribute to bringing out those interrupted trajectories, which might even re-emerge in future and reflect legitimate past practices and ideas all the same. The usefulness of this specific historical approach may be precisely this: to *normalize* our relationship with digital media, purge it of clichés, mythologies and facile enthusiasms and allow us to observe it in a more detached and objective way.

LEARNING MATERIALS

Key Points to Focus on

- Analog and digital media: definitions.
- Digitization in politics, society and culture.
- Theoretical approaches to the history of digital media:
  - The history and media studies.
  - The political economy of communication approach.
  - The science & technology studies approach.
  - The cultural studies approach.
- The newness ideology.
- The alienation inherent in constant change and constant continuity.
- The winning technologies narrative.

Questions to Answer

- Explain at least two reasons why it is important to study digital media from a historical perspective.
- How can we sum up the theoretical contributions of Science & Technology Studies (STS) to the study of digital media?
- What does studying digital media with a political economy of communication background mean? Give some examples.
- Why is interpreting the evolution of digital media as "revolutionary" controversial?
- What do we mean by "newness ideology"? Why is it a concern in the understanding of digital media? How can a historical approach overcome this problem?

A Video to Watch and Discuss

Watch the video on YouTube, a recording of Steve Jobs' public iPhone launch on January 9, 2007 (you can find it easily on YouTube and you may also read an excerpt in Box 4.4). While watching the video, reflect on how Steve Jobs' presentation sustains a *newness ideology* and a *revolution rhetoric* in relation to digital media.

A Few Books for Further Study

Bolter, J.D., & Grusin, R. (1999). *Remediation: Understanding New Media*. Cambridge, MA: The MIT Press.

Brügger, N., & Kolstrup, S. (Eds.). (2002). *Media History. Theories, Methods, Analysis*. Aarhus, Denmark: Aarhus University Press.

Edgerton, D. (2007). *The Shock of the Old: Technology and Global History since 1900.* London: Profile-books.

Gillespie, T., Boczkowski, P.J., & Foot, K.A. (Eds.). (2014). *Media Technologies: Essays on Communication, Materiality and Society.* Cambridge, MA: The MIT Press.

Gitelman, L. (2006). *Always Already New: Media, History and the Data of Culture.* Cambridge, MA: The MIT Press.

Mosco, V. (2004). *The Digital Sublime: Myth, Power, and Cyberspace.* Cambridge, MA: The MIT Press.

Parikka, J. (2012). *What Is Media Archaeology?* Cambridge: Polity Press.

Peters, B. (Ed.) (2016). *Digital Keywords. A Vocabulary of Information Society and Culture.* Princeton, NJ: Princeton University Press.

---

2 The Computer

2.1 The "Mother" of All Digital Devices

Computers are rightfully seen as the "mother" of all the digital media with which the world of communication is so replete. It was first and foremost in their personal computer incarnation, popularized from the 1980s and 1990s onwards, that computers developed into a mass digital phenomenon, used by ordinary people and later identified with internet use. However, almost half a century after the PC's first appearance, the centrality of personal desktop computers would now seem to have come of age in social terms, to leave the floor to a world characterized by *ubiquitous computing*, where not only all people carry a powerful computer in their pockets (i.e. our smartphones) but, potentially, also each object will be automatically interconnected, without the intervention of humans, in the so-called *internet of things*.

A downturn in personal computer sales has been evident worldwide for some years now, as global PC sales have in fact decreased from an all-time high of 351 million in 2012 to 269 million in 2016. This has been the result of the growth of other kinds of digital devices revolving around the *mobility paradigm*, such as tablets and especially smartphones, whose global sales increased in the same time frame from 680 million up to 1.5 billion (see data appendix, Figure A.3). It is for this reason, too, that, in recent years, the definition of *post-PC age* is frequently heard in debates on market trends for such devices to denote a period in which personal computers—for years symbol of digitization itself—are now simply one of many computing devices and interfaces available for the contemporary digital citizen.

Even if the presence of computers in today's society is increasingly characterized by light and mobile devices, cloud systems and interconnected things and our experience with computers relates more to smartphones than desktop computers, the history of both large calculating machine and personal computers is nonetheless crucial to put in perspective the evolution of our contemporary digital lives. Mid-twentieth century gigantic computers are indissolubly linked with the social incorporation of computing devices in routines, with the fact that the internet has turned into a daily necessity and, ultimately, with the emergence of the digital society itself. Unexpected historical links emerge, too: for example, the current popularity of cloud computing is, in many ways, a return to a model of use characteristic of the computers of the 1960s: indeed, as this chapter will highlight, with mainframes and time-sharing, work stations without processors and memories were used to access the calculation and filing capacities of great centralized machines.

Via a number of phases, then, computer history is synonymous with the digitization trajectory as a whole. The computer's social and technological evolution can thus be divided up into four distinct ages. The first is the age of *mechanical calculators*, in a sense computer "pre-history", a process stretching back several millennia during which social, cultural and economic demands for calculation and the automation of certain processes and activities took shape. The second computer history age relates to the birth of the first full-blown *digital computers* and encompasses the period from the 1930s to the 1970s, which saw the first of the great computers for military and then scientific and working purposes being built. It was in this context that the ARPANET project developed and the first foundations of the internet were laid down (see Chapter 3). Beginning in the mid-1970s, the third age was the *personal computer for the*

Table 2.1 A summary of the four phases in the computer's socio-technical history

Ages	Time frame	Distinctive features
1. Mechanical age	~2500 BC–mid '30s	The long-term social need for calculation achieved with mechanical machines and then fostered by the birth of the nation state, industrial revolution and mass society.
2. Mainframe age	mid '30s–mid '70s	Innovations generated by military needs and by the expansion of increasingly large corporations and global commerce.
3. Personal computer age	mid '70s–2000s	The adoption of computers by ordinary people for everyday family and personal needs later fostered by the popularization of the internet.
4 Post-PC age	2000s–today	Personal computers have been knocked off their main-digital-device pedestal encouraged by increasingly mobile and individualized lifestyles, social network communication and ubiquitous computing.

masses era in which computers moved out of the work tools for large organizations sphere becoming individual, home devices central to the everyday lives of ordinary people. PCs were also agents of change for the entire digital (and even analog) universe: it was precisely thanks to the presence of PCs in private homes that the internet and other systems were able to take on their current central importance in contemporary social life from the mid-1990s to the onset of the new century. The fourth and last phase might be called the *post-PC age*, which has seen personal computers being knocked off their dominant-digital-tool pedestal, as the mobility paradigm in internet use comes to the fore and a reconfiguration of the global geography of computer manufacturing and use, now increasingly individual, mobile and global, takes place.

2.2 The Mechanical Computer Age and the Social Need for Calculation

Computer history pre-dates the invention of digital languages and technologies and harks back to an extremely old concept in human culture, the availability of automatic machines to do calculations and perform complex operations (Goldstine, 1972). The link between computers and calculation machines highlights two important implications. First and foremost, computers have shared part of their history with calculators or, in other words, they were long considered tools whose main function was to perform calculations rather than to communicate. Second, this initial phase of their history, which lasted several millennia, was exclusively mechanical. It might, in fact, be said that computers are not *digital natives*—as we will see—but rather electronic and digital evolutions of pre-existing social and technological functions, which took shape in the mechanical world.

Machines to do calculations have thousands of years of history. Think of the first *abacus*, the first calculation device, used by the Sumerians (the ancient inhabitants of Mesopotamia), dating back at least 4,500 years, and the *astrolabe*—an astronomical tool thanks to which it was possible to locate celestial bodies and tell the time—was used a few centuries BC by the Ancient Greek mathematician Hipparchus (Ifrah, 2001). At the end of the medieval age, in thirteenth-century Spain, Catalan philosopher Ramon Llull invented a device called *Ars magna*, a system based on a logical process designed to generate ideas and concepts with which to disseminate the Christian doctrine among the *infidels* of the Spanish peninsula (Bonner, 2007). The seventeenth century saw the theoretical considerations around calculation machines come of age prompted, above all, by advances in mathematical science. It was mathematicians Blaise Pascal and Gottfried Wilhelm Leibniz, who invented two different calculation machines. The former applied clock mechanisms to number calculations, while the latter invented the *step reckoner*, a device capable of carrying out mathematical operations in the belief—expressed in 1668—that "it is beneath the dignity of excellent men to waste their time in calculation when any peasant could do the work as accurately with the aid of a machine" (quoted in Martin, 1992, p. 38). However, the important theoretical advances conceived of by Pascal and Leibniz did not come to practical fruition because mathematics was much more advanced than mechanics and also because a strong political and social demand for calculation was yet to become a priority.

The misalignment between political aims, technical capability and the scientific work is well exemplified by the case of an early calculating machine designed by the British mathematician and inventor Charles Babbage in the mid nineteenth century. In 1822, Babbage started to design a mechanical calculating machine called the *difference engine* and, in 1832, he also crafted a small prototype, but the project was then aborted because metalworking techniques at that time were not so advanced to make the required and precise tools.

Consequently, Babbage shifted his efforts on an evolved machine, on which he started to work in 1837, called the *analytical engine*. This second mechanical calculating machine is considered either the first modern computer able to calculate and store data or one of the greatest failures in the history of computers (Dasgupta, 2014). Indeed, while this machine is today considered to be technically similar to the architecture and design of modern computers, Babbage was unable to build a working machine, he was abandoned by his main sponsor (the British Government, which spent about £17,000 on the machine, equating to about $2 million in today's terms) and his work was even rejected by the British scientific community. As a result, his pioneering efforts went forgotten for more than a century and one of his mechanical calculating machines was only finally built in 1991 by the London Science Museum.

Among the few people that recognized the potentiality of Babbage's analytical engine was one of the early female mathematicians, Ada Lovelace (daughter of the poet Lord Byron). She not only understood that this kind of calculating machine could in the future become an all-purpose computer (for example a device able to create original music; see Gleick, 2011, p. 112), but also contributed to the development of the idea of "programming" and, together with Babbage, conceived what is considered the first algorithm, i.e. a recursive set of operations for the computation of a mathematical entity through a machine (Dasgupta, 2014, p. 25).

Simultaneously with the pioneering, but apparently unproductive, work of Babbage and Lovelace, the nineteenth-century modern world was evolving rapidly, improving the technical ability to build complex machines and fostering socio-economic demands of devices able to perform complicated calculations.

Technical ability and socio-economic demands, which laid the foundations for the actual development of calculation machines, and later full-blown computers, were strongly linked to some of the most significant turning points in the development of Western society: the development of *industrial capitalism* and the affirmation of *democratic mass societies*.

The primary historical process to have profound consequences in this field was the nineteenth-century Industrial Revolution, during which the need for machines capable of performing calculations and automatic operations came powerfully to the fore, first to support the capitalist manufacturing system and then to increase the efficiency of the modern nation state. A first determinant innovation occurred in a sector that apparently had nothing to do with mathematical calculation: weaving. In 1801, French engineer Joseph-Marie Jacquard introduced a new type of *automatic loom*, which was made up—in modern parlance—of hardware (the loom itself with all its mechanical components) and software. Its innovative quality consisted, in fact, in the use of a roll of punched paper containing certain instructions, which the machine was to perform to make a specific model. Substituting the roll of paper (and thus in a sense its software) also changed the clothing model produced.

In the latter half of the nineteenth century the concept of automatic looms and punch sheets was applied to calculation and to the organization of labor. Indeed, the Industrial Revolution also ushered in the need to calculate manufacturing time frames in a quasi-scientific way and promoted a progressive automation and rationalization of working tasks, a system defined as *Taylorism*, which culminated at the beginning of the twentieth century in *Fordism* and in the adoption of the assembly line in factories, which were created to answer to the increasing demand for consumer goods by the raising mass society.

The second historic process with manifold implications for calculation demands, too, was political in character, namely the affirmation of the nation state as a model of modern political organization with the consequent need, by the state administration, to calculate and measure social activities in order to tailor economic and political decisions to them. To give a few examples, just think of military service and the need to calculate available soldier numbers, measurements of the industrial production of individual countries (which still today supplies fundamental economic indicators such as GNP) and finally, the most apparently obvious but also one of the most fundamentally important functions for a state, counting its population by census.

The response to these pressing calculation demands generated what James Beniger (1986) has called a "control revolution", namely a series of technological and logistical transformations developed from the nineteenth century onwards to deal with the increased organizational complexity of the modern world. Already at the beginning of the twentieth century, certain applications had

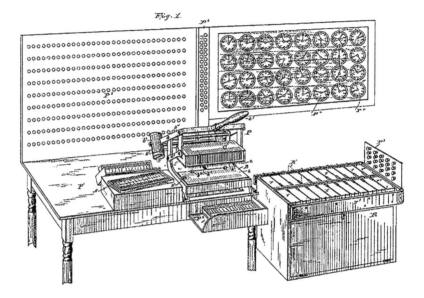

Figure 2.1 The very first punch card machine, in the drawing presented by Herman Hollerith to the US patent registry in 1889

Source: Pat. nr. 395781, Jan 8, 1889

begun to emerge, which were to be significant in computer history. Thus, in 1889, in order to carry out a census of the US population, two former Interior Ministry employees–Herman Hollerith and James Powers–developed new equipment capable of reading the information contained in punch cards automatically with no human intervention required (Anderson, 1988) (see Figure 2.1). Starting from this invention and together with a number of colleagues, in 1911 Hollerith set up a calculation machine company called CTR (*Computing-Tabulating Recording* Company), which changed its name to IBM in 1924 becoming what was later to be the most influential company of the IT world for much of the twentieth century (Pugh, 1995).

This control revolution was a crucial economic, political and social backdrop to twentieth century computer developments and the whole first generation of digital technologies. It was, in fact, with the diffusion of the first calculators in the US census office in the 1930s that a variegated commercial sector based on the invention and sale of calculation machines, cash registers and other automatic devices made its first appearance. The social and economic groundwork for the popularization of the first computers had thus already been done and only the most complex passage was required: the invention and construction of digital calculation machines.

2.3 The Mainframe Age

The Military Paradigm of Mainframes

The birth of the first digital computers was once again closely bound up with a further central event in global history, World War Two, an event which, to a greater extent than any other in the mid twentieth century, laid bare the global interdependence between the various regions of the planet. For the first time a grand total of 56 nations from all five continents fought in a single war. There is thus nothing surprising about the fact that all the projects that breathed initial life into the computer revolved precisely around the demands of war. This historic event ushered in the second of the socio-technical computer eras, the *mainframe age*: the period in which computers were large and complex machines used exclusively by governments, research centers and large firms to fulfil their military, political and manufacturing requirements.

However, just a few years before the outbreak of World War Two, a fundamentally important step in the evolution of digital computers came from a purely theoretical contribution to the field of mathematical sciences. In 1936, English mathematician Alan Turing wrote an article in which he adapted the principles of mathematical logic to the functioning of an automatic machine capable of carrying out complex operations on the basis of a binary code (Hodges, 1983, p. 112). What was called the *Turing machine* was not a mechanical technology but rather an abstract device, namely a theoretical description of the logical principles behind the functioning of a machine capable of performing calculations using a binary code (in practice software). Its abstract nature notwithstanding, the Turing machine was the first calculator to be capable of performing complex operations from a programming language adaptable to a range of operations. This invention constituted the starting point for all subsequent attempts to create digital computers and, precisely for this reason, the ideas of this English mathematician are generally considered to have been the foundation for the whole digitization process, as well as, the cultural basis for any similarities between human beings and machines, an idea that was highly popular in the second half of the twentieth century as a result of the so-called *Turing test* (Moor, 2003).

But from the latter half of the 1930s onwards, a further determinant factor in the history of the computer can be added to this mathematical interest in calculation machines: growing militarization and prevalently European governmental pressure to find new technical solutions to apply to the military field.

There is therefore nothing surprising about the fact that the first computers were developed in parallel and in secret in the early 1940s by the principal and most powerful nations fighting in World War Two. Several countries involved in the conflict invested relevant resources to build machines able to perform complex calculations for war purposes: from ballistics to cryptography and secret communication. As a result, many prototypes and working machines

---

Box 2.1 Documents

Alan Turing, *Can Digital Computers Think?* (1951)

The extract that follows is taken from one of the few public interviews given by Alan Turing, the father of the computer, in which he describes the potential for building computers that imitate human intelligence, although, as he wrote in 1951, the necessary calculation capacity was still lacking. Turing believed that computers could imitate human intelligence but was skeptical about machines imitating the characteristic forms of the human body.

> If now some particular machine can be described as a brain we have only to programme our digital computer to imitate it and it will also be a brain. If it is accepted that real brains, as found in animals, and in particular in men, are a sort of machine it will follow that our digital computer, suitably programmed, will behave like a brain [. . .] It is cus-tomary, in a talk or article on this subject, to offer a grain of comfort, in the form of a statement that some particularly human characteristic could never be imitated by a machine. It might for instance be said that no machine could write good English, or that it could not be influenced by sex-appeal or smoke a pipe. I cannot offer any such comfort, for I believe that no such bounds can be set. But I certainly hope and believe that no great efforts will be put into making machines with the most distinctively human, but non-intellectual characteristics such as the shape of the human body; it appears to me to be quite futile to make such attempts and their results would have something like the unpleasant quality of artificial flowers. Attempts to produce a thinking machine seem to me to be in a different category. The whole think-ing process is still rather mysterious to us, but I believe that the attempt to make a thinking machine will help us greatly in finding out how we think ourselves.

Source: Turing, A. (2004). Can Digital Computers Think?

In J.B. Copeland (Ed.), *The Essential Turing: Seminal Writings in Computing, Logic, Philosophy, Artificial Intelligence, and Artificial Life* (pp. 483–486). Oxford: Oxford University Press

featuring slight differences and architectures were experimented in parallel in different countries at the same time, thus making it difficult to establish the priority on the invention of "the first computer". This is a "classic" problem of media history and, moreover, it must be noticed that assigning the honorific title of "first computer" mainly depends by the definition assigned to the word "computer" itself: mechanical or digital, fully programmable or not, actually built and used or just designed, etc. This is the main reason why there is not a real "first computer", but rather a dense timeframe during which several different machines came out in several countries, each featuring distinctive aspects of what later became commonly associated with "the computer".

Among the first computers, there is a machine created by Turing himself, who worked on the development of Colossus, one of these first digital computers, built in 1943 by English military laboratories then totally absorbed by research into new devices with which to decipher Nazi encrypted messages. While the various versions of Colossus are now considered to have been the first programmable digital computers (by means of cables and connectors), the existence of such devices was totally forgotten until the 1970s, as these were destroyed at the end of the war thus sabotaging at birth the potential for the development of a British IT industry in the post war period (Copeland, 2010). The same fate awaited what was another potential first digital computer, invented in Nazi Berlin by German engineer Konrad Zuse between 1938 and 1941, the Z3 (later renamed S3). The Nazi government did not consider the project of strategic military importance at the time and denied it funding and, consequently, S3 was destroyed during the war and it too was forgotten (Rojas, 2000). The history of digital technologies, like that of media as a whole, is also a patchwork of technological solutions abandoned and forgotten and then rediscovered in historical research, as John Durham Peters (2008) has argued: communication history is an emerging process, which constantly evolves in the light of new discoveries and interests evolving in a given social context.

Both British and German errors of judgment on the importance of computers were not replicated in the United States, which applied automatic machines to the war effort on a massive scale, above all as air raid defense devices capable of calculating the trajectory of aircraft and missiles in movement. Certain figures played a crucial role in the dissemination of the computer's potential applications, as engineer Vannevar Bush, for example, also responsible for the Manhattan atom bomb Project, and mathematician Norbert Wiener, who published a crucial book entitled *Cybernetics* in 1948, thus contributing to popularizing the subject of scientific research into the application of calculation machines to social life.

Despite the huge funds pumped into it, the first American computer was not, however, developed in time to be of wartime use. It was only in the winter of 1945, when the war had just ended, that a first computer, called ENIAC (Electronic Numerical Integrator and Computer), was completed. It was a huge device, weighing around 3,000 kilograms and occupying a room measuring more than 150 square meters, which cost around $0.5 million to build in the prices of the day. ENIAC was the first of a series of computer models called *mainframe*s and was soon used in other military activities including for feasibility calculations on the first hydrogen bomb made in 1952 (Agar, 2003, p. 202). Despite being the first digital calculator in the modern sense of the term, ENIAC was very different from today's personal computers: it was enormous, very slow and required a whole team of programmers, often dressed in white coats and later nicknamed satirically the *priesthood* (Levy, 1984, p. 5), for the rituality implied in the work of inputting questions and data into the form of punch cards.

As we may symbolically see in Figure 2.2, the invention and use of this first computer had also something to do with the gender differences in the society

Figure 2.2 ENIAC's creators working in the room containing the computer, 1946 ca

Source: Image property of the United States Army, Courtesy of the University of Pennsylvania Archives

of the day. While IT emerged in the second part of the twentieth century in prevalently male environments, such as the military and scientific ones, women played a relevant, and often unnoticed, role as well. As we have seen, in the invention of the first Babbage machine in the nineteenth century, Ada Lovelace contributed to the development of the analytical engine and to the conception of the first accredited algorithm. But women's roles were also very important during the early stage of the first mainframes era, although their contribution was long swept under the carpet. Science historian Jennifer Light (1999) has, for example, unveiled that many women with high-level mathematical training were employed in the construction and functioning of the first ENIAC computer and, above all, in important software operation management roles.

Looking at the British history of the computer, historian Marie Hick has shown that, while in the 1940s computer programming and computation were mainly women's tasks, from the 1950s a "technological (and gender) switch" in the software management occurred, as part of a top-down program by the British government. The outcome of this switch was that "once computing started to become a more desirable field for young men, women were largely left out, regardless of what they might have been capable of or what they might have preferred" (Hicks, 2017, p. 3). In the decades that followed, in fact, in a majority of countries, the computer field turned into a prevalently male universe until women became a fundamentally important commercial target for the popularization of personal computers in the 1980s. This historical switch was so relevant in influencing the fields of computing in contemporary societies. If we consider statistics on women in informatics university degrees and carriers in tech firms today, inequalities of access are still relevant: in Europe, women represent about one fifth of all the graduated students in computer sciences (Pereira, 2016), while in a major ICT firm like Google in 2016 only 20% of employees in tech positions were female (Google, 2016). This is another telling example of how decisions taken in the past can influence the use and development of contemporary digital media or, in other words, how history matters because it shapes the present and in a way the future, as theoretical tradition of path dependency argues (David, 1985; Arthur, 1989).

A great many of the mainframe computers made in the late 1940s and the 1950s were built with funding from the US government and by the end of the latter decade there were approximately 250 of these. These included the first computer to emerge from the secret military experimentation rooms and make its way onto the market, the 1951 UNIVAC, which was funded by the American census office to make population calculations, a civil application that echoed the nineteenth-century use of punch cards. In 1952, this first commercial computer achieved some public fame for its ability to forecast the result of the American elections won by Dwight Eisenhower (a key president also in the history of the internet, see Chapter 3), even if initially the results elaborated by the computer were not believed. This story increased its popularity and public familiarity to such an extent that for some years the term UNIVAC was synonymous with computers in general (Chandler, 2005, p. 84 onwards). The dissemination of these first great calculators into other parts of the world took place later. In Chile, for example, one of the earliest mainframes, IBM 360, was brought in 1966 to the American firm's local branch office to be used by a private sector firm (Medina, 2011, p. 58), while this type of machine took even longer to make its way to India with one of the first mainframes, IBM 370, being set up in the Indian Institute of Technology in Madras only in the early 1970s (Banerjee, 1996, p. 127).

As the applications of these early computers were mainly military, institutional and commercial for calculation purposes, computers were mainly associated with the military and political worlds until the 1960s and for this reason they were also the preferred targets of intellectual criticism and political activism. Of these critics, one of the first was social technology scholar Lewis Mumford (1970), who described computers–as heir to a common belief in the American society of the day (see Hughes, 2004, p. 90 onwards)–as a tool designed to subjugate human freedom in the pursuit of *technological rationality* (see Box 2.2). In these years, then, computers were not simply tools to be made use of but also a cultural image replete with the frequently negative connotations, which had begun to be such a feature of the emerging IT society.

Box 2.2 Documents

Lewis Mumford, *Authoritarian and Democratic Technics* (1964)

Lewis Mumford (1895-1990) was an American historian and philosopher of technology and one of the fiercest critics of the increasingly dominant role of technology in modern Western society under the influence of an authoritarian ideology. In this excerpt from a public speech he gave in 1963, Mumford places computers at the heart of his concerns about the emergence of authoritarian technologies that could, in his view, lead to human extermination.

> Let us fool ourselves no longer. At the very moment Western nations threw off the ancient regime of absolute government, operating under a once-divine king, they were restoring this same system in a far more effective form in their technology, reintroducing coercions of a military

character no less strict in the organization of a factory than in that of the new drilled, uniformed, and regimented army. During the transitional stages of the last two centuries, the ultimate tendency of this system might be in doubt, for in many areas there were strong democratic reactions; but with the knitting together of a scientific ideology, itself liberated from theological restrictions or humanistic purposes, authoritarian technics found an instrument at hand that has now given it absolute command of physical energies of cosmic dimensions. The inventors of nuclear bombs, space rockets, and computers are the pyramid builders of our own age: psychologically inflated by a similar myth of unqualified power, boasting through their science of their increasing omnipotence, if not omniscience, moved by obsessions and compulsions no less irrational than those of earlier absolute systems: particularly the notion that the system itself must be expanded, at whatever eventual cost to life.

Through mechanization, automation, cybernetic direction, this authoritarian technics has at last successfully overcome its most serious weakness: its original dependence upon resistant, sometimes actively disobedient servomechanisms, still human enough to harbor purposes that do not always coincide with those of the system.

Like the earliest form of authoritarian technics, this new technology is marvelously dynamic and productive: its power in every form tends to increase without limits, in quantities that defy assimilation and defeat control, whether we are thinking of the output of scientific knowledge or of industrial assembly lines. To maximize energy, speed, or automation, without reference to the complex conditions that sustain organic life, have become ends in themselves. As with the earliest forms of authoritarian technics, the weight of effort, if one is to judge by national budgets, is toward absolute instruments of destruction, designed for absolutely irrational purposes whose chief by-product would be the mutilation or extermination of the human race.

Source: Mumford, L. (1964). Authoritarian and democratic technics. *Technology & Culture, 5*(1), 2

Mainframes Evolve: Desktops, Time-Sharing and Micro-Processors

As we have already seen, technically speaking, mainframes were very different from modern personal computers. In particular, these large devices used by whole research teams within out-and-out laboratories were as far away as possible from the devices used by individuals in their own homes for communication and leisure purposes today. Between the late 1950s and early 1970s, however, a series of technological ideas and innovations shifted the mainframe paradigm in the direction of the personal computer concept. These innovations consisted principally of three elements: *desktop computers, time-sharing* and *micro-processors.* As often occurs in technology history, in fact, this change of paradigm did not take place in great leaps and bounds but by means of a slow, cumulative trial and error process without a fixed objective in view or the explicit goal of creating a computer, which could be used by ordinary people.

A first transformation was one relating to the potential for computer use by individual users on a desktop and no longer by teams of researchers as had been the case with ENIAC. One of the earliest computers designed to be used by a single individual using a keyboard on a desk was model 610 made by IBM in 1957, a firm whose main but not sole field of activity was supplying technologies to public offices and departments. Initially designed at the Watson Scientific Computing Laboratories at Columbia University and released onto the market at a cost of $55,000 (more than $450,000 in today's money) only 180 of these computers were actually made. Smaller than ENIAC and UNIVAC, the IBM 610 was still a large computer with a main unit approximately one meter high and a meter and a half wide containing all the main components, which were controlled with a keyboard (Allan, 2001, p. 1/15). One of the first truly desktop computers was a calculator called Programma 101 and sold by Olivetti, an Italian based firm, in 1964. For the first time the size of this digital device was similar to that of a typewriter but in actual fact the P101 was more a calculation machine than a full-blown computer (it had no screen, for example) although it was capable of performing small sequences of pre-programmed calculations memorized on magnetic supports (Ceruzzi, 2003, p. 213).

Although the second innovation, *time-sharing,* was designed to optimize mainframe functioning it had a decisive impact on conceiving computers as tools to be used individually and in communication. Not only were they large but mainframes were also designed for collective use by groups of technicians coordinating the calculations required by a range of scientists and departments. The time-sharing idea consisted essentially in the opportunity to divide up the calculation capacity of the mainframes in such a way as to enable them to be used simultaneously at various work stations called *terminals*, thus sharing out calculation capabilities between different users (see also Chapter 3).

The first effective demonstration of time-sharing took place at Boston's MIT in 1962 using IBM mainframes. While the terminals with which mainframe use was shared out were not truly independent computers because they depended on a central terminal for calculations, this dividing up of work technique was a window onto the practical possibility of using computers in an alternative way from the collective use made of the great processors (Ceruzzi, 2003, p. 154). The time-sharing model flourished for nearly 20 years from the mid 1960s to the early 1980s becoming one of the most significant applications in the IT sector at least until the personal computer age (Campbell-Kelly & Garcia-Swartz, 2008). But the fact remains that the concept grew out of and was implemented as a form and optimization of mainframe computers and not as an innovation for the purposes of creating a different type of computer. Rather than *disruptive*, then, time-sharing can be seen as an incremental and *conservative* innovation. On the one hand, this type of use represented a follow-on development from the reference standards of the day (namely mainframes), while on the other, it introduced, however involuntarily, a very different computer use concept.

The third idea that would later turn out to be central to the creation of today's PCs consisted of the integrated circuit microprocessor technology, which opened the way to small sized computers and constant performance improvements. As early as 1965, Intel's co-founder Gordon Moore had forecast that processors would get smaller and more powerful expressing the so-called *Moore's first law*, which was to be self-fulfilling over the decades that followed guiding the pace of innovation in the IT field: "processor performance and the number of transistors relating to it will double every 18 months". The invention of microprocessors in 1971 enabled an essential computer part to be reduced to a few centimeters in size, one which performs the calculations at the basis of all modern digital devices and which, prior to this, had been very large and also extremely costly to make. Microprocessors' base components are integrated circuits, a technology invented in the early 1960s for Intel by Italian engineer Federico Faggin, who before moving to California had trained initially at the company, Olivetti, which had created the Programma 101 calculator. Faggin and Intel had created the first microprocessor, the 4004, in response to requests for components by Japanese firm Busicom, then active in the desk calculator sector, demonstrating once again the time worn link between calculation machines and computers. Although even Intel itself had not understood the microprocessor's importance, considering it of use only in calculators (Fransman, 1995, p. 168), this first 1971 Intel 4004 model was effectively the springboard for the first mid-1970s PC prototypes and the progenitor of all subsequent micro-processors including those used to build the first Apple PC in 1976.

Box 2.3 In-depth Theory

Technological Frame and *Relevant Social Groups*

Developed as part of the Social Construction of Technology approach (SCOT) by Wiebe Bijker and Trevor Pinch (1987), which we considered in Chapter 1, the concept of *technological frame* refers to the fact that social groups attribute different meanings to new technologies on the basis of their pre-existing conceptions, practices, theories and habits. The concept was developed in particular by Bijker who wrote that:

> A technological frame is composed of, to start with, the concepts and techniques employed by a community in its problem solving. [. . .] Problem solving should be read as a broad concept, encompassing within it the recognition of what counts as a problem as well as the strategies available for solving the problems and the requirements a solution has to meet. This makes a technological frame into a combination of current theories, tacit knowledge, engineering practice, such as design methods and criteria), specialized testing procedures, goals, and handling and using practice.
>
> (1987, p. 168)

Thus, the technological frame concept refers to "ways of thinking" and "fixed patterns of interaction" around specific technology that emerge and are stabilized within a specific community. The way technologies are conceived influences the choices innovators make regarding the needs such technologies should respond to and consequently affects the design of these new technologies themselves. In computer history, people working in the mainframe industry often shared a specific technological framework: the beliefs that computers were to be designed for the office context, that innovation in the field consisted of responding to corporations' needs and that laypeople would never need to use a computer at home. More generally, one of the uses of the concept of technological framework is that it helps us to understand that innovations are not simply the outcome of technical work but are profoundly embedded into innovators' core social, economic and cultural perspectives.

And this brings us to consider a second notion, strictly connected to technological framework: that of *relevant social groups*. This is another fundamental concept of the SCOT approach and serves to highlight the fact that there are recognizable groups of individuals, both producers and users, who tend to gather around an innovation process, having alternative visions of a technical artefact's evolution. As Bijker and Pinch have argued, the relevant social group concept:

> is used to denote institutions and organizations (such as the military or some specific industrial company), as well as organized or unorganized groups of individuals. The key requirement is that all members of a certain social group share the same set of meanings, attached to a specific artifact. In deciding which social groups are relevant, we must first ask whether the artifact has any meaning at all for the members of the social group under investigation.
>
> (1987, p. 23)

Each relevant social group has its own ideas on the needs that a new technology must respond to and consequently acts as exponent for a specific new technology design. The example of the creation of the first personal computers in the USA is paradigmatic of the emergence of a new relevant social group around mainframe computers, the amateurs, hackers and activists. They identified new needs and uses for computers providing an alternative technological frame from that of the mainframe industry and were thus able to develop an entirely new type of technology for the era: the personal computer. Furthermore, the development of new technologies is interpreted as a social process in which various social groups with diverse abilities to shape a new technology play a part. In the case of personal computers, for example, there is no doubt that at the outset the mainframe industry had more power than the various groups of enthusiasts in shaping the new computers. But this did not halt the innovation trajectory, which led to the invention of the first personal computers.

Further Reading

Berker, T., Hartmann, M., Punie, Y., & Ward, K. (2005). *Domestication of Media and Technology*. Maidenhead, UK: Open University Press.

Bijker, W.E. (1997). *Of Bicycles, Bakelites, and Bulbs: Toward a Theory of Sociotechnical Change*. Cambridge, MA: The MIT Press.

Pellegrino, G. (2005). Thickening the frame: cross-theoretical accounts of contexts inside and around technology. *Bulletin of Science, Technology & Society, 25*(1), 63-72.

Pinch, T., & Bijker, W.E. (1987). The Social Construction of Facts and Artifacts: Or How the Sociology of Science and the Sociology of Technology Might Benefit Each Other. In W.E. Bijker, T.P. Hughes & T. Pinch (Eds.), *The Social Construction of Technological Systems: New Directions in the Sociology and History of Technology* (pp. 17-50). Cambridge, MA: The MIT Press.

The creation of the microprocessor required the construction of what science and technology studies define a socio-technical *network* (Latour, 1987), an assemblage of heterogeneous elements including people and institutions, technologies and cultural visions. It is thus clear that while the earliest micro-processor was effectively the product of one of Silicon Valley's main IT firms, its supporting socio-technical network was much larger: on the one hand, the engineer responsible for the Intel project had been trained in a country—Italy—on the side-lines, relatively speaking, of IT evolution but it was, however, also a context that had developed the first desktop calculator a few years earlier. On the other hand, the demand for the first microprocessor came principally from Japanese companies, which played a substantial role in the creation and dissemination of this new technology. Post-war Japan had undergone a pro-cess of profound industrial transformation characterized by an openness to Western ideas and technologies. From 1957 onwards, the Japanese government supported its embryonic computer industries by levying a tax on foreign com-puter imports in order to protect it from prevalently US competition. It was also this commercial protection that enabled Japanese firms to achieve leadership of the digital calculator sector (yet another conservative technology that essentially digitized an earlier technology without revolutionizing it) from which they acted as the principal suppliers of microprocessor components worldwide over the next decade (Forester, 1993; Fransman, 1995).

The roots of desktops, time-sharing and microprocessors—three innovations later to play a fundamental role, both directly and indirectly, in the birth of the first personal computers—lay in a traditional *technological frame* (Bijker 1987, see Box 2.3): the earliest desktops and microprocessors were initially applied to a partly different sector, office calculators, while time-sharing was designed entirely within the dominant mainframe paradigm. Other socio-technical ele-ments required for the creation of personal computers were still to emerge in the 1970s.

2.4 The Personal Computer Age

The time was almost ripe, then, for a paradigmatic change in cultural visions of the computer. This is the third era in our history, the *personal computer age*. But, as we will see, the birth of the personal computer was neither straight-forward nor linear and from the late 1960s to the late 1970s a number of national governments and private companies created PC prototypes each with their own characteristics. In these years, however, the majority of these prototypes remained in the embryonic phase, above all, because their true application was not yet clear and neither a market for these devices nor consumer interest in them yet existed. From a science and technology studies perspective the personal computer was an innovation, which had yet to "enroll" its users (Callon & Law, 1982) and be supported by its *relevant social groups* (Bijker, 1987).

While the most influential models in the history of personal computers were American, many other countries also produced personal computer models that then vanished. At the end of the 1970s Soviet scientists at Kiev Institute of Cybernetics came up with a computer, MIR, one of whose versions consisted of a monitor and a rudimentary graphic interface to be managed with a light pen and designed for engineering calculations (Rabinovich, 2011). In the early 1960s in Poland, scientist Jacek Karpiński created a small computer, K-202, together with a British firm, of which only 40 were made and that were never truly released on the market (Targowski, 2016, pp. 207-210). A better known personal computer was the French Micral, credited with being the first computer to be equipped with a microprocessor and sold ready assembled and ready to use but with neither keyboard nor screen. Micral was not adopted beyond the industrial applications market because its creators marketed it mainly as a further form of the office mini-computer rather than the progenitor of a new generation of devices (Mounier-Kuhn, 1994).

In fact, while these first prototypes were a new development compared to mainframes and digital office calculators, they were not presented as devices designed for novel uses and especially for a mass market but as mainly professional or scientific applications. The persistence of an "old" dominant technological frame as the inspiration for the developers of these early "failed" personal computers was thus one of the reasons for their lack of commercial and social success.

Of the range of attempts with which 1970s personal computer history is so replete, a place of honor goes to the Xerox Alto terminal created in 1973 by US company Xerox. Several thousand were made of this model, most of which were used in the Xerox plant itself and other American campuses linked to the firm, known prior to this for photocopier making–as we saw in relation to calculators, the core business of many of the earliest digital media producers was in other media and non-media sectors leading to a sort of *intermediality* (see Box 5.1) or inter-technological interest between old and new media, analog and digital. Xerox Alto was a terminal rather than a PC, i.e. it did not perform programs independently but used the calculation capabilities of a central server. While it was not a full-blown PC, Xerox Alto did bring in two innovations that were of fundamental importance later to the success of modern personal computers although these found no applications for at least a decade. These were the *mouse* and a *graphic user interface* (GUI) managing the computer's functions based on the desktop metaphor, all of which were factors in the success of the IBM, Apple and Microsoft computers of the 1980s onwards.

Figure 2.3 A MITS Altair 8800, released between the end of 1974 and the spring of 1975. It was the first personal computer based on an Intel 8080 micro-processor available on the market

Source: Photo and courtesy by Matthew Ratzloff, taken at the Living Computers Museum in Seattle, Washington

A further important PC, Altair 8800 (see Figure 2.3), appeared on the market in spring 1975 as an affordable computer for assembly, first targeting electronics hobby enthusiasts through specialist journal advertizing. This computer was sold by correspondence as an assembly kit at the affordable price of around $400 (around $1,800 in today's money). Altair's special feature was that it consisted of a "box" containing its principal components but had no screen or keyboard or, at least initially, even an operating system or a machine language of reference and was based on the idea that it was to be the hobbyists themselves who would create the necessary software and applications. It was in fact precisely the absence of essential functioning components that made Altair so attractive to so many of the young IT hobbyists, enthusiasts and hackers in the mid 1970s, who vied to come up with solutions to fill in these gaps. A group of Kansas City enthusiasts found a way to save programs inserted into Altair using audio tapes as support, thus opening the way to the use of this analog audio format as a tool for archiving digital data (Ceruzzi, 2003, p. 213). Then in 1975, two young engineering students, Bill Gates and Paul Allen, developed their first software, Microsoft Basic language, precisely for Altair, allowing them to launch a small firm focusing exclusively on software design. It was an innovative idea because at the time the truly profitable IT sector was held to be the manufacturing of the machines themselves while software was considered an accessory or an additional service to be offered free-of-charge with the computers themselves (Freiberger & Swaine, 2000, p. 55 onwards).

By the mid 1970s, then, the main technologies that were to contribute to personal computer development in later years were already available: microprocessor, mouse, graphic interface and the programming language required to make individual machines work. Moreover, the IT industry could boast of firms—such as IBM, Hewlett Packard and NEC—capable of making large-scale investments in the market for a potential new personal computer designed for ordinary people rather than offices. But one essential ingredient in personal computer popularization was still missing: a cultural vision of its potential social role or, in other words, a new technological frame capable of supporting its creation and popularization. As we will see, the emergence of this new technological frame was triggered at the crossroads between previously distinct social spheres: IT enthusiasts, the hippy counter-culture and the civil rights movement (Turner, 2006). The success of personal computers was due as much to the counter-culture vision of a new social role for computers as it was to specifically technical innovations because the former contributed to generating new expectations, which were very different from the established visions shared among the IT industry of that time. This is a further proof of the fact that all new technologies are profoundly dependent on the social expectations and cultural constructions, which nurture their creation and popularization.

The Birth of the PC: Hacking, Amateurs and Counter-Culture

The influence of hobbyists and enthusiasts on the development of technologies destined for mass use is not a novel phenomenon and neither is it limited to the case of the PC. As various historians of technology have highlighted, in the twentieth century hobby culture has played an important role in the development of a range of devices, such as amateur hams for wireless telegraphs and radio in the 1920s and 1930s (Haring, 2008) or musical synthesizers in the 1970s (Pinch & Trocco, 2002). Before the personal computer, hobbyists and hacker culture had already exerted direct influence when adaptations and modifications to computers had been experimented with in the mid 1960s (Gotkin, 2014), especially at MIT in Boston, where the early *hacking ethic* began to take shape, a first step towards subtracting computers from governmental and bureaucratic control (Levy, 1984).

The best known and most influential group of hobbyists in the history of the personal computer was probably the Homebrew Computer Club based in Palo

Alto, a town in the southern part of San Francisco Bay. Young enthusiasts and hobbyists influenced by libertarian political ideas met at the club on a weekly basis and had fun assembling and dismantling calculators and computers (Levy, 1984, p. 153 onwards). The Club's inspiration was the idea that people should be able to build and use computers on their own without the limitations and costs imposed by large firms like IBM and Hewlett Packard, thus translating the cultural and political ideas behind the civil rights movements, then underway in many countries, into technological terms.

If the idealism and culture embodied by the goal of freeing computers from the grip of the bureaucracy and the large corporations was undoubtedly common to the first computer enthusiasts, this was also partly due to the fact that from the 1970s onwards San Francisco Bay was one of the epicenters of the US civil rights movement and youth counter-culture. It was at the University of California in Berkeley, a few kilometers east of San Francisco, that the Free speech movement was launched in 1964, the first student movement to place the issue of freedom of political expression center stage. Those taking part included engineering student Lee Felsenstein, later one of the leading lights of the Homebrew Computer Club and the man who, in 1973, set up Computer Memory at Berkeley, a project based on a telematic system (technically developed on the time-sharing model) aiming to share "alternative" news and information and probably the first application of computer networks outside the office and government agency context (Ryan, 2010, p. 56). In these same years, once again in San Francisco Bay in the Stanford town area, writer Ken Kesey and psychologist Timothy Leary also began collective experiments with hallucinogenic substance LSD to the rhythms of psychedelic band The Grateful Dead contributing to widening the perspectives of computer activists and enthusiasts (see Markoff, 2005).

Without an understanding of this socio-cultural backdrop it is difficult to make sense of the fact that it was precisely in San Francisco that an alternative technological frame grew out of the personal computer's social role, a new perspective that laid the foundations for the creation of the first computer for ordinary people. On one hand, in fact, personal computing required a new vision of the computer itself, intended not as a calculating machine, but as a personal communication media channeling content of interest to ordinary people. On the other, the San Francisco Bay counter-culture was especially capable of shaping a vision of the computer in opposition and alternative to governmental authority and the large computer corporations. This vision became a reference for other counter-cultural movements in different countries around the world and, ultimately, shaped many of the mythologies of cyber-culture that spread in the years to come.

Two mythological players in the construction of the personal computer were Steve Jobs and Steve Wozniak, both isolated from and marginal to the IT industry of the day, but at the same time, part of the early 1970s Californian counter-cultural scene. The first activity of the two within the IT world was as hackers, initially building and selling devices called *blue boxes* capable of hacking the telephone network to make free long-distance telephone calls invented by one of hacker culture's legends, Capitan Crunch (Thomas, 2002, p. 18; see also Chapter 3). Jobs and Wozniak were also a frequent presence at the Homebrew Computer Club where they made their first public demonstrations of their personal computer prototypes in July 1976. In contrast to other enthusiasts, who were more interested in collective experimentation than exploiting their passion commercially, they decided to found their own firm, calling it Apple and setting to work on building their computer model, Apple I, whose enclosure was an artisanal box made in wood by hand in a small garage. A little over 200 of these were built and they were sold at a price of $666.66. Thanks to the visibility generated by Apple I within the amateur world, Jobs

Figure 2.4 The advertisement used in 1977 to present Apple II, one of the first personal computers sold to be used at home by ordinary people

and Wozniak made contact with an investor who pumped $250,000 into the production of a second personal computer, Apple II, in 1977 this time for a mass market. Apple II shot to the attention of media, investors and a public opinion increasingly infatuated with IT.

It is interesting to note that the great computer firms of the day, used to selling ultra-expensive devices to governments and multinational companies, considered the development of a new mass market based on computers for the family and the home to be unrealistic. It is well-known that before founding Apple in 1976 Steve Wozniak had gone to see his former part-time employers at Hewlett Packard to discuss the idea (in fact HP owned the rights to the idea under the employment contract signed by Wozniak himself at the time). The company's management turned down the proposal, citing technical issues and the absence of a market for home computers as their reasons (Wozniak & Smiths, 2007, chap. 12). In the same year DEC's—a large company known for having successfully ridden the wave of the shift from mainframes to mini-computers *only* as large as a wardrobe—president stated that he saw no reason to believe that individuals would want to own home computers (Gelenter, 1998, p. 61). These two stories translate in practical terms into what Clayton Cristensen (1997) has referred to as the *innovator's dilemma*, namely the reluctance of large companies with a dominant position in a given market to support technologies, which could revolutionize their own sectors and thus favor the entry of new rival firms. The entire history of digital media, like media history in general, is littered with refusals to adopt new technologies and later on in the book we will also look at AT&T's pessimism in relation to the future of mobile phones and internet and its reluctance to invest in these communication technologies in their early stages.

If the large IT corporations remained skeptical and aloof in these years, it was not only Apple but other small companies as well who attempted to invest in the embryonic personal computer market. In addition to Apple II, at least two other personal computers entered the market in 1977 with the goal of gaining entry to family homes: Commodore's PET, coming from what was then a pocket calculator firm, and TRS-80, sold by consumer electronics firm Tandy as an assembly kit for hobbyists. It is worth stressing that none of these first three personal computers marketed in 1977 was produced by one of the great IT companies that had dominated the profitable mainframe and office computer markets. Although these firms had the necessary resources and skills in the processor and calculator fields, their technological frame made them completely unsuited to taking the potential of personal computers for family and ordinary use on board.

PCs Become Consumer Goods

The next steps in the popularization of personal computers were, on the one hand, greater ease of use and their definitive transformation from work tool to consumer object destined for a non-specialist user and, on the other, increased social appeal, i.e. the process of transforming them into desirable, fashionable objects. Let us consider these two issues carefully.

A fundamentally important factor making computers simpler was software and operational systems industry developments making them usable to non-IT experts. If mainframes were the preserve of highly qualified scientists and technicians, the first personal computers such as Altair and Apple II were only a partial step forward in terms of simplification and accessibility to those not fluent in software language, first and foremost because interacting with these computers required knowing how to put together complex code strings. For PCs to fully become mass consumer items an easy, intuitive solution was required enabling end users to dialogue with these machines in a simpler way. Such a solution emerged in 1984 when Apple released the model named Macintosh onto the market, the first personal computer designed for mass use to be managed with a GUI, a graphic user interface. The latter enabled PCs to be managed moving a cursor with a mouse in a virtual desk (the desktop) and so files became grouped together in a straightforward and intuitive way (in folders). As we have seen, this was not an entirely innovative solution as Apple had taken both GUI and mouse from the Xerox archives, which the latter already used for its Xerox Alto in 1973 (Hiltzik, 2000, p. 329 onwards). After its 1973 Xerox Alto, Xerox did not entirely abandon the idea, launching a new terminal model in 1981 based on a desktop interface designed exclusively for office use, Xerox Star, which, however, turned out to be extremely complex and costly and thus joined an already long list of commercial IT failures. Apple itself had brought out a further computer model called Lisa a year earlier, in 1983, once again based on a graphic interface but in this case with limited commercial success. The story of the introduction of GUIs–still used today in a form that is only a minor evolution from the first version presented by Apple–is an interesting case in point of the way innovations are frequently non-linear, tortuous processes and the extent to which the ability to align several already existing elements in the right way and sell a product frequently plays a determinant role in the success of new technologies on the consumer market.

A second factor required for personal computers to succeed was their transformation into socially appealing objects, i.e. attractive consumer products for a consumer society increasingly influenced by TV advertising and popular culture. The press, advertising and also films undoubtedly contributed to modifying public perceptions of personal computers. In 1983, for example, the

Figure 2.5 The cover of the first 1983 issue of *Time*, featuring the computer as "Person of the Year": the first time this title was conferred to a non-human as the "Machine of the Year"

US weekly *Time* fomented great interest in computers, devoting its traditional "Person of the Year" cover award to the personal computer (see Figure 2.5), forecasting that "in the fairly near future, home computers will be as common-place as TV sets or dishwashers" (Friedrich, 1983).

The success of the first Macintosh was not purely a matter of its technical innovations but also of the huge marketing campaign that developed around this model, especially with one of the best known and most expensive TV ads of the day and one that is still remembered to this day as a key moment in the history of advertising (Scott, 1991; Friedman, 2005). This TV ad was broadcast just once, on January 22, 1984 during a Super Bowl advertisement break, the most popular TV program in the US. Entitled *1984* the ad echoed George Orwell's famous novel and was filmed by director Ridley Scott, following on from his recent success with the 1982 sci-fi movie *Blade Runner*. The ad showed images of a shadowy, threatening Big Brother symbolizing IBM, then Apple's main rival. In the ad, Big Brother-IBM is routed by a multi-colored and dynamic female athlete in a sport hammer throw (indirectly conjuring up the pending Los Angeles Olympic Games of the next summer). The ad's rhetoric made its own the innovative idea that the computer could be a tool for individual freedom and social growth, transforming this vision into a powerful marketing strategy

(Magaudda, 2015). It had a notable impact on both public and consumers and was an important factor in the computer's cultural perception redefinition process in the American society of the day and in its transformation into an attractive object of desire for an ever-wider consumer segment.

In the early 1980s, the computer's cultural transformation process was given a further boost by the popular media culture and films in particular. Concerning the collective imagination, up until then computers had been indissolubly linked with HAL 9000, the military computer that had played the villain in Stanley Kubrick's well-known film *2001. A Space Odyssey* (1968). From the first half of the 1980s onwards, not only were computers' appearances in starring roles in films multiplying but they began to be shown in alternative use scenarios, not simply in military or work contexts but also in scenes of everyday life or teenage experience. An emblematic example of this shift is *War Games* (1983), a film where a boy playing on his PC at home comes close to triggering a nuclear war between the USA and the USSR. A year later, in 1984, the comedy *Electric Dreams* featured a love triangle with a personal computer in the middle. A further contribution to the construction to a new vision about the computers was *Tron*, produced in 1982 by Disney, featuring a virtual reality scenario where a young video game programmer takes on a large software corporation. Thus, alongside a series of technical innovations and the introduction of new computers onto the mass consumer market, the dissemination of the first personal computers was also accompanied by a process of transformation in the cultural connotations associated with it in which both advertising and film played a significant part.

Both *War Games* and *Tron* highlighted clearly what was a further, determinant boost to the popularization of the first personal computers for private, home use, the video game world, popular since the early 1970s in the form of consoles for the exclusive use of video games. In actual fact, the history of video games dates back even further as the earliest such games came out in the mid 1960s when leisure use software designed for the great computers present in universities and institutions began to circulate. There is thus nothing random about the fact that the first known video game, *Spacewar* dating to 1962, reflected the space research and war context that was one of the main focuses of US government research in those years. Indeed, *Spacewar* was created at Boston's MIT by a team of researchers interested primarily in testing to their limits the new generation of minicomputers but with direct influence from the emerging hacker culture (Graetz, 1981). In 1972, a console designed specifically for video games was sold, Magnavox Odyssey, which became the first mass digital device to enter private homes, beating private computers to it by a few years. Not only were the original consoles the first digital computers to cross the threshold into private homes but they also opened the way to an intermedia convergence between video games, computers and TVs, which were initially popular terminals for some of the first consoles and PCs.

From the mid 1970s onwards, game consoles were all the rage in the United States and a small but dynamic industry specializing in both devices and game software programming was dominated by Atari, set up in 1972 (Kirriemuir, 2006). But the latter lost control of the sector in 1983 when the US video games industry collapsed and this event marked a shift in the video games industry heartland from the USA to Japan (Montfort & Bogost, 2009). Japan has remained the leading player ever since thanks above all to Nintendo but subsequently opened the way to a globalization of the gaming industry via the emergence of small independent firms scattered across a number of countries such as Finland, Lebanon and Scotland (Wolf, 2015).

As Leslie Haddon (1988) has noted, in the British context, in the early 1980s the teenage passion for video games gave the popularization of some of the earliest computers such as Sinclair ZX81 and Commodore 64 a massive boost. In these same years, however, one of the limits to the vision of computers intended as game machines emerged: the fact that it hinged on a limited circle of consumers—generally young, teenage and male—and furthermore projected an idea of personal computers as mainly frivolous and fun focused.

In the mid 1980s a further event marked the fate of the personal computer sector for decades to come: the emergence of the Microsoft operating system called Windows. In contrast to Apple whose sales strategy had revolved around hard and software integration, Microsoft had decided to focus exclusively on computer program creation in an approach that Gates and Allen had adopted as early as 1975, when they supplied a base functioning language for Altair 8800. These two young engineers were convinced, in fact, of an idea that was novel and innovative in its day, namely that to make headway in a computer industry, then dominated by IBM, what was needed was to produce software rather than actual machines. In those years, making a profit from software sales was at least as alien to the sector's business practices as the idea of developing a new computer market for families had once been to mainframe manufacturers (Zachary, 1994). By contrast Bill Gates was convinced of the idea's potential and had begun a battle for safeguards on software copyright some time earlier. As far back as 1976, in a letter addressed to the Homebrew Computer Club, Gates had advised hobbyists and enthusiasts to pay for and not simply copy the software he had written for Altair with the rhetorical question: "Hardware must be paid for but software is something to share. Who cares if the people who worked on it get paid? Is this fair?" (quoted in Johns, 2009, p. 483).

Thanks, then, to the experience derived from the language created for Altair (incidentally modelled on yet another language, which had circulated openly in the hacker community since the 1960s) in 1980 Gates and Allen developed a first

Box 2.4 Documents

Italo Calvino, *On Software and Hardware* (1988)

In the 1980s, computer and digital technology themes made an appearance in public debates and in the literary field, too. The brief excerpt is one of the lectures Italian writer Italo Calvino was scheduled to deliver at Harvard University in 1985 but he died before he could do so, in September that year. Here Calvino sets out the relationship between lightness, software and hardware in literary terms and, more generally, shows us how a literary work can constitute an important historical source for an understanding of media's socio-cultural history, both digital and otherwise.

> Then we have computer science. It is true that software cannot exercise its powers of lightness except through the weight of hardware. But it is software that gives the orders, acting on the outside world and on machines that exist only as functions of software and evolve so that they can work out ever more complex programs. The second industrial revolution, unlike the first, does not present us with such crushing images as rolling mills and molten steel, but with "bits" in a flow of information traveling along circuits in the form of electronic impulses. The iron machines still exist, but they obey the orders of weightless bits. Is it legitimate to turn to scientific discourse to find an image of the world that suits my view? If what I am attempting here attracts me, it is because I feel it might connect with a very old thread in the history of poetry.
>
> Source: Calvino, I. (1988). *Six Memos for the Next Millennium.* Cambridge, MA: Harvard University Press, p. 8.

operating system for personal computers called Xenix, on this occasion too adapting a further pre-existing system, Unix, created around ten years earlier in the Bell laboratories. A decisive moment in Microsoft's history took place in 1981 when the company introduced MS-DOS, a new operating system designed to be installed on all IBM personal computers and for which IBM itself agreed to pay Microsoft a percentage on its computer sales. An interesting feature of this agreement between IBM and Microsoft relates to the fact that the latter was left free to sell its operating system to other computer manufacturers too, a clause IBM accepted in the mistaken belief that no-one would ever make a profit distributing software alone. Thus, when other companies began making personal computers with technical architectures similar to those of IBM (the so-called

IBM PC compatible) these, too, adopted MS-DOS as their reference operating systems and were happy to pay Microsoft a small percentage for software supplies. This agreement laid the foundations for Microsoft's domination of the global personal computer market in the three decades that followed: a great many hardware machine producers that functioned, however, thanks to a *single* operating system sold by Microsoft, which thus practically acquired a monopoly of the personal computer sector (Wallace & Erickson, 1992).

In 1985, a year after the Apple Macintosh came out, Microsoft introduced the first version of its Windows operating system borrowing its graphic interface, mouse and desktop metaphor from Macintosh. It was a highly-simplified operating system, especially when compared to today's. For example, only one program could be used at a time and the system had in any case to be launched using brief text commands, which required the use of MS-DOS language. From the second half of the 1980s onwards, Microsoft reinforced its dominant position in the personal computer world with dedicated software for specific activities, too. In 1988, it created a "package" called Works and then proposed an even more complete program in 1990 calling it Office. These packages contained not only the Word word-processing program (an initial version of which was created in 1983 and very soon became a *killer application*) but also Excel calculation sheets, in 1985, and the PowerPoint presentation program launched in 1987 (Campbell-Kelly, 2003, p. 253 onwards). By renaming its package Office in 1990, the interpretative framework, which Microsoft was appropriating, was twofold: on the one hand supplying a software package, which allowed computers to carry out the normal office functions performed by typewriters (and thus aiming to replace them) and on the other, to maintain some sort of familiarity, including metaphorically, with the objects normally found in offices and homes (desks, files, bins, etc.). It was thus a way of translating what had been one of the most complex and alien languages to most people—programming code—into iconic and user-friendly language.

The next step in simplification for non-expert users took place in 1995 with Windows 95, which finally no longer required the use of MS-DOS text codes for launch and represented a significant step forward from its predecessors on a graphic level too. Made available precisely at the time when the internet was becoming popular, Windows 95 almost immediately integrated a browser program for surfing the Web, Internet Explorer, thus transforming personal computers based on Microsoft software into the main Web access points for millions of home users. Yet again, contributing to Windows 95's socio-cultural popularity was a huge advertising campaign where Microsoft invested around $300 million, placing software center-stage in an advertising strategy for the first time, while the OS's sounds were entrusted to famous musician Brian Eno, then one of the most popular composers of electronic ambient music.

With its operating system and office software Microsoft consolidated its IT sector leadership and had gained control of more than 90% of the global personal computer software market by the late 1990s. Contrary to IBM's forecasts—which had, and not by chance, used a mainframe technological framework in its reasoning—selling software turned out to be more profitable than selling actual computers. In many ways, the PC business had thus come to resemble certain old analog media sectors, with their rigid distinction between content production (vinyl records or TV programs for example) and hardware firms marketing machines capable of "reading" them (record players and TV sets).

Personal Computers Come of Age: Internet, Laptop and Linux

In the 1990s, personal computers achieved an extensive market in the majority of developed countries and were being made by a now mature industry. A sign of the maturity of the computer industry came with the first effects of globalization on the hardware industry, which had remained focused on the USA and to some degree Japan since its beginnings. One of the earliest consequences of globalization was thus that the manufacturing of PCs and some of their components began inexorably to move toward countries such as Taiwan, South Korea and China. The Taiwanese manufacturers, led by the Asus and Acer brands, played a central role in this shift, achieving 70% of world PC sales in 2004 (Dedrick & Kraemer, 2005) and Acer even achieved second ranking in global PC sales for a brief period in 2009. As we will see below, the most significant takeover occurred in 2005, when Chinese firm Lenovo bought up IBM's computer division thus becoming the top producer worldwide in the space of just a few years.

From the mid 1990s onwards personal computers began to definitively make their way into the majority of family homes especially in the US, Europe and the advanced economies of East Asia, thus bringing to fruition the seemingly futuristic forecast by *Time* just a decade earlier that personal computers would in the future be "as commonplace as TV sets or dishwashers". Seventy million computers were sold in 1996 doubling to 134 million in 2000 and doubling once again in 2007. In the year 2000, the average family access to personal computers in the world's principal countries was 45%, a figure that grew constantly to 59% in 2005 and 77% in 2012 (OECD, 2015). From the year 2000 onwards, even many countries that had been immune to computers in the previous decade—such as Russia, China and Brazil—saw use expand achieving figures of approximately 50% or more of families using these devices in the second decade of the new millennium. Nevertheless, more than in the case of the internet and especially of the mobile phone, marked differences remained in countries with strong economic and social inequalities. By 2005, in a country as populous as India, for example, only 2% of the population had a home computer and in South Africa–where Apartheid was coming to an end in 1991 and did not cancel out socio-economic differences–only 13% of the population had access to a computer (see extended data in the appendix, Table A.6). Obviously, the poorest part of the planet, Sub-Saharan Africa, was almost entirely excluded from the spread in computer use. Significant differences notwithstanding, in any event, with the onset of the new millennium personal computers became a stable presence in the lives of the majority of citizens in some way linked to globalization processes including, thanks to the dissemination of the internet and the importance of e-mail, for example, both New York brokers and sub-proletarian immigrants from underdeveloped countries, however great the differences.

As we will see in the next chapter, 1995 was a crucial year for the development and popularization of the internet and thus, from the mid 1990s onwards, PCs became increasingly synonymous with the internet with the latter starting to transform them both technically and in terms of the social role they began to play in people's every day and working routines. In the first place, the mid 1990s marked the beginning of a process where PCs became frequently more portable and suitable for use outside the home in line with the emergence of a social model based on what English cultural studies scholar Raymond Williams (1974) had coined *mobile privatization*, characteristic of post-Fordist societies (on this concept, see Box 4.5). The first portable computers were sold in the early 1980s but it was only in the decade that followed that certain functions identified with today's laptops emerged: limited weight and easy trans-portability, trackpad integrated into the keyboard and color screen large enough for them to aspire to substitute desktop models. It was also thanks to these innovations and cost reductions that laptops began to be bought not only by professionals but also by families and students in the early years of the new millennium and soon began to overtake desktop computers in annual sales figures, first in the US and then, from 2008 onwards, in the global market as a whole.

Culturally speaking an especially significant portable computer was Apple's 1999 iBook, whose success hinged on an aspect previously considered unimportant in the personal computer world: attractive appearance and design. Until then computers had generally been grey or black in a squared off shape with very limited aesthetic appeal. The new Apple portable computer had, by contrast, been designed by young designer John Ive who had also been responsible for its new 1998 desktop computer model, the iMac–the first colorful, oval-shaped computer encompassing all components and accessories including the speakers into a single object. In the years that followed, emulating Apple's example, other manufacturers began to offer consumers more eye-catching computers with the attractiveness factor emerging as a centrally important dimension in tablet and smartphone evolution too (see Chapter 4).

In the latter half of the 1990s, at least one new feature contributed to supplementing the social implications of personal computers adding a more directly political dimension to its social use and role. Microsoft's *de facto* software monopoly raised fears and political unease, which promoted, among other things, an EU inquiry into its dominant position (Case no. COMP/C-3/37.792), which began in 2000 and ended with two major rulings in 2004 and 2008 that ordered this Seattle-based firm to pay 500 and 900 million Euros respectively for its anti-trust rule violations. This negative climate for the company and the increasing political relevance of computer use contributed to the dissemination of an alternative operating system called Linux based on the *open software* philosophy, a product of the collective work of the programmers and activists who had founded the *free software movement* in the years prior to this (Kelty, 2008, p. 93 onwards).

The movement was born in 1983 when the GNU (*GNU is Not Unix*) project was founded at Boston's MIT by programmer and software activist Richard Stallman, with the goal of creating an operating system similar to the already common Unix but that was not "owned" and thus could legally be modified, adapted and transformed by users (Williams, 2002). The philosophical origins of the free software concept were rooted in the Californian hacker milieu, which had contributed to the creation of the first personal computers but it was not until the early 1990s that an open operating system became available to all. Beginning in 1990, an engineering student from Finland, Linus Torvald, together with other IT activists contributed to the creation of this new free operating system capable of ongoing user improvement and called Linux (Himanen, 2001; Moody, 2001). While Linux use in personal computers has never reached significant levels—stabilizing at 1-2% of total individual computer installations—it has been successfully re-adapted to a range of different applications, ranging from *supercomputers* (computers with huge calculation capacities, a sector that Linux has taken by storm) to portable devices and smartphones (one of the most common systems, Android, was developed using Linux as its base platform, see Chapter 4). In addition to its effective dissemination, over the years Linux has taken on an important symbolic role with direct political implications of computers and network use. Think of the crucial role Linux had in boosting the open software and more recently open culture movement's visibility in a multiplicity of social fields ranging from design to the world of scientific research as well as making it one of the most significant metaphors to emerge from the digitization galaxy that later expanded into the rest of society (Delfanti, 2013; Söderberg, 2015).

2.5 The Post-PC Age

The fourth and last era in the computer's history, borrowing a commonly used label in IT marketing, might be called the *post-PC age*, a phase in which personal computers have lost their primary-digital-tool-for-ordinary-people hegemony and a multiplicity of (mainly mobile and Web-connected) digital devices have emerged as major digital devices for an increasing set of everyday activities.

The year 2001 was a symbolic breakwater in this transformation process. On the one hand, 2001 was a very negative year for the personal computer industry. For the first time since the 1970s world computer sales slowed down, dropping from 134 to 128 million units sold over the course of the year. It was partly the effect on the sector of the bursting of the so-called *dotcom bubble* around the dissemination of the Web and the dotcom firms in a sudden, radical crash in the early years of the new millennium (Doms, 2004; see also Chapter 3). From the start of this crisis in the noughties, a number of frequently-failed attempts were made to offer consumers alternatives to the by then prosaic personal computer. In 2001, for example, Microsoft brought out the first tablet computer, a device enabling users to write on the screen with a pen but this soon emerged as a commercial flop. This was in part due to the fact that Microsoft did not present this device as a radical departure from the computer (it had, for example, the same operating system as a desktop) but rather limited itself to a conservative traditional portable computer framework with added touch screen functions. A further two models were essentially influenced by a new digital development paradigm popularized from the early noughties onwards and still dominant—mobile use. Canadian company Rim, initially active in the pager sector, introduced the BlackBerry in 2003, a mobile telephone equipped with an integrated keyboard and an e-mail function. Palm, a US leading electronic agenda company, launched a new type of telephone in 2005, which combined telephone functions with the functions and calculation power of an electronic agenda. In these years, a range of firms making electronic agendas adopted a Microsoft software produced from the year 2000 onwards, initially for electronic agendas, with which it hoped to emulate the domination it had achieved in the personal computer sector. However, neither Rim, Palm nor Microsoft succeeded in taking up the mobile device gauntlet thrown down in the second half of the noughties by the manufacturers of two firms, once again from the computer and internet world: on the one hand the iPhone smartphone made by Apple in 2007 and, on the other, the Android operating system (based as we have seen earlier on the Linux OS) developed by Google in 2008 to be used by mobile devices made by other brands.

A further attempt, in 2007, to go beyond the traditional PC format was a conservative commercial strategy aimed at revitalizing the sector with small, affordable and low performance laptops, the outcome of the commercial strategies of mainly Taiwanese PC companies and especially Acer, whose activities had expanded in the 1990s–the so-called netbooks. In the 2008-2009 two-year period, in fact, netbooks achieved a 20% share of the portable market as a whole and Acer, thanks precisely to this short-lived success, shot to second ranking status in the PC manufacturing world in 2009. It was, however, a fleeting trend that was superseded by the arrival on the market of a new generation of tablets. Once again it is evident that digital device innovation is a trial and error process consisting of fleeting successes and sudden market changes of direction.

Of the great many companies engaged in this fresh market challenge it is Apple that has seemed to be coming out on top once again in recent years as

---

Box 2.5 Documents

Steve Jobs, *Digital Lifestyle* (2001)

Steve Jobs envisaged a new perspective on personal computers in 2001 at a time at which the industry was pondering decreasing global personal computer sales. In that year, Jobs unveiled Apple's Digital Hub Strategy, which was connected to the imminent introduction of the iPod, the very first of Apple's portable ecosystem devices. Steve Jobs' words make it clear that his computer strategy and the release of the iPod were part of a wider social and cultural vision of the role of digital media in peoples' everyday lives: the so-called "new digital lifestyle".

> We are living in a new digital lifestyle with an explosion of digital devices. It's huge. And we believe the PC, or more importantly the Mac, can become the digital hub of our new emerging digital lifestyle, with the ability to add tremendous value to these other digital devices. And we saw that the benefit here was a combination of a bunch of things. It was hardware, the computer and other hardware, the operating system, the application, the Internet, and marketing to create this solution. So, we thought this was very important and it took all these components and we realized that Apple is uniquely suited to do this because we're the last company in this business that has all these components under one roof. We think it's a unique strength. And we discovered this with iMovie 2, that it could make a digital device called the camcorder worth 10x as much. It's 10x more valuable to you.
>
> Source: Steve Jobs, January 9, 2001, *Speech at the Macworld Expo*, San Francisco, CA

the company whose brainchild personal computers were and which played such an important part in making a consumer item of them. In the 1980s, Apple contributed to transforming the computer's cultural role within families not simply with its new look models but also with its innovative vision of these media in the home context. In January 2001, on the occasion of one of his customary product presentations, Steve Jobs told the story of Apple's change of direction on computers describing the PC's shift from productivity tool to veritable digital lifestyle building icon. In this approach computers were no longer to be seen as free-standing, self-sufficient tools but rather management centers—hubs—linking together an increasing set of new personal digital devices that had shot onto the scene in these years such as camcorders, MP3 players and cameras (see Box 2.5). The 2001 launch of a new music reader called iPod (see Chapter 5) was part of this same digital life style building strategy.

In 2007, this California-based firm introduced what was then presented as a hybrid between mobile phones and iPods calling it the iPhone. Here we will limit ourselves to noting that it was important for Apple, also and above all, because it supplied it with a sales model, which it returned to in 2010 with its new iPad tablet. In contrast to the tablets created by Microsoft at the beginning of the decade, the iPad was explicitly marketed as an entirely novel, "revolutionary" device destined to substitute PCs in certain central digital communication activities such as surfing the Web or watching films. It was a computer-smartphone hybrid, which achieved vast success because it also conjured up the same fashion and lifestyle trends that had been such a feature of iPods and iPhones (Magaudda, 2015). With this new device—rapidly brought out in similar format by its main market competitors including the Korean Samsung—the evolution of personal computers into alternative tools based primarily on the mobile, individual use model began to take concrete shape.

For all these reasons, over the second decade of the new millennium the personal computer market has begun showing signs of crisis above all in several of its heartlands. In Sweden, for example, PC home penetration started to drop, decreasing from a peak of 92.3% in 2012 to 88.3% in 2015, as well as in South Korea, where PC penetration declined from 82.3% in 2012 to 77,1% in 2015, while in Japan the decreasing has been even more visible, going from 87.2% in 2009 to 79,7% in 2015 (Source: ITU; see also data appendix, see Table A.6). In other countries where computers were still not yet as commonplace as TVs, PC take-up stabilized. This was the case for both still-developing countries, fulcrums of political unrest such as Turkey—where computer home penetration rates have remained stable over the decade at around 50%—and economically and politically "mature" countries such as France where computer take-up has remained more or less constant at around 80% (OECD, 2015). Thus, although personal computer take-up by the various countries of the world appears stratified and diversified, the last decade effectively seems to highlight a tendency to saturation in the traditional PC market in favor of the dissemination of other kinds of devices. While global PC sales fell 23% from 2012 to 2016, smartphone sales increased in the same period by 109% (see data appendix). As we will see in greater depth in Chapter 4, mobile networks and smartphones would seem to lend themselves better than personal computers to the needs of many African, Asian and South American countries where traditional infrastructure is lacking and in which individual smartphone use has much more potential, for example, than collective public PC use.

The preference for smartphones in large areas of the so-called Global South offers an opportunity to open up linear visions of innovation, for which underdeveloped countries should adopt the same digital technologies already common in Western ones. In the early noughties, in fact, the issue of the so-called digital divide (i.e. the effects of inequalities in PC and internet use between developed countries and other regions of the world—see Box 3.4 on the theme of the internet digital divide) was brought to the public attention. In order to take on this problem, in 2005 the founder of MIT's Media Lab, Nicholas Negroponte, launched a non-profit project called One Laptop per Child (OLPC) whose objective was to disseminate an affordable laptop in Africa at an initial cost of $100 (at the time less than a twentieth of the going price, but which had increased to $399 by the time the project launched). Although around 3 million of these computers were distributed between 2007 and 2015, the project had a limited impact and was criticized for a variety of reasons. In particular critics emphasized that the idea of resolving the problems of countries as complex as the African nations (where access to drinking water and electricity, for example, remain more serious issues) by transferring a technology calibrated to the post-Fordist work demands of developed countries was a characteristically colonialist and Western-centric error (Fouché, 2012).

The transformations and contradictions generated by globalization in the post-PC age also translated into a change in the economic and productivity paradigms that gravitated around these devices. Nothing epitomized the transformation of the political geography of the computer industry better than the 2005 acquisition by Chinese firm Lenovo of the hardware division of the historic US firm, IBM, by then synonymous with computers themselves. Lenovo was founded in China in 1984 and initially focused on a technological sector, which was on the increase in China, the TV sector, specializing subsequently in *chinesifying* Western IBM computers and programming them for use with Chinese characters. In 1996, Lenovo became the main producer of computers for the domestic Chinese market and, in 2002, decided to expand internationally taking its current name and buying up the IBM computer division for $1.25 billion (together with $0.5 billion of debts generated in the meantime by sector crisis). In part thanks to this acquisition and in part to growth in the Chinese domestic market (where the number of PCs sold per year went from 20 million in 2005 to 70 million by 2012), Lenovo became the primary worldwide personal computer manufacturer in 2013. Thus, as we will see in our chapters on the internet and mobile telephones, the computer's historical trajectory highlights a recent tendency to de-Westernize the production and consumption of digital media. The parts of the world that are growing today—and will probably continue to do so tomorrow—are thus not those which historically dominated the analog media markets of the twentieth century.

However, the current post-PC era implies more than a general end to the personal computer's main digital device hegemony. More recent trends in the obsolescence of the personal computer pass through a series of concepts, definitions and labels, which blend innovation rhetoric, marketing definitions and actual transformations in people's everyday lives. One of the concepts that have catalyzed interest around the computer's new lifespan scenarios is the notion of *ubiquitous computing*, i.e. the idea according to which computers are increasingly pervasive and no longer dependent on a single device that—as one of this sector's early 1990s founders wrote—is destined to "disappear. They weave themselves into the fabric of everyday life until they are indistinguishable from it" (Weiser, 1991, p. 78). If on the one hand it is true that our relationship with computers today is profoundly different from that of the 1990s and that our use of them is increasingly interwoven into our daily lives, as Dourish and Bell (2011) have argued, the idea of ubiquitous computing perfectly integrated into our lives is more a myth capable of feeding the digital ideology than an actual outcome of computer evolution. In fact, while computers are more and more frequent, smaller and more habitually connected, a better definition of our experiences with them than "ubiquitous" or "seamless" would be inherently messy. Just think, for example, of the difficulties often experienced by users attempting to connect to public Wi-Fi networks or of the compatibility problems between different hardware manufacturers, OS versions and distribution platforms.

In any event the growing presence of different types of computers in our daily lives is also sustained by the success of forms of cloud computing, i.e. computing systems based on shared remote computer processing resources and data, made available to client computers and other devices. Undoubtedly, the growing number of cloud computing systems supported now by all the main digital service providers—from Apple to Google, Microsoft to Amazon—are an ever increasingly characteristic trait of our everyday use of computers, smartphones and other devices. The definition of "cloud computing" is a bearer of a metaphorical implication that supports the development of the services offered by these large corporations whose marketing strategies rely on low-impact rhetoric, the availability of our data wherever we are and the belief that we are "immersed" in an integrated data, problem-free environment (Peters, 2015, p. 332). This too is a partial truth because, as Starosielski (2015), for example, has argued, the apparently low impact and immaterial cloud system is actually based on cable and server infrastructures, which are anything but low impact and even less environmentally friendly. The cloud rhetoric, then, also shores up our adhesion to a specific model of computer and device use, which is increasingly dependent on the integrated services offered by the digital multinationals frequently in exchange for its clients' data.

Thus, while it is true that computers have a golden future ahead of them, this future is still to be written and will certainly to some extent depend on the technological frames, innovation myths and rhetoric that have accompanied computers in all their forms to our own day.

LEARNING MATERIALS

Key Points to Focus On

- Four stages in the computer's development.
- The digital computer's historic mechanical origins.
- Democratic systems, the industrial revolution and social pressure to calculate.
- The role of women in computer history.
- The shaping of the computer as a tool for war and productivity.
- The cumulative innovations that lead to the creation of the personal computer.
- The differences between the mainframe and personal computer "technological frames".
- Changes in social perception of computers and counter-cultural views on its social role.
- The PC's transformation into a consumer item promoted through marketing and advertising.
- The role played by software and operating system development.
- The role of the internet in familiarizing PCs at the global level.
- The post PC age, the globalization of PC production and China's role.
- The end of the PC as the most popular digital device.
- The myth of ubiquitous computing.

Questions to Answer

- Explain why the computer was seen in negative terms after the Second World War, especially with relation to the ideas of Lewis Mumford (see Box 2.1).
- What was the hippy movement's main contribution to the social shaping of the personal computer?
- In what sense was the personal computer actually "personal", compared to previous generation of computers?
- Explain the consequences of the globalization process on the computer industry and the adoption of these devices in underdeveloped countries.
- In what sense is the idea of ubiquitous computing a myth?

A Song to Listen to and Discuss

In 1981, right at the moment that large scale commercialization of personal computers was beginning, German electronic band Kraftwerk released its album *Computer World*, the first popular music album devoted to the topic of the social rise of computers. Listen to the album and look up the lyrics of some of the songs contained in this album—for example *Computer Love*—and reflect on the themes emerging from these songs. In the light of this work and the other examples proposed in this chapter, try to explain the role popular cultural representations have played in computer history.

A Few Books for Further Study

Agar, J. (2003). *The Government Machine, A Revolutionary History of the Computer*. Cambridge, MA: The MIT Press.

Campbell-Kelly, M. (2003). *From Airline Reservations to Sonic the Hedgehog. A History of the Software Industry*. Cambridge, MA: MIT Press.

Ceruzzi, P. (2003). *A History of Modern Computing*. Cambridge, MA: MIT Press.

Friedman, T. (2005). *Electric Dreams: Computers in American Culture*. New York: New York University Press.

Lally, E. (2002). *At Home with Computers*. Oxford: Berg.

Kelty, C.M. (2008). *Two Bits: The Cultural Significance of Free Software*. Durham, NC: Duke University Press.

Turner, F. (2006). *From Counterculture to Cyberculture: Stewart Brand, the Whole Earth Network, and the Rise of Digital Utopianism*. Chicago, IL: University of Chicago Press.

----

3 The Internet

3.1 What We Mean by the *Internet*

The most all-encompassing of the many and controversial definitions of the internet is perhaps *network of networks* in accordance with the meaning first supplied in December 1974 in the *Specification of Internet Transmission Control Program* document on which TCP/IP protocol is based. But the internet's history began long before 1974, stretching at least as far back as the 1950s with the Cold War technological battles and to the 1960s with the creation of early computer networks and the American ARPANET project in particular. Over the decades, this network of networks has evolved and now expanded globally to such an extent as to be generally perceived as an enormous unitary and homogeneous system (which it actually isn't), a single network of computers and increasingly of other devices such as smartphones. There is nothing coincidental about the fact that a synonym of the internet in common parlance is precisely *the Net*. And even this is not entirely accurate. There are, for example, nets that permit communication within a firm (intranet) or between firms and suppliers-sellers (extranet), which are not part of the internet galaxy.

Therefore, the question "what is the internet?" is an entirely legitimate one. From a technological point of view, as we have already seen, it is a network that brings together a range of technologies—telecommunications and computers in particular. The internet is thus, first and foremost, a network linking millions of other mini networks across the globe. The network's technical infrastructure derives partly from the old telecommunications (and telephone networks in particular) and was partly created specifically to carry data using fiber optic, undersea cables and wireless technologies. All in all, the most interesting aspect is the fact that the internet brings non-homogeneous and diverse networks together and gets them interacting thanks to shared protocols, namely interaction languages and procedures allowing different hardware and software to be linked up. Second, the internet is also a network of computers that, despite being very different from one another, can interact without compatibility problems thanks precisely to the existence of this network.

This network of old and new nets and of computers is the internet's *infrastructural* and *material* dimension, a topic that is right at the heart of infrastructure studies and increasingly the subject of media studies debate (Parks & Starosielski, 2015). On the one hand, this means that the internet is a historically designed infrastructure: Bowker et al. (2010) have called this durable process as the "long now", a perspective looking at the formation of digital networks and infrastructures as a long process (lasting more than 200 years) against the short and often inaccurate time span of the "information revolution". On the other hand, as we have already noted in Chapters 1 and 2, the ethereal and immaterial cloud metaphor notwithstanding, the internet is actually made up, above all, of huge physical servers that require cooling space, undersea cables transporting the bulk of international data, and devices like computers or smartphones to surf contents, all tools that pollute considerably, contrary to the internet's "green" rhetoric.

The internet is, however, more than an infrastructure and a series of technologies. It is also a political object and a range of cultural meanings. Over the course of its history it has, for example, become replete with ambivalent political implications. Various world governments have interpreted the internet as a crucial resource both in the development of new forms of democracy or in controlling its citizens, as both a new socio-cultural space for communication and a place to be monitored and exploited to its own advantage, as both driving force indispensable to the economy of the future (frequently defined the IT or knowledge economy) and negotiating table between a small number of ultralarge corporations such as Google, Facebook and Amazon.

Internet is also a commercial and financial medium, in fact. Just think of the increase in economic importance of Net-based firms (which has sometimes even been overestimated prompting the bursting of a series of financial "bubbles") but also of the fact that the internet has recently been turned into a gigantic virtual shopping mall open 24 hours a day and just a click away from billions of clients. Furthermore, the internet is also a personal communication medium, a characteristic that is inherent to the whole of its history but has accentuated over recent decades. The–historically determined–"social" nature of the web has also contributed to the dissemination of new forms of human relationships activating virtual networks and interest communities made up of countless millions of people across the globe.

All these meanings have now become part of what we see as internet today, a medium that today almost half the earth's people consider part of their everyday lives. Slowly, over the course of the decades and with significant differences between the various parts of the world, this communication medium has moved to the heart of contemporary culture and is now dreamed of, contested and even claimed as a right in the half of the world where it has not yet penetrated.

This chapter is about the history of the internet from a global perspective and this is a challenging proposition for three fundamental reasons. Internet historiography is still embryonic and relatively little research work exists on which to base it—this is something that is probably going to change in the near future as the establishment of specific journals like *Internet Histories* testifies. The majority of the very few academic publications focuses on the evolution of the internet in one specific country, the United States of America—and this also makes sense because for much of its history the internet was primarily American and, even when emerging in other countries, the US was seen as the reference model. The very few non-American internet histories are almost all nationally based, recounting the internet's development in one specific country and mainly neglecting the trans-national dimension.

To reconstruct the history of the internet we have partially chosen, from the many potential options, James Curran's 2012 framework, which divided up the internet's development into five *formative influences*, each characterized by tensions between various relevant social groups. These social groups were able to introduce specific meanings to internet history in specific moments, creating military, scientific, counter-cultural, public service-related and private/commercial influences. Starting from the late 1950s and running through to the present day, these influences are not interpreted solely in diachronic and consecutive terms but as different dimensions, which have built up layer upon layer and continue to co-exist: for example, while military influence is no longer at the center of the internet's developments, some of the ideas that emerged in that period are still crucial to the structure of the contemporary internet and co-exist with other influences, which are more evident today (e.g. commercial or social influences). In other words, even if they are apparently no longer extant, its formative influences have played a determinant role in the internet's political, economic, technological and cultural development contributing to *co-building* some of the meanings that are still today at the heart of what we call the internet. In a word, history matters.

Nevertheless, this framework has three main flaws, which we will attempt to correct here. First, it is largely based on US internet history and, for this reason, we will expand it with examples of the evolution of the internet in other countries whose experiences enrich the original model. Second, Curran's model is mono-dimensional, presenting specific influences as the only ideas in a certain period. Nevertheless, there are also other (losing or winning) ideas that appeared at the same time and had partial influences on the way the internet was imagined. We will look at some of these non-dominant and not-so-influential influences too in order to analyze majority and minority internet ideas over history symmetrically. Finally, Curran's reconstruction does not take sufficient account of the internet's recent development and we will add an additional

Table 3.1 A summary of the 6 formative influences in the internet history

Formative influences	Time	Distinctive features
1. Military	Since 1960s	Internet mainly financed by military departments and seen as a strategic tool for defense.
2. Academic	Since 1960s	Internet as a network of computers mainly hosted by universities in order to improve scientific exchange between scholars.
3. Counter-cultural	Since 1970s	Internet seen as a household utility combining personal computers and telephone networks to be used by people to create alternative realities.
4. Public service	Since 1980s	Development of digital networks as an extension of telecom monopolies and CERN World Wide Web; internet seen as a repository of knowledge with civic relevance.
5. Commercial	Since mid-1990s	Internet as a marketplace, the internet bubble and its bursting, the contemporary dominion of US companies.
6. Social	Since mid-2000s	Web 2.0 and the rhetoric of participation; from freedom to political control; globalization of internet users.

"social" influence to Curran's five, in which many of the contemporary internet's contrasting tendencies originated.

3.2 The Military Influence

In October 1957, plum in the middle of the Cold War, the USSR launched its first artificial military satellite into orbit. Sputnik 1, as it came to be called, upset US public opinion and military circles because it showed that the Soviet block was technologically further ahead than had been believed. This prompted in February 1958 the American president Dwight Eisenhower to set up an agency in the Department of Defense–ARPA (Advanced Research Projects Agency)– whose purpose was to fund scientific research in the technological sphere which was, at the time, largely directed at extra-terrestrial space. The new department's first idea was, in fact, to develop a network of telecommunications satellites but, when a specific space study agency (called NASA) was set up at the Department of Defense, ARPA had to justify its own existence.

Computer scientist Joseph C.R. Licklider, hired by ARPA in 1962, came up with a bright idea: connecting computers up to one another into a network for the purposes of reciprocal information exchange (see Licklider & Taylor, 1968). As we saw in Chapter 2, at least until the 1970s computers remained costly, were used above all for military purposes and by research centers and were inactive for much of the time. To obviate this problem the time-sharing concept was introduced (see also Chapter 2). Time-sharing made single computers available to multiple users by means of linked terminals, each of which employed just a portion of a mainframe's total calculation capacity. The creation of a network of "temporary" users around a single super computer became so popular that it was soon one of the computer industry's most promising business sectors until the 1980s when it was obscured by the arrival of personal computers (Campbell-Kelly & Garcia-Swartz, 2008). This business developed primarily in the United States but it spread rapidly to other countries too (including the United Kingdom where the first non-American time-sharing system was set up in the late 1960s). Licklider's brainchild—soon re-named ARPANET—was approved by ARPA in 1963 and made the time-sharing logic the basis of a specific belief: connecting up a limited number of the agency's computers and those of other research agencies would enable researchers to communicate and share information thus increasing scientific work productivity (Hafner & Matthew, 1996).

One of the internet's *myths* is that this first network concept was conceived to defend the US against a potential Soviet nuclear threat. This legend originated from the overlapping of the ARPANET project with another idea, which was in fact prompted by political and strategic concerns and also emerged in the early 1960s in both the United States—where it was the work of Paul Baran, an engineer at the private Rand Corporation—and the United Kingdom independently, the latter thanks to the work of an IT division of the National Physical Laboratory (Russell, 2014). Two ideas that later became key characteristics of the internet did, in fact, emerge from the political-military context: Net structure and packet switching communication.

The former was the *distributed network* concept whose purpose was to ensure communication even in the event that a nuclear attack damaged some nodes, by adopting a new center-less network structure. This was achieved by linking up each and every communication node—i.e. the network's nerve centers into which its points flowed—to at least four other nodes using the neurons of the human brain as a model. This distributed and redundant structure meant that if one node were to be destroyed or damaged communication could continue on other routes (see Figure 3.1).

The second of these innovations related to the circulation of messages, which were no longer to travel as single information units from one node to another but broken up into a number of packages (hence the name *packet switching*) sent via diverse routes and reassembled only once they had reached their destinations. According to internet historian Johnny Ryan (2010), the historical sources

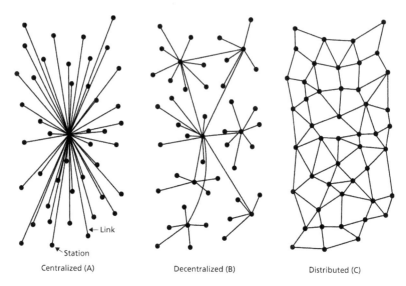

Figure 3.1 Centralized, decentralized and distributed networks according to Paul Baran

Source: Baran, 1964, p. 2, Courtesy of Rand Corporation

throw no light on the extent of Paul Baran of the Rand Corporation's influence on the ARPA project but packet switching and the distributed networking concepts remained distinct projects until early 1968 when they intersected to the benefit of both. Consequently, the ARPANET project's objectives shifted from a network designed primarily to increase research productivity to one facilitating military control and capable of resisting—by then—a potential Soviet nuclear attack (Edwards, 1996).

This first phase of the internet's history, characterized by American military interests and investment, is indispensable to an understanding of at least three influences that impacted on the internet's development over the years to come. In the first place, distributed networks became the theoretical, and mainly mythological, reference to how the internet networks should be built. In the popular imagination, moreover, distributed networking means horizontal networking in which all nodes (i.e. all users) are at the same level and thus have the same importance—it is thus a profoundly democratic network concept. In reality (as can clearly seen from Figure 3.2), ARPANET's architecture was not based on a distributed and redundant logic and also architectures of other internets were (and still are) more often similar to both traditional telecommunications and broadcasting networks, where more important nerve centers determine communication flows. In other words, the first influence of the military era is more symbolic than real one. A second military influence on the internet was ARPANET's flexibility and the idea of integrating different networks and computers in reciprocal dialogue. This concept is still today the core of the internet. Finally, packet switching has remained the main transfer method for data on the internet. In sum, the distributed and horizontal internet concept, as well as the dialogue between different calculation machines (and then growing numbers of other devices) based on packet switching are all influences—and what Richard Barbrook (2007) calls forms of imagination about the future internet—born in the military realm in the 1950s and 1960s and still shaping contemporary internet's ideology and narrative.

In the majority of countries, the early computer network development was stimulated by military investment and needs but could also take unexpected directions. Perhaps the most interesting case, in direct opposition to the US in the Cold War period, is the Soviet system (see Gerovitch, 2008; Peters, 2016b).

In the 1950s and 1960s, in the Soviet Union, three network projects that never came to fruition succeeded one another (Peters, 2016b, chap. 3): the 1959 Anatoly Kitov project, whose purpose was to build a civil use network based on the pre-existing military network; the 1962 Aleksandr Kharkevich project, whose objective was technological standardization and the unification of the country's various communication methods; and the third idea by N.I. Kovalev, again in the early 1960s, whose objective was to build a computer network for Soviet economic planning.

The most ambitious and best known of the Russian networks, however, was that formulated by the director of the Kiev Institute of Cybernetics, Viktor Glushkov and called All-State Automated System (in Russian OGAS). Developed in the 1960s and then progressively abandoned in the 1970s and 1980s, this project was as unsuccessful as its predecessors but was initially supported by certain political elements. Its objective was "to connect tens of thousands of computer centers and to manage and optimize in real time communications between hundreds of thousands of workers, factory managers, and regional and national administrators" (Peters, 2016b, p. 5). It was probably the most ambitious computer network project in the world at the time and was based on the idea—characteristic of the cybernetics' liberal vision of the day—that it would favor rational, even-handed, manageable and, last but not least, horizontal political and economic management and socio-cultural control of the country. All these projects were abortive, however, because they met with resistance from various social forces for diverse reasons. Soviet industrial managers and bureaucrats (for example, at the central statistics body and GOSPLAN, the state planning committee) feared that the new system might underscore their inefficiency and undermine their power. The project was also accused of draining a huge quantity of funds (the plan was not, in fact, for a gradual growth in the network but its wholesale construction) then used for economic reforms in favor of a system whose efficiency remained to be tested. Even Western liberal reformers interpreted this Soviet IT network as a way of perpetuating the previous power hierarchy and an attempt to recentralize economic control. For all these reasons, Soviet internet construction projects failed and remained on paper until the 1990s at the earliest when a network was developed by private enterprise in the new Russia, emerging in the wake of the collapse of the Soviet Union.

The Russian case is exemplary for at least three reasons. In the first place, as we have seen, because this network alternative idea was not military in nature but based on a different vision of Soviet society and economy, one which was rational and computer-controlled with IT networks. In the USSR, the national network idea was dictated by political economy demands charged with technological determinism: computer networks could prompt consequent, linear evolutions of a socio-economic nature (mainly the effective management of a decentralized, large scale economy). Second, the Russian case is a classic example of technological failure. It was, however, a failure that was not inherent in the idea itself—i.e. using the internet to plan a country's economy—as a network created for this purpose was one of the great achievements of Allende's Chile (Medina, 2011). Its failure also had nothing to do with the country's closure, as a form of "local" internet was successfully implemented in France, as we will see later. Very often technological failures are to be attributed to the political, economic and social context in which media develop and, in this sense, the opposition of certain groups to the new project was probably the cause of its abortive outcome. Finally, it shows how computers' networks in the 1950s and 1960s were not developed in the US only, but other countries were experimenting with them at the same time and independently.

3.3 The Academic Influence

The academic influence is probably the most common in global histories of the internet. John (2017, pp. 91-92) claims that "as was the case with the diffusion of the internet to many other countries outside of United States, the first connections were made between academic institutions" and he quotes the examples of Israel, South Africa, Ghana and India (among others). As in other nations, in the United States the computer network for military purposes logic intersected right from the start with the *academic internet*, namely a network built around the needs and expectations of the academic community. As we have seen, even the ARPANET project was initially seen as a tool with which to boost academic productivity.

There were three specific convergences between the academic world and the military. First, neither were in favor of adopting a centralized network structure, but for different reasons: the military were worried about keeping communications working during enemy attacks while the academics were worried that the centralized network might potentially transmute into some form of control over their work.

Second, a key military concept adopted in the academic universe was *flexibility* by integrating different networks and computers but modifying the structure of the network itself. This idea led the way in the creation of a series of protocols favoring intercommunication. Working for ARPA (which had, in the meantime, adopted the acronym DARPA in which the D for defense underlined the agency's new military character) in the 1970s, Vinton Cerf and Bob Kahn created a protocol, which is still today at the heart of the internet's functioning and, as we have seen, was the first time the word internet was used—the so-called TCP/IP. One part of the protocol (TCP, Transmission Control Protocol) deals with managing information flows between two nodes on the same network while another part (IP, Internet Protocol) enables data to be resent to the computer/user requiring it, assigning each terminal in the network a single name. Finalized in 1978 and adopted by ARPANET in 1983, TCP/IP is important for an understanding of the current internet architecture and the influences exerted on it by demands from the academic community. This protocol made it possible both to integrate very different networks and computers into a single environment and to implement an idea of centrifugal network, characterized by a structure of computers on the same hierarchical level (Townes, 2012). This model openly contrasted, however, with the networks conceived by the telephone companies of the day—and in particular American Telephone and Telegraph (AT&T) with its oligopoly on the American market—who were historically in favor of a centripetal framework on the grounds of its greater reliability and controllability. It was for this reason that, as the 1970s wore on, two profoundly different network models began to conflict, triggering the so-called *standard wars*, which saw the centrifugal-computer protocol TCP/IP competing with the centripetal-telephonic X.25 (Abbate, 1999, p. 150 onwards).

A third element on which military and academic influences converged was the physical building of the ARPANET network (once again see Abbate, 1999). Funded with military money, the initial 1968 project involved the creation of an *ad hoc* network linking four research centers at American universities: the Stanford Research Institute, the University of California in Santa Barbara, the University of California in Los Angeles and the University of Utah. The project was in place by the end of 1969 but the network then rapidly expanded. By 1971, there were already 15 nodes, while in 1973 ARPANET broke out of its American borders and used satellite links (SATNET) to connect to European research centers in Norway and England (see Figure 3.2).

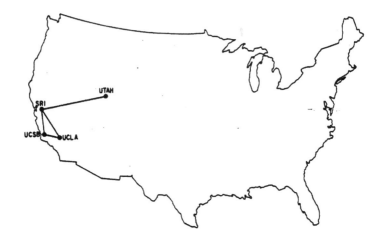

Figure 5:   The ARPANET in December 1969

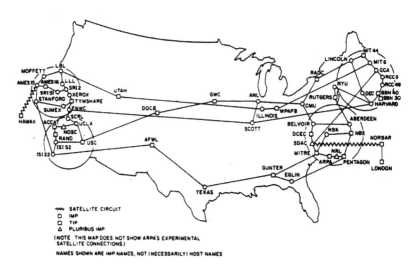

Figure 15:   July 1977

Figure 3.2 ARPANET networks in 1969 and in 1977

Source: BBN Report 4799, retrieved from http://walden-family.com/bbn/arpanet-completion-report.pdf

The 1970s were a decade of certain decisive changes in network funding, too. In the first half of the decade ARPANET management was offered to the national telephone company AT&T, which turned it down mainly because of the very different network architecture from the telephone network (as we saw previously) and because the computer network business model was a difficult one for a telecommunications firm to grasp. While AT&T's refusal may seem a colossal blunder today, media history is a catalogue of such errors right from its beginnings, testifying to the uncertainties and difficulties in understanding experienced by media firms. Remaining with digital history AT&T did not believe in the potential of mobile phones in the 1980s, accumulating considerable delays in developing this sector (see Chapter 4).

DCA–the American Department of Defense (once again the military context)– on the other hand, did believe in ARPANET and came to an agreement with DARPA in 1975 for a three-year management period, which actually continued until 1983. In the same year a significant disagreement between the military and academic spheres on the subject of security (Rosenzweig, 1998) and the fading of the military objectives on which it had been built led to ARPANET being divided into two: a minimalist, inexpensive network for military use (called MILNET) funded by the Ministry of Defense and a further network for civilian and research purposes (practically the lion's share of ARPANET) funded by the National Science Foundation (NSF). ARPANET was closed down in February 1990 and the NSFnet network took its place, a network that NSF had, in the meantime, been constructing and making increasingly accessible.

Security standards were not, however, the only difference in outlook between the military and academia and a second tension arose in relation to envisaged uses and users. The main example of this relates to the use of e-mail. Launched in 1971, e-mail was one of the first and most popular tools with which ARPANET users began to exchange information. We should also remember that e-mails were not exactly what we think of today and, for some considerable time, reading e-mails involved printing them out in a typical analog-digital interplay.

ARPA's original intentions were for e-mail to promote scientific research progress but it immediately went well beyond purely scientific communication especially with the use of mailing lists. Some of the most popular talking points among researchers via e-mails and mailing lists were, for example, sci-fi, wine and the winetasting, outcomes of the inter-connections between human relationships and society, and much more (Hauben, 2000). The popularity of these non-academic discussions obliged ARPA's managers to suspend certain discussion forums as they took up band width needed for more "serious" matters. The military opposed this unforeseen use of the technology also because it clashed with the Department of Defense's motives for funding the

Box 3.1 Documents

John McQuillan, *Why Have Emails Had Such a Sudden Success?* (1980)

In this short text, John McQuillan, an employee of Bolt Beranek and Newman Inc. (one of the first private ARPANET affiliates), explains the reasons why electronic mail was such a rapid success and reminds us that unexpected uses of technologies can sometimes be killer applications.

We have used electronic mail when our bosses have. Electronic mail is useful when communicating with your colleagues and clients (the well-known advantages of speedy delivery, delivery across time zones, etc.). It becomes necessary or even critical to use electronic mail when your boss does so. [. . .] on the ARPANET as a whole, the flash point occurred around 1973 or 1974 after one or two years of initial growth. After this date, most communication within our company and between us and other organizations on the ARPANET took place by means of electronic mail. [. . .] Computer technology changes quickly, but people change very slowly. When the technology of electronic mail was introduced (unannounced) in relatively crude form, it was immediately adopted by the early users as a replacement for telephone or the post. [. . .] To this day many people do not take much advantage of the other features that electronic mail systems provide (for example, a data management systems for one's correspondence, interface with reminder or calendar systems, etc.) but instead continue to treat it as a simple replacement for the postal service. [. . .] The ARPANET as a whole was designed for one purpose (resource sharing) and has been used for quite another (electronic mail). It is very significant that the network was not used as predicted and that it is used in a way that was not predicted. We assumed that people change more quickly than they do. [. . .] The immediate success of ARPANET mail was due in large part to the fact that it used the existing worker computers on the network. The mail experiment flourished because most ARPANET researchers have their own terminal, log into a computer daily, have informal communications with each other regularly and need a lot of information on a timely basis. In this setting, it was easy to introduce electronic mail using the same terminals and computers as the researchers were using already; and without changing the social interaction patterns or the hardware technology to affect a great change in how people accomplish their work.

Source: McQuillan, J. (1980). A retrospective on ARPANET electronic mail. *ACM SIGOA Newsletter archive*, *1*(1), 8-9

project. Instead, it was tolerated and even promoted in academic circles above all on the basis of the informal, joint working and overall freedom in which the earliest ARPANET programmers (mainly young researchers from the best American universities) lived and worked.

The ARPANET network became the reference point for the development of IT communication in other countries worldwide too as Goggin and McLelland (2017, p. 5) have asserted, pointing out that

> the beginning of computer networks involved signing up for a connection with the infrastructure already established in the US. This necessarily required those nations [...] to accept the protocols and terms of use already established there. [...] many histories of the internet outside of North America have emphasized these first connections with the US technological backbone in their own local histories.

For many national research centers worldwide, then, ARPANET embodied the tangible opportunity to access a computer network as well as a model for the development of such network systems in their own countries. There were, of course, exceptions: France, Japan and China, for example, favored the development of closed national networks or privileged relationships with other countries and research centers. For instance, diffidence to and from the American government (export of computers from the US to China was forbidden by the US government for long time) and a special relationship with Germany (China imported various mainframes manufactured by Siemens over the years), moved the Chinese academic community to connect up to the international Net for the first time in 1987 by means of the Karlsruhe Institute of Technology in the German Democratic Republic (Hauben, 2005; Zorn, 2007).

While the main protagonist of the internet's early history, ARPANET was not the only model designed to build computer networks for academic research purposes. Europe, in particular, was very active from the 1970s onwards in the–not always successful–programming and structuring of a series of international research networks. One of the best known examples was in the early 1970s when the European Economic Community funded a research project whose purpose was to set up a European Informatics Network (EIN) based on the ARPANET model to link research centers in Italy (Politecnico of Milan and the EURATOM Centre in Ispra), Switzerland (ETH Zurich), France (Institut national de recherche en informatique et en automatique in Paris) and Britain (National Physical Laboratory in London) (Gillies & Cailliau, 2000, pp. 56-60; see also Figure 3.3). On one hand, EIN was not especially successful because monopolistic telecommunications firms and, more generally, difficulties in agreeing shared standards and processes acted against its creation. On the

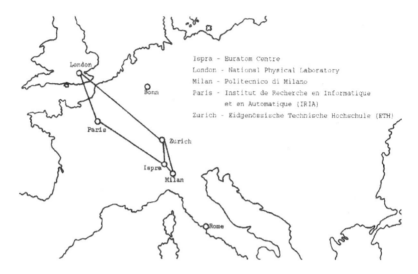

Figure 3.3 The European Informatics Network in 1973
Source: Courtesy of NATO Advanced Study Institute

other hand, when the network was closed down in 1980 it had in fact achieved an important objective. It had created a model for future European networking and thus set dialogue in motion for the achievement of shared standards between different European states. There is nothing accidental about the fact that, in the 1980s, pan-European academic networks such as EUnet in 1982 and EARN in 1983 gained ever greater importance in the academic world to the extent that research centers elsewhere in the world began to connect to European networks (Shahin, 2006; Davies & Bressan, 2010).

Countless academic centers around the world saw computer networks as an opportunity to make research progress using shared calculation resources. But the tangible upshot and practical shape of academic influence on the internet took the form, in particular, of its openness and flexibility logic, which then became ingrained in the internet's popular image (Flichy, 2001/2007, chap. 2). The most important consequence of this openness and flexibility logic is, however, to be sought in the very architecture of the internet that emerged in the 1970s: an open, distributed network, the heart of whose "intelligence" was not in the center but at the margins of the network itself (so-called end-to-end). It was a network that sacrificed solidity and security in the name of compatibility and favored shared and constantly changing codes (the so-called running codes) to fixed and relatively un-innovative ones (Russell, 2014). As we will see later on, this infrastructure and information flow model changed radically with the WWW and then with the commercialization of the Web—the fourth and fifth influences of our history. Nevertheless, the relevance (and a plea for a return) of distributed networks is still debated in contemporary internet literature (Musiani & Méadel, 2016) and this clearly shows how the academic formative influence had long-term consequences for the evolving shape of the network.

One last influence that apparently conflicted with the priorities of the academic age was the discovery of the internet's playful side. The fact that researchers used mailing lists for their sci-fi conversations was actually the first concrete sign of an alternative to the internet's "serious" and "productive" side, one that was later reworked and modified in the counter-cultural stage: computers in the 1970s and the internet later were tools to get people talking and keep them entertained and having fun.

3.4 The Counter-cultural Influence

Alongside ARPANET's military and academic uses, from the 1970s onwards a new community of *bricoleur*, political activists, young students, hackers and straightforward internet fans began to proliferate bringing different and alternative visions to the Net. This was the very same counter-cultural environment referred to in Chapter 2 where the home computing idea took shape.

This third vision of ARPANET differed from the previous two in at least two ways. In the first place, if ARPA's objective right from the start was to link up powerful calculation resources (mainframes), the counter-cultural milieu saw internet as a network capable of linking up the first personal home computers, which were appearing on the scene. In the second place, ARPANET could not supply universal access because the terminals connected to it were, for the most part, situated within large research centers in selected university campuses. These counter-cultural environments, and hackers in particular, by contrast, planned to use a pre-existing network available in the majority of homes for their data exchanges—telephone networks.

There is nothing coincidental about the fact that hackers put forward the use of the telephone network for data transmission and computer link-up, as they had been using the AT&T network for personal interests and against the firm's directives for at least 20 years. It is well-known that they had long been making free long-distance calls thanks to a specific frequency produced with a whistle (see also Chapter 2). Naturally, until then the telephone networks had supported analog type communication and their progressive digitalization began only in the 1980s on different time frames in the various countries. In other words, the use of analog telephone networks as the backbone for connecting digital computers is just another case where analog and digital merged and hybridized–and as an aside it should be noted that this is one of the least studied periods in telecommunications and digital history (see Franke, 2014).

Until the 1970s, AT&T robustly defended its telephone network, blocking the dissemination of unauthorized use in the name of the potential for damage to the system as a whole. From the end of the 1960s onwards, however, the political climate changed to the extent that over the next decade, the firm broke up and a century long dominance in the telecommunications sector came to an end. Consequently a 1975 ruling by the Federal Communications Commission (FCC) enabled telephone users to connect any technological device to the telephone network on condition that no damage was done to the latter's functioning (Ryan 2010). Thus, in the second half of the 1970s, the first modems were used allowing for the development of the so-called public bulletin boards or BBSs (ubiquitous in Asia–Japan and Taiwan in particular; see Li, Lin & Hou-Ming Huang, 2017). One of the first and best-known BBSs was probably Community Memory, set up in 1973 in Berkeley, a network of computer terminals whose purpose was to link up a range of counter-cultural organizations via telephone networks, which very soon became a message exchange and information retrieval system, a kind of "social media's dial up ancestor" (Driscoll, 2016; for a broader overview on BBS see also Driscoll, 2014). It was thanks to public bulletin boards and BBSs and via the normal telephone network that the first message and file sharing services became accessible *de facto* launching amateur telematic communications. The technological structure of the counter-cultural network had thus been born.

The consequences of the counter-cultural concept became clear, however, only in the 1980s and these were not so much technological as social. It was, in fact, in this decade that the Net's structure was used by the first electronic communities initially in the United States and then in Europe and the rest of the world in the 1990s. It was in these places that the "mythological" internet's main counter-cultural values and ideologies came to full fruition. These values emphasized an empathic, mutually understanding attitude based on informal and horizontal relationships, the breakdown of a series of social conventions in "real" society, which had no *raison d'être* in the "virtual" world, and, finally, a general conviction that certain classic political and economic power logics were shifting in favor of cyber-citizens (Streeter, 2010, chap. 2). The first electronic-virtual communities were geographically localized, an aspect that has persisted into the modern day in some cases. Two famous examples are the WELL (Whole Earth 'Lectronic Link) community, created by Stewart Brand and Larry Brilliant in 1985 in the San Francisco area (Turner, 2006), and De Digitale Stad (DDS, Amsterdam's Digital City) in Holland, whose pilot project was launched in 1994.

Another form of more lasting virtual community, which has become an indelible part of the internet-related popular representations, was (and is) geographically dispersed taking advantage of the real-time distance communication facilitated by the internet: some of the best-known cases are UseNet, BitNet, FidoNet and PeaceNet (on the history of the virtual communities see Rheingold, 1993; Naughton, 1999). William Gibson's cyberpunk novel *Neuromancer* published in 1984, also contributed to popularizing the ideas and ideologies of the virtual communities, becoming a full-blown digital society manifesto and inventing the term *cyberspace*, which gradually made its way into the collective imagination. Over the course of the 1990s, this virtual community enthusiasm spread into scientific research too with the latter long interpreting cyberspace as a sort of alternative virtual space to the real world, a juxtaposition that has gradually faded in the most recent research into the digital media.

What has the main legacy of counter-cultural influence and, more generally, of these alternative network ideas on the modern-day internet been? First, the so-called computer geeks transformed the internet from a primarily military-scientific project to the embodiment of social community with PCs seen as a sort of TV (one in every home) and internet information as a leisure activity (retaining the TV metaphor, like the shift from the public service broadcasting's educational focus to commercial TV's fun-entertainment logic). The idea of the Net as a leisure time tool, second, contributed to shifting the way computers themselves were seen from "serious" calculation machines to vehicles for entertainment, fun and sociability generating online cult activities in the 1980s and 1990s (Turkle, 1995). Beyond the new terminal concept, the American counter-culture influence also delivered a new concept of physical network—no longer great colossi designed by the military apparatus linking up mainframes in university or army laboratories but one made up of the telephone network already present across the land and in every home. The internet still uses great swathes of telephone network (and in particular the so-called *last mile*—the final portion of the telecommunications networks that physically deliver services to end-users' houses) today.

Two further influences from the counter-cultural phase have become clear only in the latter stages of the internet's evolution. On one hand, services like BBS inspired founding characteristics of contemporary social networks and, in particular, their flexibility as sources of information and communication exchanges between subscribers. On the other, the key counter-cultural "vision" of a new digital and freer society was paradoxically appropriated by and incorporated into the narratives of large corporations such as Google, Facebook, Tencent or Alibaba in our own times. This is unsurprising because the counter-cultural movement and neo-capitalism *à la* Silicon Valley also shared a number of key figures such as Steve Jobs, whose attractiveness was such as to prompt their emulation in the digital rhetoric, which then pervaded many countries worldwide: this is the so-called "Californian ideology" mixing apparently opposite aspects like freedom of hippies and corporate yuppies (Barbrook & Cameron, 1996). Some of these arguments have been elaborated by social theorists Boltanski and Chiapello (1999/2005) to illustrate the ways in which the anti-authoritarianism and "obsession with flexibility" embodied by the network metaphor turned into crucial elements in the shaping of the new spirit of capitalism after the 1960s.

All things considered, the counter-culture influence shows that an alternative internet idea to ARPANET was feasible. But seen from a global perspective it was neither the only alternative idea to ARPANET nor the only one that aimed to reuse the telephone network to transfer digital information. The French Minitel is perhaps the most interesting example of such an alternative vision. In the early 1970s, France was one of the most active in following the American ARPANET and implementing a network capable of linking up non-homogeneous computers made by diverse manufacturing firms, most of which were French. In 1972, the state research center INRIA, in fact, launched an avant-garde project named Cyclades that fell victim, however, to progressive loss of public interest and closed down in 1979 (Griset & Schafer, 2011; Russell & Schafer, 2014).

In the late 1970s and early 1980s France Telecom, then the national mono-polistic telephone company, launched a further project, which had a more conservative spirit and outcome—the Minitel network. Launched onto the market in 1982 Minitel was popular for at least a decade—from 1984 to 1995—and consisted of a network of video terminals all identical to one another (not, then, full-blown computers but simply low-tech terminals with limited memory capa-cities) linked via the telephone network. This concept, like the counter-cultural formative influence, intended to make use of the already extensive, decades-long telephone network and lacked two elements of the internet as we are used to conceiving of it: a network of networks status (as the only network used was the already established, homogenous telephone network) and linking up different types of computer (terminals were all identical). The use of the tele-phone network as the principal connection infrastructure was not, however, confined to France. As we will see, most European governments handed over setting up projects designed to extend their national internet networks to public telecommunications companies in the 1980s and 1990s.

Manuel Castells (1996) has argued that Minitel owed its success to its ease of use and to the fact that it was strongly supported by the Ministry of Post, Telegraphs and Telephones. The Ministry was implementing the well-known Nora and Minc's report, that in 1978 foresaw the advent of a telematic society; France needed to prepare for it, also in order to defend its cultural differences

Figure 3.4 The French Minitel 10 used by children at home in a 1994 advert
Source: Courtesy of Orange Archives

from the onslaught of the American media, and this idea mobilized the French government to set up Minitel as well (Eko, 2012, chap. 8). France Telecom even went as far as to deliver a Minitel terminal free of charge to all telephone subscribers requesting it instead of the normal phone book. Furthermore, seeing Minitel as an opportunity to diversify telephone network use, this same company opened up the system to advertisers and suppliers of private services as producers of specific contents for Minitel.

Minitel was well received in French society with services offered via a *kiosk* system in which various types of information could be browsed: for example, weather forecasts, transport information and later tele-shopping and tele-banking. The two killer applications, however, were its telephone directory and messaging service. Users could use the former to source telephone numbers including those of friends they had lost touch with some time ago and was, in this sense, a sort of *ante litteram* Facebook model. *Messageries*, experimented with in the early 1980s and launched in the second half of the decade, were used by approximately five million users in the early 1990s (Schafer & Thierry, 2012, chap. 3). Structured as chat lines they were very soon monopolized by erotic or even pornographic content (to be then called *messageries roses*, pink chats) but their popularity diminished from the second half of the 1990s onwards partly as a result of the explosion of the WWW. As is frequently the case in media history, however, the "new" technologies did not succeed in killing off the "old" ones quite so easily. The Minitel service actually only closed down in 2012 and retained a certain following even in the WWW era. On the other hand, researchers agree that the success of the videotext service contributed to slowing down the development of the internet in France—a classic and in some ways typically French trajectory according to which the success of one medium slows down the dissemination and breakthrough of other, perhaps more innovative media (see the case of the electric and optical telegraph in Flichy, 1991/1995).

The Minitel story is thought provoking on many levels. First and foremost, it is an example of a national political economy guiding media choices and success: Cyclades fell from grace when it lost government support, while Minitel's success was to some extent due to the political support of the French Ministry of Post, Telegraphs and Telephones. Second, Minitel—especially compared to the Cyclades project—was a simple and conservative technology using "stupid" terminals similar to TVs linked up by traditional telephone lines. In other words, Minitel showed that less advanced and even old media-based technological solutions can sometimes be more popular because they have already been metabolized and so come across as closer to users' everyday lives. A third interesting aspect is network structure. As we have seen, internet is frequently envisaged as distributed and non-hierarchical in nature, while Minitel revolved around a hierarchical network designed more for vertical than for horizontal communication (Kramer, 1993). Users opted to take advantage of this structure, favoring the more horizontal of Minitel's services, i.e. chats. This highlights the fact that, far from being 'natural', media can develop their own characteristics only as the result of a *co-production process* (Jasanoff, 2004) involving technological potential and social demands. Like the American counter-cultural phase, French Minitel saw the internet as a social and home-based medium, favoring household to household dialogue and thought exchange—basically some, still relevant characteristics of the contemporary internet concept.

3.5 The Public Service Influence

The fourth formative influence on the modern internet did not come from the United States but from Europe and European welfare and communications public service traditions. Seeing the internet as a public service essentially meant two things in the 1980s and 1990s: first, contextualizing the new medium in the long tradition of nineteenth- and twentieth-century telecommunications (telegraph and telephone) and broadcasting, which in most countries were run as

Box 3.2 In-depth Theory

Public Services in Communication History

Public service is a long-lasting idea in communication history. In the realm of electric media, it emerged as early as the mid-nineteenth century in the debate on how to regulate the telegraph networks. Here, two models were identified: private management via concessions or direct management (generally monopolies) by state bodies. The latter model saw telegraphs as an essential public service and foresaw entrusting management to the state for two reasons. First, because state investment would be nation-wide and not simply in the most profitable areas in contrast to private firms. This enabled a universal service to be provided capable of covering city dwellers and those living in the remotest valleys equally–in telecommunications economic theory this was called equalization or, from French, *perequation*. Second, it was believed that leaving telecom management in private hands would soon result in just one or two private corporations creating monopolistic or oligopolistic cartels (as in fact occurred in the United States with the Western Union telegraph company). This idea was linked, in both telecommunications and transport, with the concept of *natural monopoly*, i.e. the first actor to set up a network acquires a competitive advantage over its rivals who, for example, have nothing to gain from building a second motorway alongside an already fully functioning one. The political reasoning was thus as follows: in the light of the risk of natural monopoly, state management of telegraphs was to be preferred to private management.

Many of these nineteenth-century logics were taken up and re-worked in the 1920s with radio broadcasting and, from the mid-twentieth century onwards, with TV. Public service broadcasting (abbreviated to PSB) came, alongside healthcare, to symbolize the European public service concept. The reasons for which the bulk of European nations chose to regulate broadcasting as a public service first as a monopoly and then, from the 1980s onwards, in competition with private bodies, were manifold. From a technological point of view, given the scarcity of available frequencies for radio in the 1920s, it was decided that this limited spectrum should be managed and monopolized by the state to avoid the overlapping of the different channels–the validity of this logic progressively diminished over the twentieth century with the abundance of channels deriving from satellites and then new digital distribution models. From a political economy perspective, the two logics cited for telegraphs were reworked for the new media: radio and TV were seen as universal services to be provided to all citizens in a state as a common good supplied by (theoretically impartial) government bodies, in order to prevent broadcasting falling into the hands of just a few firms. These logics derived partly from early recognition of the fact that PSB could be influential as it in fact was: think of the extensive use of radio made by totalitarian regimes in the first half of the twentieth century or the nation building role TV played in the second half of the century in democratic countries.

This cultural backdrop to the European public service logic was also applied to the internet in the 1980s and '90s. On one hand the internet was seen as a classic form of telecommunications, subject to the same equalization and natural monopoly dynamics that characterized telegraph and telephone networks. On the other, as already recalled in this chapter, the World Wide Web resembled PSB, taking information, entertainment and culture into people's homes. There is thus nothing random about the fact that tensions between public and private space and between government control and commercial interests are still today central to an understanding of digital technology's development and that of the internet in particular.

Further Reading

Hills, J., & Michalis, M. (2000). The internet: A challenge to public service broadcasting? *International Communication Gazette, 62*(6), 477–493.

Scannell, P. (1989). Public Service Broadcasting: History of a Concept. In A. Goodwin & G. Whannel (Eds.), *Understanding Television* (pp. 11–29). London: Routledge.

Starr, P. (2004). *The Creation of the Media: Political Origins of Modern Communications.* New York: Basic Books.

public services and, second, making information available free of charge via the internet with the so-called World Wide Web.

The bulk of European policy making in the 1980s and early 1990s applied the same policies adopted hitherto by other forms of communication—telegraphs and telephone but also broadcasting (see Box 3.2). The model followed had a series of well-defined characteristics (Ricker Schulte, 2013, chap. 4). In the first place, apart from the academic networks referred to previously, the various 1980s European projects were nation based. They dealt, that is, with developing and organizing networks solely in one country without taking much interest in international links—a model that has also recently been coming powerfully to the fore with the Chinese and Russian *intra-net* (see Section 3.7). Second,

European governments adopted protectionist policies and favored national network firms, internet service providers and manufacturing companies. The network firms identified were, on a continuum with the past, telecommunications and mainly telephone monopolist companies funded to expand their internet providership services. Thus regulated, the *European style* internet was to become a new public utility, a shared space for political debate, for expressing personal opinions and disseminating relevant news to citizens (like De Digitale Stad in Amsterdam). This logic, too, was borrowed from public telephone services and radio-TV broadcasting and based on equal, universal access to the network just as electricity, water and railway networks had been throughout the nineteenth and twentieth centuries. Following the European public service logic, on the other hand, meant governments could control the contents circulating in their countries as had been the case with public service broadcasting (as the 1990s-battle against internet pornography in some countries such as Germany and France exemplified).

In contrast to the policy pursued in the United States with ARPANET, this strategy turned out to be a failure in most countries with the sole possible exception of Minitel in France, as we saw earlier. In response to this and the simultaneous rise of neo-liberal policies in the telecommunications sector, European internet policies gradually changed tack. In the (predominately analog) media environment of the 1970s and 1980s, radio and TV monopolies gradually came to an end and, in the 1990s, publicly owned telephone companies were privatized and a number of rival firms sprang up in each country (this was true for both landline telephones and, to an even greater extent, mobile phones; see Chapter 4). Simultaneously, the trans-national directives issued by the European Union also gradually increased in importance, supporting digitization seen in a determinist way as the revolutionary force capable of generating a brighter future (Mansell, 2014): the 1990 Bangemann report and the 1993 European Commission white paper entitled *Growth, Competitiveness, Employment* placed the digitization of telecommunications infrastructure—and telephone networks in particular—on the top of the true information society agenda.

But the best known of these projects was *eEurope 2005*, launched in 1999, with which the European Union aimed to promote the creation of a European internet integrating and harmonizing national policies and networks developed in the previous decade. This project aimed also to give Europe the opportunity to carve out an important space for itself in the internet's global geopolitics. Rather than using public money the idea was to encourage fierce rivalry between internet firms following the American liberal model, which had shown its effectiveness to date. Thus, while a commercial logic was making its way into European management network policies in these years, the public service internet notion was, by contrast, progressively coming to the fore in the United

States especially in the wake of the publication of the well-known Clinton administration document *The National Information Structure: Agenda for Action* in 1993. This report placed the information networks, better known as the *information superhighway(s)*, at the center of US economic and industrial policy to guarantee American citizens access to circulating services and contents (the metaphor of circulation and mobility is central to this document) and American digital and non-digital firms a speedy and efficient national infrastructure enabling them to compete in, and potentially dominate, the international market (Kozak, 2015, see also Box 3.3).

Box 3.3 Documents

US Government, *The National Information Infrastructure: Agenda for Action* **(1993)**

All Americans have a stake in the construction of an advanced National Information Infrastructure (NII), a seamless web of communications networks, computers, databases, and consumer electronics that will put vast amounts of information at users' fingertips. Development of the NII can help unleash an information revolution that will change forever the way people live, work, and interact with each other:

- People could live almost anywhere they wanted, without foregoing opportunities for useful and fulfilling employment, by "telecommuting" to their offices through an electronic highway;
- The best schools, teachers, and courses would be available to all students, without regard to geography, distance, resources, or disability;
- Services that improve America's health care system and respond to other important social needs could be available online , without waiting in line, when and where you needed them.

[...] Our efforts will be guided by the following principles and objectives:

- Promote private sector investment [...]
- Extend the "universal service" concept to ensure that information resources are available to all at affordable prices. Because information means empowerment—and employment—the government has a duty to ensure that all Americans have access to the resources and job creation potential of the Information Age.

- Act as a catalyst to promote technological innovation and new applications. [...]
- Promote seamless, interactive, user-driven operation of the NII. As the NII evolves into a "network of networks," [...]
- Ensure information security and network reliability. [...]
- Improve management of the radio frequency spectrum, an increasingly critical resource.
- Protect intellectual property rights. [...]
- Coordinate with other levels of government and with other nations. Because information crosses state, regional, and national boundaries, coordination is critical to avoid needless obstacles and prevent unfair policies that handicap U.S. industry.
- Provide access to government information and improve government procurement. [...]

The time for action is now. Every day brings news of change [...]. The benefits of the NII for the nation are immense. An advanced information infrastructure will enable U.S. firms to compete and win in the global economy, generating good jobs for the American people and economic growth for the nation. As importantly, the NII can transform the lives of the American people—ameliorating the constraints of geography, disability, and economic status—giving all Americans a fair opportunity to go as far as their talents and ambitions will take them.

Source: Information Infrastructure Task Force. (1993, September 15). *National In-Formation Infrastructure Agenda for Action*. Washington, DC: National Telecommunications and Information Administration

The internet's second incarnation as *public service* also emerged in Europe. In the late 1980s and early 1990s, at the CERN European Particle Physics Laboratory in Geneva (Switzerland), Tim Berners-Lee, Roger Cailliau and a group of other researchers came up with the idea of the World Wide Web, i.e. transforming a part of the internet into an information and document consultation, and not simply exchange, space (Gillies & Cailliau, 2000). It was not an entirely new field of thought. For several decades, a range of scholars and researchers had been debating the re-organization of human knowledge. In 1945, for example, Vannevar Bush had imagined a (never to be built) mechanical system designed to speed up information retrieval by linking up different sources by means of intersecting commands based on semantic resemblance. Memex, as this analog filing system was called, was in turn inspired by the functioning of the human brain and, in particular, the ways in which information searches in the cerebral cortex take place (Bush, 1945; Nyce & Kahn, 1991). In 1960, Ted Nelson (1974) elaborated the hypertext concept in the unfinished Xanadu project coming up with the idea of applying Bush's mechanical processes to the digital world. In the wake of Bush's and to an even greater extent Nelson's studies, Berners-Lee formulated two of the WWW's key concepts: making the Web into a repository of computer knowledge contents (the CERN computer initially and then worldwide) and creating a system that allowed text documents and worksheets to be published on the network's nodes and then modified constantly by users (Berners-Lee, 1999).

It is worth clarifying that Berners-Lee had not in mind what we consider WWW today because his objective was essentially to resolve a circumscribed problem, which had emerged within CERN, namely difficulties researching and locating information scattered throughout the center's network and combating what he called "information loss". Similarly, the technical structure underlying WWW was not entirely new as it essentially consisted of putting together old and new elements, which had emerged in studies of the IT network to date (Bory, Benecchi, & Balbi, 2016; Brügger, 2017). Nevertheless, right from the start the WWW was to be primarily a way of locating documents and the new idea was to assign a personal name to each worksheet entered into the CERN network and then on the WWW (the so-called URL). Navigating these pages occurred—as it still does—by means of browsers, namely programs enabling users to locate the information they are looking for rapidly. The first commercial browser was Netscape Navigator, introduced in 1994 and then followed by a Microsoft-created version called Internet Explorer. The two systems were bitter rivals and launched what was later called the *browser war* (Bresnahan & Yin, 2007). A further two characteristics were: all documents had to be written in a standard-ized script (HTML) and hosted on servers, which users (clients) accessed to source them.

Let us take a closer look at this latter aspect because it was a radical departure from the structure and communication logic of earlier network concepts (for military, academic or counter-cultural purposes) while echoing old analog mass media. The client/server model adopted for WWW, in fact, fundamentally modified the horizontal, distributed network idea inherited from previous internet influences. In the client/server model, instead of com-municating reciprocally or building contents, multiple user-clients request access to a large quantity of contents stored in a small number of supplier-servers. Take Google for example: every day billions of internet users (clients) access this search engine to access contents kept at huge databases (or servers) controlled by Google itself. Musiani and Schafer (2011) have argued that WWW set in motion a *broadcastization* process involving transforming content access methods from a point-to-point (horizontal information exchanges) to a one-to-many or many-to-many logic thus resembling radio and TV forms of communications in which a small number of channels supply content to millions of users (the audience). As Roscoe has argued, "WWW was seen principally as something you watched, rather than something you built a small corner of yourself" (1999, p. 680). When we use the Web, we are often users of contents pre-prepared by others like TV audiences are, rather than the empowered and active users of internet rhetoric. As already mentioned before, a more recent critique of the distributed network has come from Tang-Hui Hu (2015) who has argued that this sort of network has never existed for two reasons. First, the number of cables (and thus of channels and routes) that data can follow in the internet is limited and based to a considerable degree on pre-existing telegraph and telephone lines. Second, a small number of providers has often concentrated and centralized network power into their own hands effectively dominating structures and dynamics as occurred in the past for other large technical systems such as railway or telephone networks.

While the WWW idea seems effective and successful today to the extent of being commonly and misleadingly used as a metonym for the internet as a whole (think about the word *the Web*), the project initially prompted no interest at CERN (the pen note "vague but exciting" on the original Berners-Lee 1989 presentation is well-known) and was set aside twice. One cause of friction between the CERN hierarchy and Berners-Lee related to the commercial exploitation of the new software. Berners-Lee defended the need to release the WWW source code to the world community free-of-charge while the research institute's management planned to exploit it commercially via a private firm or stimulate some sort of competition (Berners-Lee, 1999). Berners-Lee's idea came out on top, however, and in April 1993 CERN released the WWW software as a gift to the international community to be freely used and improved in a collective effort. This was exactly what the French government had done a century and a half earlier in 1839 when it released the photography patent thus triggering a feverish amateur experimentation period, which contributed notably to the dissemination of the new patent-free medium (Flichy, 1991/1995). Releasing WWW for free use had a comparable outcome in every way to the extent that in the 1990s the WWW and extensively the internet itself expanded and slowly came to the fore globally.

The public service influence had a profound impact on the later development of the internet and conceptions of it. In the first place, some of the logics typical of public telecommunications and broadcasting services (including universal services) have recently been re-applied to the internet at a historical juncture witnessing a range of national, macro-regional and trans-national plans to develop so-called broadband networks capable of transporting large quantities of data rapidly (on this subject, see Hilbert, 2016). Second, as we noted previously, WWW is now generally misleadingly seen as synonymous with the internet itself while it is actually only one of the services offered by the internet, however important it might be, on a par, for example, with e-mail. Third, the broadcastization of the internet that emerged with the WWW is apparently a growing trend. Increasingly great servers seem to be achieving predominance over other parts of the internet and have become the infrastructure's new nerve centers—the exact opposite of the decentralized network notion that has not, however, entirely vanished especially as a mythological inspiration (see Musiani & Méadel, 2016). Fourth, today's internet is still a battlefield between public service and business logics. While the business logic that we will examine in the next section envisages the Net as dominated by large private corporations, the former believes that co-operation, non-profit (think of free software), information sharing and public debate make the internet a vehicle for a culture and human knowledge revolution. This public/private tension can be unexpectedly solved by large corporations such as Google, Facebook and Twitter in the sense that these manage "to conflate the economic logics typical of platforms with the public interests and quasi-universal services formerly characteristic of many infrastructures" (Plantin, Lagoze, Edwards, & Sandvig, 2018, p. 306). In other words, the large corporations have powerful global and imperialistic interests typical of private firms while at the same time increasingly acting as infrastructure providers, performing certain forms of public service—think of Facebook Internet.org or Google Loon projects aiming to combat the digital divide (see Box 3.4.) by bringing internet connections technologies to the African continent. In sum, the early 1990s public service formative influence has also expanded to non-governmental bodies making one of its main narratives commercial: people should have the *right* to access the internet because it (and more in general digitization) has become an indispensable service in contemporary cultures.

3.6 The Commercial Influence

Government, business and technical internet zeal peaked in the mid 1990s and public interest soon followed. Military influence had apparently fizzled out by the beginning of the decade and the internet was then a combination of academic, counter-cultural and public service values, which had breathed life into a seemingly decentralized and interactive public space. In this context, in the United States, parts of Europe and gradually other countries too commercial interests started to grow and seemed to be having a positive impact from various points of view. It was the private firms that supported and promoted the adoption of user-friendly interfaces, browsers and search engines for the purposes of encouraging a definitive popularization of the Net. These corporations saw the internet as a new source of profit right from the start generating a sometimes-naïve enthusiasm, which slowly faded in the early noughties. Finally, the commercialization of the Net seemed capable of making novel opportunities such as the ability to compare product prices available to users and translated into one of the foundation stones of capitalism as much as the framework to today's internet is widely seen as neo-liberal.

The year 1995 marked a watershed in internet history. In the first place, two relevant essays on internet and digital culture were published–*Being Digital* by Nicholas Negroponte (1995) and *The Second Media Age* by Mark Poster (1995)–and both argued that the internet would trigger a "democratic revolution" and herald the end of the communications monopoly era with distributed forms of knowledge. It was precisely from the mid 1990s onwards, then, that the internet became the driving force behind the digital revolution idea, whose genesis we referred to in Chapter 1. Once again in 1995 John Perry Barlow, a leader of the Electric Frontier Foundation, wrote an article placing the internet among the most important (perhaps *the* most important) revolutions in communication history:

> With the development of the Internet, and with the increasing pervasiveness of communication between networked computers, we are in the middle of the most transforming technological event since the capture of fire. I used to think that it was just the biggest thing since Gutenberg, but now I think you have to go back farther.
>
> (Barlow, 1995, p. 36)

A technological revolution, then, a paradigmatic change held to be more significant even than the impact of printing on human culture and society and on a par with the prehistoric discovery of fire.

Alongside this mid-1990s cultural vision of the internet, and once again in 1995, the rapid commercialization of this "legendary" space began in the US and elsewhere (Greenstein, 2015). On January 1, internet retail–hitherto banned on the basis of *Acceptable Usage Policy*, a series of usage rules issued by the NSF– was legalized. On April 30, the NSF sold its academic structure (the NFSnet referred to above) to a number of private firms ending the direct American governmental funding and control of the internet era, which had begun with ARPANET. On August 9, the Netscape Corporation, producer of the era's main browser, was listed on the stock exchange and its initial public offer created a sensation in financial circles and triggered a surge in this dotcom firm share value. On September 3, eBay, still today one of the most important e-commerce sites, was set up. But it was not only in the US that 1995 was a watershed year for internet commercialization: in that same year CHINANET launched online retail services in China (Tai, 2006, p. 130), the Brazilian government decided to open access to the internet infrastructure at Telebrás and then to gradually privatize the Net (Dutta-Roy & Segoshi, 1996; Knight, 2014) and many other systems emerged elsewhere. The fact that NSF had endorsed internet sales thus had a knock on, "freeing up effect" in other countries too.

Immediately after 1995 internet-related companies began attracting huge capital investments and the speculation bubble, which burst in the mid noughties with serious consequences for the American and world economies began forming. Economic growth in the internet sector from 1996 to 2000 was as dizzying as its later nose-dive. Two American market events are exemplary of this. NASDAQ, the main American stock exchange index for technology firms, peaked in March 2000 (at 5,132.52 points on March 10) thus increasing internet sector value fivefold. A network and Net device company of secondary importance in the 1990s, Cisco Systems, shot to third place in the US company rankings of the year 2000 (Nolan, 2001). This fervor was partly and primarily due to the fact that the internet was now becoming a huge virtual marketplace users could access at any time of day and pay for by credit card with a standard and secure use protocol emerging for the latter in 1997.

The myth of the internet's apparently infinite growth suffered a crushing blow in 2000–2002 when a rapid, generalized economic crisis undermined the certainties of previous years. Once again it is NASDAQ figures that best capture the essence of the situation: in October 2002, the index's value plunged to mid-1990s levels effectively nullifying the digital growth boom and it was only in 2015 that the index recovered its 2000 5,000-point level (see Figure 3.5). A symbol firm that struggled in the aftermath of the bubble bursting was *Yahoo!* whose share price plunged from $138 to $4 triggering, among other things, the onset of Google's world search engine primacy.

Of the many reasons for the dotcom share price crunch, two are the most important. The first relates to the business mentality of the firms, which had thrown themselves into the new and little-known internet world. Many of these believed that doing so required abandoning consolidated economic models in the name of a new approach designed to breakdown hierarchies and oriented to joint working (another logic which derived in part from the hacker and counter-cultural milieu). But in actual fact only those companies capable of integrating more traditional business models and new network based business ideas survived. A second element in the sector's crisis was the backwardness of the late 1990s and early noughties internet. Despite the extremely high (and

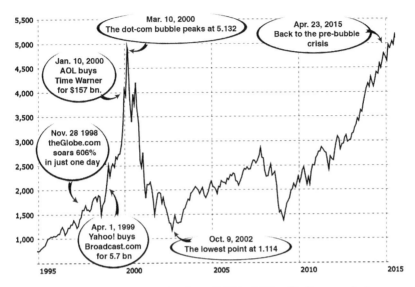

Figure 3.5 Curve of Nasdaq index from 1995 to 2015, with the so-called "internet bubble" around 2000

Source: Nasdaq; authors' artwork

clearly over-inflated) expectations of the companies investing in it (Gadrey, 2003), at the time the internet was still a work in progress; a lack of broadband networks meant online surfing was a slow and difficult process and user numbers were still low as was the willingness to buy online.

The bubble bursting in the early noughties was accompanied by a parallel puncturing of the whole internet mythology. Debate on the future of the internet began in many countries who questioned the value of policies supporting the internet and in the UK, for example, doubt was cast on the creation of broadband networks and services at least until 2003 (Dutton, Gillett, McKnight, & Peltu, 2004). In addition to a digital skepticism, which was to last for some years, internet commercialization began to show its darker side. Gambling and pornography were some of the most popular contents. Advertising had reached intrusive levels from the earliest banners to the increasing presence of spam (Brunton, 2013) to recent surfing tracing systems via cookies. The business models of the new corporations were (and to some extent still are) non-transparent and based on the paradox of a network where the bulk of the information circulating was and is free at the center of a market economy. Rather than encouraging competition, starting from the late 1990s the market has gradually privileged the dominant positions of some of the largest global firms as was already beginning to be the case for Google and Amazon. Finally controlling users' preferences, interests and purchases—also by means of the main search engines—gave rise to the widely known phenomenon of internet surveillance, a social trend that David Lyon (1994) first envisaged in the mid 1990s and that it is still at the centre of the contemporary internet society, especially after the so called Snowden case (Lyon, 2015).

Despite all this, the influence of commercialization is perhaps the most characteristic feature of the internet over the last 20 years and one which has left a series of specific legacies, some of which have yet to be fully assessed. First, it is unlikely that the internet would have been able to grow to the extent it has without its business interests. In other words, the internet owes its popularization and accessibility to a worldwide public to the fact that it is attractive to business. Second, a commercial internet also means an internet on which economic transactions are reliable and shared protocols are stable. It is a tendency that is diametrically opposed to that of the first phase of internet history when flexibility and collective protocol building were preferred to reliability (see Section 3.3). It is, at the same time, a further demonstration of the way in which evolving political, economic and technical interests and user habits prompt constant changes in internet architecture and, consequently, to information flows transiting through it. Furthermore, as we will see in the next section, the firms that have effectively acquired oligopolistic, dominant market positions originated during the "creative destruction" period in which the bubble was forming (Google and Tencent were founded in 1998, Alibaba in 1999, Baidu in 2000) or in the period immediately following on from this (Facebook in 2004 and YouTube in 2005, to cite just two examples). Finally, a close-up view of the contemporary internet shows that its commercial side is probably its most important and visible with increasingly sophisticated advertising techniques using algorithms: note that many of today's platforms "learn" user preferences and target them with products tailored to earlier online searches. This is one of the consequences of what has been called the "filter bubble" (Pariser, 2011), i.e. one of the Web's contemporary tendencies which, a number of scholars have argued, has encouraged us to stick with what we know, with those we already agree with, with products we already like in some way (in the sense that we have chosen something similar in the past) and which suit us. The filter bubble is a socio-economic concept, which largely emerged from the fact that the internet is first and foremost a business space.

3.7 The Social Influence

This last of our internet history influences does not, as we noted at the outset of this chapter, appear in James Curran's framework. It is a phase that began in around the middle of the noughties (we will take 2004 as our symbol date, when the expression "Web 2.0" was coined and Facebook was launched) and, as the most recent and thus still evolving, it is probably the most difficult to judge also because of its many paradoxes and counter-tendencies. In this section, we will use the key adjective "social" in at least three different ways. First, recent internet history can be christened social as a result of the birth of so-called Web 2.0 and the–real or presumed–active involvement of users in *social network sites* such as Facebook. This first meaning deals with the etymology of *socius* as "companion", "ally" or "follower". Second, an apparent user freedom has been matched by ever-greater *social control* of the information circulating, and so the second meaning of "social" considered in this section deals with the limitations and regulations of social interactions on a political and cultural level. Finally, expanding in more and more countries and *societies*, the internet has been, on the one hand, increasingly globalized in terms of governance and users and, on the other, confronted with the growing political and economic dominance of a few ultra-powerful American firms. This third meaning of social focuses more on the large scale and global spread of the internet in differentiated social settings that, at the end, mostly benefited large corporations. These are the three macro-themes, which will structure this section.

Web 2.0 and the Participation Mythology

In 2004, Dale Dougherty, vice president of American colossus O'Reilly Media, coined the term *Web 2.0* to describe a new internet phase apparently different from earlier phases. The expression Web 2.0 was first and foremost a rhetorical resource, indirectly echoing other internet history phases, in an attempt to differentiate this new period from the commercial phase of a hypothetical Web 1.0. At the same time, it aimed to return to and implement some of the founding internet "parables" and mythologies embedded in collaborative and counter-cultural values in the golden age of the horizontal internet (implicitly marked as a sort of Web 0.0). It is precisely this tension between the Web's past and present that has prompted Matthew Allen (2013, pp. 269-270) to argue that the Web 2.0 rhetoric contained a high degree of historicity, i.e. one deliberately intended to focus on a diachronic, long term trajectory cutting through the internet's history as a whole.

The need to mark out a historic breakwater is directly linked to the Web's need to recapture its economic and cultural respectability after the bursting of the dotcom bubble, which, as we have seen, led to growing digital diffidence in many world economies. Moreover, the commercial phase seemed to have placed the economic interests of a small number of firms, which dominated the Net's development in a hierarchical way, center stage. The new Web 2.0 paradigm, by contrast, proposed a return to the Net's "traditional" values–joint working, co-creation, connecting up human beings. According to this rhetoric, these were the main characteristics and vocations of the Net's military and academic influence (improving researcher communication and collaboration), of the counter-cultural BBS and virtual community phase (whose aim was to get people dialoguing in new cultural spaces) and, finally, of the public service logics, which saw the Net as an immense human knowledge repository.

The Web 2.0 metaphor has become so powerful over the last decade or so that it is now applied to non-communications fields too. For example, the well-known "small world" and "degrees of separation" theories emphasize the extent to which nodes in different networks require just a few steps for access and what emerged in communication studies was then applied to biological, physical and mathematical phenomena (Barabási, 2002). This means that the Web 2.0 notion has stimulated theories in accordance with its main rhetoric emerging as a metaphoric resource adopted to address many and differentiated social phenomena.

The defining narrative of Web 2.0 and, more in general, of the social phase is undoubtedly that of the active, participatory user creating contents re-christened "user generated contents" (UGC, see Han, 2011). This idea was (and partially still is) so popular that a new term to refer to new digital users who are simultaneously producers and consumers was coined–prosumer–borrowing a neologism introduced by Alvin Toffler as far back as 1980. Like the word "prosumer", creating *bottom-up contents* is neither exclusive to the social phase nor to digital media. Swedish based scholars Anders Ekström, Solveig Jülich, Frans Lundgren and Per Wisselgren (2011) have argued for a historical perspective in participatory media to move beyond the simplistic Web 2.0 narrative as the starting point for audience engagement in media co-construction. In their book, they collect examples from the eighteenth to the twentieth century such as the printing press, sound media such as phonographs, photography, exhibitions, TV, photocopying and other (analog and digital) technologies in order to show that audiences have been always frequently taken part in media history. In recent years, then, the UGC historical perspective has been booming in digital culture too. A recent and interesting example is the work of Michael Stevenson (2016) who has argued that the 1990s-digital version of *Wired* (Hot Wired) has shown that a new publication paradigm narrowing the gap between media professionals and user participation in content creation was already being talked about at that time.

Alongside this historical trend, two other paradoxes or juxtaposed tendencies have emerged in recent years in relation to user participation. The first is a matter of the effective degree of user participation. On this issue Nielsen's (2006) theory of participation inequality argued that 90% of users make "passive" use of Web contents with 9% taking a limited part and only 1% doing

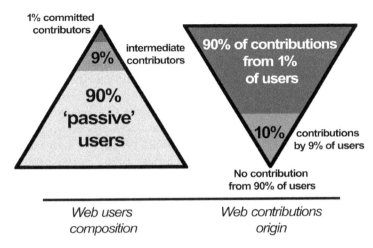

Figure 3.6 Graphic representation of Nielsen's participation inequality
Source: authors' artwork

so to a significant degree (see Figure 3.6). In other words, in a world in which social network sites and new digital practices of hyper-socialization have yet to spread significantly, according to Nielsen the majority of user generated contents were the work of a tiny minority of the most active users.

In light of a new, post social network site context, it is often argued that this theory requires re-evaluation. Indeed, Facebook claims to have around 2 billion monthly "active users" worldwide, WhatsApp and WeChat are intensively used by 1 billion people to share contents and data every month and, more generally, our everyday lives seem to be more and more actively engaged with digital platforms. Nevertheless, recent research has substantially confirmed low and poor user participation. Despite booming reader figures, for example, the number of active contributors to Wikipedia has been declining for years (Halfaker, Gieger, Morgan, & Riedl, 2013). Recently, then, Nielsen's research has been substantially confirmed: Gonzalez and Cox (2012), for example, confirm that only 10% of digital contents are users generated and so that a minority of the user population of online community participates actively even in the "new" social media environment. It is not a coincidence that studies on *lurkers* have become very popular in recent years: this is a term coined in the BBS period, which then occasionally re-emerges to define online users who visit online communities without posting messages—in this apparently resembling *passive* broadcasting audiences more than *active* digital users (Crawford, 2011). A further contemporary digital keyword is *slacktivism*: coined from the word slacker, it reminds that the quality of user participation is low and limited to "lazy" forms of action such as commenting, "liking", posting photos, all elements that denote poor, superficial and unfocused participation by the majority of users (Keen, 2007).

The second *user participation paradox* is the fact that the Web is free to use but, at the same time, generates economic or social value. This has generated positive examples of full-blown *collective intelligence* development, which were seen in the 1990s (Levy, 1994/1997) as an internet human knowledge development opportunity. The case of Wikipedia mentioned previously, founded in 1999 but which only established itself in 2001 is perhaps the most significant example (on the history of Wikipedia, see Sanger, 2005). There is, however, a flip side to this coin: the fact that large private firms such as Facebook, Twitter, You Tube and other social network sites are effectively making profits from user generated contents (written posts, videos, photos, etc.) at no expense to themselves. This is the so-called exploitation of free labor, which, while it was present in earlier forms of analog communication, seems to be a key and worrying feature of digital media according to influent critical observers such as Evgeny Morozov (2011) and Christian Fuchs (2014).

All in all, one of the main characteristic features of the social internet history phase–user participation–seems to be more a mythology and a narrative construction than a reality. First, "participation" is an unclear concept that requires careful re-consideration. Second, arguing that it has emerged in the digital environment alone is historically inaccurate. Third, it is a practice involving a minority of digital users while, according to recent research, the majority of these are still adopting traditional mass media practices–those targeted by the digital rhetoric. Finally, the corollary of participation, collective intelligence, is historically turning into another form of dominion and exploitation of users by big corporations. These are all mythologies and counter-hegemonic narratives (see Conclusion) that are deeply debated today and would certainly benefit from a historical perspective.

From Freedom to Social Control

In the 1990s and early noughties, the internet was regarded as a realm of freedom: cyber space was juxtaposed to physical "real" space precisely because it enabled users to be and do what they really wanted but could not be and do in the real world. This was at length the idea behind the creation of multi user dungeons (MUDs), anonymous chats and role-plays initially taking only written and then increasingly graphic form in which users made contact with strangers and played whatever characters they wanted (see Turkle, 1995). Perhaps the best-known and most interesting example of MUDs is Second Life, a virtual platform set up in 2003 that offered (and still offers) users the chance to create their own made-to-measure worlds and also to integrate real and virtual worlds in concerts, electoral committees and even religious ceremonies. This platform's user figures peaked at over 9 million in 2007-2008 and then declined sharply by the end of the noughties. A significant factor in this contraction was the success of social network sites such as Facebook and YouTube, which proposed a very different model: no longer a rigid separation between real and virtual but rather the merging of the two. Both set up in the mid noughties (Facebook in 2004 and YouTube in 2005), these two social networks offered users the chance to "connect and share with the people *in your life*" and "broadcast *yourself*", proposing users' continual osmosis between their physical and online lives to the extent of there being no distinction between the two.

This also implied recognizing that cyberspace is simply integrated into and part of everyday life, a concept with its own historicity. From a political economy perspective, in the 1990s cyberspace was considered a fully separated space, which governments could not control. The most telling formulation of this ideology was probably *A Declaration of the Independence of Cyberspace* written by John Perry Barlow in Davos, Switzerland, in 1996. In a significant extract Barlow argued thus:

> Governments of the Industrial World, you weary giants of flesh and steel, I come from Cyberspace, the new home of Mind. On behalf of the future, I ask you of the past to leave us alone. You are not welcome among us. [. . .] I declare the global social space we are building to be naturally independent of the tyrannies you seek to impose on us. You have no moral right to rule us nor do you possess any methods of enforcement we have true reason to fear. [. . .] Cyberspace does not lie within your borders. Do not think that you can build it, as though it were a public construction project. You cannot. It is an act of nature and it grows itself through our collective actions. [. . .] In China, Germany, France, Russia, Singapore, Italy and the United States, you are trying to ward off the virus of liberty by erecting guard posts at the frontiers of Cyberspace. These may keep out the contagion for a small time, but they will not work in a world that will soon be blanketed in bit-bearing media.
>
> (Barlow, 1996)

Despite this declaration of independence, in the space of just a few years it became clear that, in actual fact, cyberspace *could* be controlled and regulated for political ends too. In the year 2000, a well-known legal case saw *Yahoo!*– then the most popular American search engine–pitted against the French government with the latter complaining that Nazi propaganda sites violating French laws were accessible in France via the portal. This legal battle revolved around one key element. *Yahoo!* argued that it was unable to identify user connection locations and that contents were difficult to regulate by country of access. However, the trial showed that the exact opposite was true and it was thus established that the French government had the right to regulate or censor contents on *Yahoo!*'s American (and European) servers if these broke national laws (Goldsmith & Wu, 2006, chap. 1).

Governments have always been interested in subjecting the media to their laws and the internet is no exception. The issue was actually how a medium designed to avert any form of control or censorship, interpreting these as obstacles to be bypassed on a par with nodes destroyed in a nuclear attack (see Section 3.2), could be controlled. The solution adopted in many countries has been controlling the so-called "intermediaries" (internet service providers, search engines and financial middlemen) who must have a national physical location by their nature and these latter have frequently given in meekly to national government demands. In the 1990s, Germany put pressure on one of the largest German service providers, CompuServe Deutschland, to block access to Web pages with child pornography contents. The United States has demanded more than once that Google block contents which, while present on foreign servers, are contrary to American law. In 2016, the Indian government asked Google, Microsoft and *Yahoo!* to block research key words leading to the Web pages of companies offering fetal gender tests. This decision was taken to conform to an Indian law that banned fetal gender tests in 1994 to prevent female fetus abortions.

From this perspective, an interesting case is undoubtedly China. As we have seen, the Chinese government is certainly not the only political institution to have filtered the information its citizens can access within national borders. But China is one of the most interesting examples both of how a one-party state considered authoritarian interacts with a medium universally held to be libertarian and for the variety and ingeniousness of its internet content filtering.

China's internet beginnings are deferred but not very different from those of the US: in particular in terms of the key role played by the military apparatus and academia in the late 1980s and early 1990s, and then the relevance of BBS and virtual communities in the mid and late 1990s (Yang, 2009; 2012). In the mid 1990s, the Chinese government began both to recognize the key role of the internet in the country's future development and to control a medium capable of weakening central power and facilitating dissidents' access to information. For this purpose, at least five principal filtering strategies were experimented with (Harwit & Clark, 2001; Negro, 2017).

The first of these strategies was the Golden Shield Project better known as the Great Firewall of China. Designed in 1994 and implemented in 2002-2003 by American Cisco Systems, it was a filter system capable of blocking access to the Web sites the government considered undesirable by generating technical errors, the classic "site not found" message. Observers (Ensafi, Winter, Mueen, & Crandall, 2015) have noted that, despite its symbolic scope, the Golden Shield Project showed significant technical inefficiencies and limitations especially related to the ease with which national control can be bypassed thanks to the so-called Virtual Private Networks (VPNs), which enable users to connect up to foreign servers. A second and more effective strategy, exerted since the mid 1990s in accordance with what has been said of other countries, has concentrated on national internet service providers who frequently then self-censor contents or exclude users on government request for fear of political reprisals. A third form of control is applied to users and even thanks to users themselves. On the one hand, for example, bloggers have been asked to register with the central government and those attending popular internet cafés have been required to supply ID for Web use. This is the so-called *real name registration system* (*shimingzhi*) policy and this too has not been entirely effective because such rules are not always obeyed. On the other hand, users have been brought into online content controls awarding points to those promptly reporting dangerous contents or other issues to the government. A fourth strategy is fostering *rumors* and what has been called the *50 cents party* is a good example of this. These are armies of low-cost moderators—it is, in fact, said that these commentators are paid 50 cents for every post favorable to the party—whose task it is to report, comment negatively or distract Web attention from anti-government sentiments or dissent. The more contrary or unrelated comments are posted, or in other words, the more noise is made, the more this dissent is buried. A fifth and last strategy deals with media law: the Communist Party has avoided drawing up a well-defined legal framework controlling Web contents in favor of a freer hand in online content control. This is a political strategy that is definable as deregulation for the purposes of maintaining high levels of action flexibility.

The history of the internet in China once again shows that the Net depends on the political directives and choices of national governments. In this case, as already said, it is worth noting one more time that China is certainly not the only country to control and filter internet content and that other nations have shown varying degrees of tolerance and adopted a range of specific strategies in this regard. For example, in recent years the United States has also been accused of implementing covert mass surveillance strategies as the revelations of former NSA analyst Edward Snowden made public in 2013. The rhetoric and hope of the 1990s has turned into a false mythology: the illusion that the internet is open, free and global, that everyone can access the same contents from wherever they are and finally that it is an inexorable liberating and democratizing force (Morozov, 2011). It can be the diametric opposite because, contrary to Barlow's 1996 ideas, the internet has no intrinsic nature but is geographically located and constantly renegotiated over time and space.

The Globalization of the Internet and the Persistent Dominance of US Companies

A third characteristic of the internet's social influence is again a paradox: at a historical juncture at which a growing number of countries and cultures can access the internet, the oligopolistic tendency that originated in the commercial era has culminated in a small number of mainly American firms dominating the whole of the Web's space and traffic.

Let us begin this last section by mentioning three statistical data. In May 2016, seven of the top ten internet companies by revenue and market capitalization were American (Amazon, Alphabet/Google, and Facebook were the top three) and three were Chinese (source: Kleiner, Perkins, Caufield, & Byers). Amazon, for example, was founded in 1994 and was launched as an online-bookshop in 1995. It soon extended its product range, however, and expanded internationally building warehousing, delivery infrastructure and national sites (in Canada, the UK, Germany, Australia, France, Italy, Spain, China, Brazil, Mexico, Japan, Holland and India) and is now a global company delivering products all over the world. An even more interesting fact is that eight of the ten most visited sites in the world at the beginning of 2017 were American and two Chinese (Baidu and Tencent, both almost exclusively domestic market based). Once again, in 2017 Google (also in its co.in version in India and co.jp in Japan) was still the most visited site in the world followed by YouTube, Facebook, Wikipedia, *Yahoo!* and Amazon (source: Alexa.com). A last thought-provoking statistic tells us that, in October 2016, 31.9% of global online visitors to Google were from the US or, in other words, that 68.1% of Google access was from outside the US: 8.5% from India, 4.5% from Japan, 3.5% from China despite its being banned, 2.9% from Iran and so on (source: Alexa.com).

These figures–subject to rapid change but capturing a situation that has formed over time–contain much food for thought. First, they make clear that one of the internet's characteristics in its social phase is its domination by platforms, which were founded in, and continue to operate from, the United States. This means that American *soft power*, a feature of US media policy at least since the end of World War Two and thus well before the onset of media digitization, is still under way.

Second, moreover, in all likelihood it highlights an unprecedented phenomenon in communication history. Many countries worldwide, including those that have historically been careful to limit the American media product invasion (think of Hollywood movies) via quota systems and restrictions on sale of audio-visual products on national territory, have imposed no limitations on the Web "giants". The fact that Google, Facebook, YouTube, Amazon and other American sites are the most visited in the bulk of the world's countries has provoked no specific reactions (with a few exceptions which we will examine shortly).

Third, in a social phase that has placed discussion, sharing and horizontality center stage in its philosophy, what we are witnessing is the reverse: a concentration of power and profit in a small number of vertically structured companies. If we think of Google and its business model it is clear that, on one hand, it resembles the TV commercial model centered on advertising and, on the other, that new forms of oligopolistic control are being experimented with. In 2015, Google restructured, changing its name to Alphabet and presenting itself as a privileged knowledge and know-how access system and a node comprising physically thousands of servers accessed daily by billions of users requiring information from almost all over the world. It is, then, a model in which one single company has acquired astonishing global importance and now the most significant of the firms that have emerged from the so-called digital revolution (Vise & Malseed, 2005).

A last paradox to be underlined is the fact that even the so-called sharing economy, with companies that might have been expected to found their business models on horizontal structure and resource sharing, is shifting to a more "traditional" (neo)liberal and capitalistic model. Uber and Airbnb, for example, began as start-ups whose aim was to break monopolies working to the disadvantage of users (taxis and transport in general the former, the large-scale hotel chains the latter) and are now themselves becoming global companies whose power and socio-economic importance is concentrated into just a few hands.

Even in this more recent phase of internet history, however, opposition to the American liberal model does exist. In a phase in which the internet is, rightly or wrongly, held to be fully global it is creating counterweights to US digital dominion—in Russia and China in particular but also, more generally, in the BRICS nations (Brazil, Russia, India, China and South Africa). Resistance to US domination derives from two main considerations. In the first place, a recognition that Web use is increasingly globalized and, in particular, that a shift has taken place from a large majority of US users (61% in 1995) to US minority status with North American users accounting for 8.5% of world users in 2017 (364 million out of 4 billion; source: Internet World Stats; see also data appendix, Table A.1 and Figure A.1). In other words, non-American internet users are now in a global minority while Asian user numbers in particular (thanks, above all, to mobile internet) have grown exponentially and now account for about 50%

Box 3.4 In-depth Theory

The Digital Divide

The expression *digital divide* is used to denote forms of inequality in access to digital media and the internet in particular that have developed over recent decades. These inequalities can take various forms: between rich countries, generally with high internet coverage rates, and poor countries with generally limited access if any at all, within a single nation, between different geographical contexts in which networks are either inaccessible or limited, typically city/countryside or center/periphery divides. A further form of digital divide is income based between users able to afford Web access and others who cannot for purely financial reasons. A generational divide can also develop and the young are generally held to be more computer literate and to gain more from internet access than the elderly. More recently, research has highlighted that the ways in which people use the internet are also relevant: the so-called second-level digital divide focuses on proficiency and ability to use and access the Net, on searching for and getting the information required.

A series of initiatives has been employed by public institutions to combat the digital divide, which is seen as one of the great obstacles to digitization's dissemination and, more generally speaking, to social wellbeing. Global institutions such as ITU or UNESCO have been combating the digital divide for decades with specific economic policies to varying degrees of success especially in Africa, frequently in the belief that the internet "naturally" leads to progressive social democratization. Other private firms such as Facebook (with the project internet.org) and Google (with the Loon project) have made equally significant investments designed to extend internet access in Africa via air balloons, drones or other wireless technologies. There have been positive reactions, on one hand, to the role played by these global corporations in supplementing public institutions but, on the other, criticisms have been made of what are perceived to be the covert aims behind these operations: the desire to extend their influence and enlarge the number of users in parts of the world which are currently excluded from them.

The digital divide still surprises today because it flows against the tide of what appears to be common sense and to the digitization rhetoric of recent decades. While digital, and the internet in particular, are frequently viewed as democratizing and liberating forces, the digital divide shows the flip side of the coin: not only has digitization not had the results hoped for, but it has actually contributed to sharpening the differences between haves and have nots in accordance with an updated version of the knowledge gap theory, which emerged in the 1970s. For example, world internet usage data (see Table 3.2) shows that 51.8% of the world population was using the internet in December 2017 but it follows that 48.2% is not using it–half the world's people. Internet penetration also varies significantly from continent to continent passing from 32% with access to the Web in Africa to 95% in North America (with significant figures in Asia, accounting for more than half the world's population, where access to internet is only 49.2%). As we have seen, in the various macro regions, penetration rates vary considerably from country to country and within these same countries, with more or less developed areas. What is even more surprising is the fact that, even in regions like North American or Europe, where penetration rates are high, a significant segment of the population is excluded from internet access. Digital divide theory is often applied to the internet alone, while especially today the use of other digital media and especially mobile phones should also be included in it. Not only because smartphones are increasingly the key Net access devices but also because the adoption of mobile phones seems to be the real digitization history success story (see Chapters 2, 4 and the data appendix).

Further Reading

Norris, P. (2001). *Digital Divide: Civic Engagement, Information Poverty, and the Internet Worldwide*. Cambridge, MA: Cambridge University Press.
Ragnedda, M., & Glenn, W.M. (2013). *The Digital Divide: The Internet and Social Inequality in International Perspective*. Abingdon, UK: Routledge.
van Dijk, J. (2005). *The Deepening Divide: Inequality in the Information Society*. Thousand Oaks, CA: Sage.
Warschauer, M. (2003). *Technology and Social Inclusion: Rethinking the Digital Divide*. Cambridge, MA: The MIT Press.

of world internet users (see Table 3.2). Consequently, internet user culture and needs may no longer accord with American platforms.

A second reason to resist US dominance emerged thanks to Edward Snowden's revelations of mass surveillance practiced by the American government with the complicity of its powerful digital corporations. As a consequence of these public revelations too, certain countries started to affirm that the moment had come to free themselves of American infrastructure, hardware and software control. The Brazilian government, for example, issued a bill specifying

Table 3.2 Internet penetration into the various parts of the world in proportion to world population, December 2017 (Our elaboration on Internet World Stats Data)

	Population in 2017 (million)	Quote over world population (%)	Internet users 2017 (million)	Internet penetration rate in the region (%)	Quote over internet world users (%)
Africa	1,288	16.9	412	32.0	10.2
Asia	4,208	55.1	1,992	47.4	49.2
Europe	828	10.8	700	84.6	17.3
Latin America	652	8.5	425	65.1	10.5
Middle East	254	3.3	147	57.8	3.6
North America	364	4.8	346	95.0	8.5
Oceania	41	0.6	28	68.3	0.7
Total	7,635	100.0	4,050	51.8	100.0

that the digital data of Brazilian citizens must be stored in Brazil. This triggered a battle (renamed the *digital cold war* and *Internet Yalta*, see DeNardis, 2014) for control and global governance of the Web fought in recent years by the US and China/Russia in particular but also by international organizations. By means of ICANN, a US-based non-profit organization set up in 1998 with the objective of assigning internet addresses and dominions globally, the US has argued for what it refers to as a *multi-stakeholder* model. This assigns an important role in governance and decision-making processes not simply to national governments and ICANN itself but also to private firms (primarily the large American firms referred to above) and civil society representatives. The alternative and so-called *multilateral* model is supported primarily by China and Russia: the fundamental idea here is that internet governance should be entrusted primarily to national governments and intergovernmental organizations such as the International Telecommunication Union (ITU), which represent the interests of the various countries in a balanced way. Daya Thussu has written: "At the heart of the debate are two competing views–the *sovereignist* where national governments take the major decision, and a market-led privatized network–on how the most significant global network should be governed" (2015, p. 249). This battle seemed to culminate in a New World Communication Order (NWCO) on which BRICS countries, which have massively expanded their internet infrastructure and user numbers over recent decades and still have considerable growth margins, will surely have an increasing influence.

A fundamental contemporary tendency is once again a "return to the past": China and Russia, but also to some extent Brazil, are today moving in the direction of more nationally based internets closed to foreign, and primarily

Box 3.5 Documents

Lu Wei, *Cyber Sovereignty Must Rule Global Internet* (2014)

This document is an excerpt from a letter sent by Lu Wei, the Director of the Chinese State Internet Information Office, to the *Huffington Post* in 2014. It clearly states the Chinese view on global internet governance and explains the relationship between China and the US on this matter.

> The relationship [between China and US] displays two features: First, deep fusion and high stakes. China and the U.S. have never been so closely interconnected as they have become in cyberspace. China is the biggest overseas market for U.S. Internet companies. Almost all leading U.S. Internet companies have made great profits in China. [. . .] Nearly a thousand U.S. investment funds have designated China as their priority, reaching to every corner of the Chinese Internet market, accounting for more than half of their total overseas investment in this field. The success or failure of some U.S. companies is closely related to the Chinese market. The U.S. is the main overseas IPO destination for Chinese Internet companies, almost 50 of which are listed in the U.S. with a total market value of nearly U.S. $500 billion. U.S. shareholders have benefited from the development of the Internet market in China. Not long ago, the IPO of Alibaba in the U.S., the largest IPO ever in the world, raised over U.S. $25 billion. Experts believe that the investments made by U.S. shareholders in Alibaba demonstrates they have great confidence in the Chinese Internet, the Chinese market and the future of China.
>
> Second, disagreements and frictions still exist. It is because of the deeper integration, more extensive exchanges and closer contacts between the Internet industries of China and U.S. that our differences are easily put under magnifying glasses and spotlights—not to mention we also have the impact of cultural differences. [. . .] For example, with regard to the cyberspace governance, the U.S. advocates "multi-stakeholders" while China believes in "multilateral". ["Multi-stake-holder" refers to all Internet participants on an equal footing making the rules and is considered more "people-centered" while "multi-lateral" refers to the state making the rules based on the idea of the sovereignty of the nation-state representing its citizens.]
>
> These two alternatives are not intrinsically contradictory. Without "multilateral", there would be no "multi-stakeholders". Exaggerating our disagreements due to difference in concepts is neither helpful to

the China-U.S. Internet relations nor beneficial to global governance and the development of the Internet.

[...] President Xi Jinping has pointed out that those who share the same idea and follow the same path can be partners, and those who seek common ground while reserving differences can also be partners. We can have disagreements but we must not stop communication. We can have arguments but we must not discard trust. We should not be confused or blinded by chaotic situations. Instead, we should look carefully at the issues with a historic perspective. We should see that cooperation between China and the U.S. benefits our two countries as well as other countries, while confrontation can only hurt both sides and even the world at large. [...]

In this spirit, I therefore put forward five propositions:

1. First, mutual appreciation instead of mutual negating. [...]
2. Second, mutual respect instead of confrontation and accusation. [...]
3. Third, mutual governance instead of self-interest. [...]
4. Fourth, mutual trust instead of mutual suspicion.
5. Fifth, win-win instead of zero-sum. [...]

Source: Wei, L. (2014) "Cyber Sovereignty Must Rule Global Internet". *The Huffington Post*, USA, December 15 (www.huffingtonpost.com/lu-wei/china-cyber-sovereignty_b_6324060.html)

American, players with a tendency to replace these latter with national operators. This is what happened in the 1980s and 1990s with the European national internets and is a form of *minitelization* of the Web, returning to a closed, national and centralized internet model. In sum, at a time at which the internet is being used by half the world's population and in which digital communications are increasingly considered a global and irresistible phenomenon, an alternative anti-American model is emerging.

The *social influence* on future internet history is not an easy one to identify. In this section, we have concentrated on highlighting recent paradoxes and contradictory tendencies: the user participation rhetoric, the tension between horizontal and vertical models, freedom and control, the economic domination of the American firms, a progressive reduction in the American share of the global users and finally growing global internet control and management tensions. Probably all these topics will be widely debated in the future. The most likely outcome of all this is, however, that this too will be simply a transitional influence and phase in internet history and that those who see the social phase as internet history's finishing and highest post will probably be proved wrong by further and unforeseen future developments.

3.8 Re-reading the Internet in Historical Perspective

The internet history presented in this chapter has adopted James Curran's five formative influences with the addition of a supplementary influence (social), global case studies and "alternative" ideas and influences in specific historical periods. Under this framework, numerous trajectories and insights have emerged and in this final section we will attempt to suggest further readings of our internet history.

In the first place, our political history of the internet has highlighted the shift from government funding (military in origin in the US and more telecommunications-related in Europe) to private funding especially from watershed year 1995 onwards. This political history has encompassed many trans-national elements such as the WWW idea, which emerged from the Geneva CERN, and the global battle for internet governance we have just described with a growing trend, however, in the direction of increasingly national internets at least in certain countries.

A second layer we have examined is the internet's business history beginning mainly in 1995 and continuing through its moment of euphoria and disillusionment in the late twentieth and early twenty-first century dotcom bubble, which—contrary to expectations—led to forms of oligopoly by a small number of firms. These mega companies have acquired global control over the internet in the first two decades of the twenty-first century: they are mainly American, but we are also facing an increasingly significant proliferation of firms in other parts of the world, in Asia and China in particular.

A third possible reading of our internet history has looked at a series of alternative cultural ideas: Russian political-economic network management in the age of the military-academic ARPANET; internet as a closed system using earlier media such as telephones, *à la* Minitel (recently fashionable once again) in the counter-cultural movement era; and internet as a world knowledge repository (WWW) when it was mainly a commercial breakthrough. These, and other, alternative ideas show that the cultural significance of the internet, and of digital media in general, is continuously changing and negotiated in different periods and cultures.

A fourth sub-reading of internet history relates to users: academics dominated the early years of computer networks and were then joined by hackers and counter-cultural figures and then gradually by generic users especially from the second half of the 1990s onwards to considerably different degrees in different cultures. Today, internet user history is increasingly shifting from Western societies to other parts of the world and to Asia in particular.

There is also a fifth reading level that brings together the internet myths and counter-hegemonic visions (on this topic see the conclusion for a comprehensive analysis), which have proliferated in the popular imagination (see also Mansell, 2012): a network enabling academic research, one that "naturally" stimulates horizontal communications, economic prosperity, active user participation, etc. In this sense, the dialectic between a network seen as freeing human beings and giving them a form of democratic communication and that focusing on its control purpose has perhaps been the most omnipresent and enduring. It is a rhetorical oscillation with a long history: first the internet dominated by the powers-that-be (military-state), followed by a vision of the internet as a stimulant to distance human contact (counter-cultural), then a network working to the advantage of the economic *status quo* (until the bubble burst), before returning to a libertarian network concept in which users can express themselves in content creation and communication (origins of Web 2.0 ideology), culminated for now in an oligopolistic network which is increasingly controlled by large groups for economic purposes. In this process, the Net's two souls—freedom and control—cohabit and clash constantly.

A diachronic and long-term approach to the internet has enabled us to grasp some of the many readings and meanings that would not have emerged by looking at the state of today's internet alone. We have seen that the internet is an unstable form of communication (Thorburn & Jenkins, 2003) whose characteristics can and have varied profoundly over time and will probably continue to do so in the future. Furthermore, the very structure and current form of the internet is the result of the sedimentation, suppression and re-emergence of ideas and visions that have cut across its history at least since the 1950s. Some of these ideas have exerted, as James Curran says, *formative influences* on the contemporary internet to the extent that in various moments of its history long term *constitutive choices* have been made, which have been difficult to revise later on (Starr, 2004). Finally, internet history clearly shows that there is not—and should not be—a single "natural" internet form. Like all media and technologies, the internet is neither democratic nor totalitarian, global nor national, inherently good or inherently bad. All historical conflicts between groups, the material limits of technologies, political, technical and economic interests, cultural re-appropriation and the ability of users to transform the internet have made it what it is today.

LEARNING MATERIALS

Key Points to Focus on

- The technical, political, commercial and socio-cultural meanings of the internet.
- Six formative influences on the history of the internet.
- Military influence:
  - ARPANET
  - Time-sharing
  - Distributed network
  - Packet switching
  - The Cold War and the alternative (and failed) idea of the internet in Russia
- Academic influence:
  - Converging and diverging visions with military
  - European academic networks
  - The role of academia in the origins of the internet worldwide
- Counter-cultural influence:
  - Different visions of the internet: personal computers linked through telephone (and so home-based) networks
  - The origins of online communities
  - The French Minitel as a low tech and (another) "telephonic" vision of the internet
- Public service influence:
  - Internet in Europe in the framework of public services such as tele-communications and broadcasting
  - The invention of WWW at CERN
  - The symbolic document *The National Information Infrastructure: Agenda for Action* in the US
- Commercial influence:
  - 1995 as a symbolic year: main reasons
  - The dotcom bubble
  - The increasing commercialization of the internet
- Social influence:
  - Web 2.0 and its historical meanings
  - Web 2.0 and the participation mythology
  - Internet as a land of freedom in the 1990s and a land of control in the 2000s
  - Globalization of the internet and the dominance of few American companies

Questions to Answer

- Explain how the internet today is a consequence of past influences or, in other words, how history of the internet matters in explaining the contemporary Net.
- What is the relationship between the development of the internet and the telephone network? How is it an example of the combination of analog and digital?
- Why is *The National Information Infrastructure: Agenda for Action* a key document explaining the internet's role in political discourse starting from the 1990s?
- What are the main influences the commercial phase brought to bear on the contemporary internet?
- In what way can the concept of Web 2.0 be considered historical? And what are the main (mythological or not) characteristics of the social influence of the internet?

A Text to Read and Discuss

In 2010, *Wired* director Chris Anderson wrote an influential piece entitled "The Web Is Dead. Long Live the Internet". Here is an excerpt from this text. Read it (and, if you like, search the full article: www.wired.com/2010/08/ff_webrip/).

> You wake up and check your e-mail on your bedside iPad—that's one app. During breakfast you browse Facebook, Twitter, and The New York Times—three more apps. On the way to the office, you listen to a podcast on your smartphone. Another app. At work, you scroll through RSS feeds in a reader and have Skype and IM conversations. More apps. At the end of the day, you come home, make dinner while listening to Pandora, play some games on Xbox Live, and watch a movie on Netflix's streaming service. You've spent the day on the Internet—but not on the Web. And you are not alone. This is not a trivial distinction. Over the past few years, one of the most important shifts in the digital world has been the move from the wide-open Web to semiclosed platforms that use the Internet for transport but not the browser for display. It's driven primarily by the rise of the iPhone model of mobile computing, and it's a world Google can't crawl, one where HTML doesn't rule. And it's the world that consumers are increasingly choosing, not because they're rejecting the idea of the Web but because these dedicated platforms often just work better or fit better into their lives (the screen comes to them, they don't have to go to the screen). The fact

that it's easier for companies to make money on these platforms only cements the trend.

While the author wrote this idea in 2010, what do you think is today's *public Web* versus *closed platforms* situation? Do you agree with Anderson's perspective? Can you think of any other examples in which private platforms prevail over Web pages?

A Few Books for Further Study

Abbate, J. (1999). *Inventing the Internet.* Cambridge, MA: The MIT Press.

Curran, J. (2012). Rethinking Internet History. In J. Curran, N. Fenton, & D. Freedman (Eds.), *Misunderstanding the Internet* (pp. 34-65). London: Routledge.

Flichy, P. (2001/2007). *The Internet Imaginaire.* Cambridge, MA: The MIT Press.

Goggin, G., & McLelland, M. (Eds.). (2017). *Routledge Companion to Global Internet Histories.* New York: Routledge.

Ricker Schulte, S. (2013). *Cached: Decoding the Internet in Global Popular Culture.* New York: New York University Press.

Ryan, J. (2010). *A History of the Internet and the Digital Future.* London: Reaktion Books.

Streeter, T. (2010). *The Net Effect: Romanticism, Capitalism, and the Internet.* New York: New York University Press.

---

4 The Mobile Phone

4.1 The Origins of the Mobile Phone

One of the themes running through this book is that digital media are at the center of a tension between the break with the past and continuity with analog media and earlier communication technologies. Mobile phones are no exception to this. While on the one hand, mobile phones have internationalized and democratized communication, on the other they are the direct heirs of two late-nineteenth-century electromechanical technologies: the landline telephone and the wireless telegraph-telephone.

Although the history of landline telephones does not concern this book (even if telephone networks were crucial in internet histories as well, see Chapter 3), scholars studying mobile phones have frequently noted just how close the symbolic and practical links between these two forms of telecommunications are. To begin with, the mobile phone's extraordinary success and fast take-up rates cannot be explained without reference to home phones. When Alexander Graham Bell patented the telephone in 1876, it was the first person-to-person communication medium allowing long-distance speech transmission and was slow to take off for this very reason, particularly in the lower classes (Marvin, 1988). By contrast, when the mobile phone concept returned to favor in the 1970s and 1980s, the phoning concept was already a familiar one. People had been using—or at least had some kind of familiarity with—point-to-point communication technologies (such as telegraphs and telephones) for decades and were already used to distance sound transmission and reception via telephones and, naturally, radio and television. People were also accustomed to using telephones and shared a number of assumptions that seem routine today but were nothing of the sort at the time (e.g. making a simple phone call). Finally, and perhaps most importantly, a body of potential users with landline phones already existed for the first mobile phone owners to call on their new devices: this is the so-called "club" or "network effect" where the more a communication

Table 4.1 A summary of the main phases in mobile phones' socio-technical history

Ages	Time frame	Distinctive features
1. First birth	1900-1960s	The radiotelephone age: connections with landline telephone and wireless telegraphy; origins of mobile telecommunications for niche markets.
2. Second birth	1970s-1980s	First analog commercial services, national and fragmented systems in Europe, US backwardness, NMT in Denmark, Norway, Sweden and Finland.
3. The boom	1990s	Digitization of 2G and adoption of GSM standard in 1992, diffusion of mobile telephone thanks also to SMS, (unsuccessful) origins of 3G and mobile internet.
4. The global	2000s-today	Mobile internet and smartphones take off diffusion (thanks to iPhone primarily), global spread of mobile telephony especially in Asia and Africa.

device is used, the more new potential users are willing to adopt it because it enables them to reach a more extensive network of people (Curien, 2005; on network effect in mobile see Birke & Swann, 2006). For all these reasons, then, pre-existing communication technologies had to some extent already set the stage for mobile telecommunications.

Given the close relationship between landline and mobile phones, there is nothing surprising about the fact that home phones and cell phones have followed similar take-up trajectories (moving from being the preserve of the "serious" professions and for emergency use to a way of keeping up with friends and family) and have prompted surprisingly similar health (electrocution and electro smog) and invasion of privacy concerns (Lasen, 2005).

Obviously, mobile telephones are different from landline phones especially because mobile phones were and are free of the wires that bound older phones, and this has been clear since the beginning of its history. Mobile communications have stimulated more personal uses than household landline phones (although there are many exceptions on this score) and have also allowed for what a number of scholars have christened *constant touch* or *perpetual touch*, making people contactable and able to communicate at all times. Furthermore, it took decades for landlines to be widely adopted, and take up rates in some countries are still low, while mobile phones have been one of the greatest success stories in media history; indeed, the number of mobile phone subscribers has nearly exceeded the total world population and this has happened in a very short space of time (see data appendix, Tables A.2 and A.5). Finally, while home phones are exclusively a matter of speech communication by means of electrical impulses—in other words, an oral medium—mobile phones added initially a written element with text messages and then other multimedia elements via the integration of Web-based services.

The second forerunner of mobile telephones as we know them today is another medium with late-nineteenth-century roots: wireless telegraphy. Wireless telegraphs innovated and improved on certain aspects of electrical telegraphy using the air waves (with low infrastructure costs) rather than wires to transmit communications, thus allowing two individuals or even vehicles in movement to exchange point-to-point written messages. Experiments were already being carried out to replace written these in Morse code with speech in the first decade of the twentieth century, passing *de facto* from telegraph to phone. The basic assumptions behind late-twentieth-century mobile telecommunications were the same as those behind these early-twentieth-century experiments, namely the idea of transmitting wireless messages (written words or speech) from person to person in movement.

Experiments were made with radiotelephones in particular during and between the two World Wars. The outcome of these experiments were two distinct media. The first was a sort of walkie-talkie used in various countries mainly by the armed forces and the police to manage emergencies and this can be considered the forerunner of the late-twentieth-century mobile phone. The second medium, by contrast, took advantage of the downside of radiotelephones—the fact that anyone could listen in on private messages—in order to disseminate information and entertainment intended for all those with receivers. Full use of this latter technique came to fruition from the 1920s onwards in the form of radio and then TV broadcasting.

The "walkie talkie" or better radiotelephone model was considered most strategic and relevant by major wireless companies from 1900 to the 1920s (Balbi, 2017b) and so experiments included media campaigns that were given plenty of coverage in the newspapers and magazines of the day and popularized it as a means of communication. One of radiotelephony's first killer applications was thus ultra long-distance communications (see the transatlantic wireless communication promoted by Guglielmo Marconi himself), which actually only came to mass fruition much later via complex roaming agreements between countries. In the 1920s and 1930s radiotelephony experiments were carried out by a number of police forces (the systems used in Chicago and Detroit are the best known) who could now hear emergency calls but not answer them. By World War Two, two-way radios had been developed—thus allowing for dialogue. They were used in civilian contexts, for example by New

Figure 4.1 The Excell Mobile Phone in a 1980s British advertisement is compared to the previous (and obviously heavier) generation car phone

Source: courtesy of www.advertisingarchives.co.uk

York taxi drivers, and, after the war, in non-emergency situations. This brought to the fore an ingrained problem with mobile telecommunications: potential congestion or overlapping of electromagnetic waves in the Hertzian spectrum, that part of the airwaves that is invisible to the human eye and enables telecommunications to be transmitted. These radios thus supplemented and interfered with a series of other wireless applications, which had been pro-liferating in the meantime such as radio-telegraphy messages, amateur radio experiments crisscrossing the airwaves and broadcasting signals (Gow & Smith, 2006, chap. 2).

How did early-twentieth-century radiotelephony differ from what we call mobile phones today? First, as we have already seen, early radiotelephones were more like walkie-talkies than ordinary telephones: users had to press a button to speak and then release it to listen, there was no full-blown public access network and such radios were thus limited to occasional and special services use. Second, while these radios were effectively portable, they were certainly not comparable to today's mobile phones as they often weighed several kilos and had to be connected to car or vehicle batteries because of their heavy and high-energy consumption (Glenn, 2006)—this connection between mobile phones and cars was long lasting in the popular imagination (see Figure 4.1). Third, radiotelephones were relatively complex to use: calls were not auto-matic and switchboard operators put callers and receivers through, again like nineteenth- and early-twentieth-century landline phones. Finally, as we have already seen, conversations could easily be intercepted by anyone listening out for them. These differences notwithstanding, however, radiotelephony's history is to all intents and purposes a chapter in the history of the contemporary mobile telephone and these earliest mobile devices contributed to popularizing the idea of mobile communication in the twentieth century popular imagination. For example, Dick Tracy, a well-known 1930s comic strip character who used a watch-radiotelephone, helped the concept of mobile (and even wearable) distance telecommunications to slowly penetrate popular consciousness.

If, historically speaking, the origins of mobile telecommunications can be dated to the end of the nineteenth century, social use and public success was to come only at the end of the next century (Ling, 2008). This delay can be explained by several interconnecting reasons: people were not yet ready for the idea; mobile communication was not yet considered useful; a consolidated business model did not exist for it and political convenience and other insti-tutional reasons did not offer this technology a favorable eco-system for its development at the moment of conception. However, rather like an underground stream, mobile phones re-emerged in a later era, as other media had in the past according to cinema scholars Gaudreault and Marion (2005). Defining this process, a *double birth*, Gaudreault and Marion claim that certain communi-cation technologies are born more than once and, after their rebirth, can take on very different uses and social values from those of their first life (see Box 4.1). In this respect, mobile phones have lived at least twice.

Box 4.1 In-depth Theory

The *Double Birth* Model

The *Double Birth* media studies model was developed by French scholars André Gaudreault and Philippe Marion with the aim of rethinking media birth and genealogy going beyond the traditional idea that media have precise and one-directional dates of birth, which generally coincide with their invention. Using the case of early cinema, the two scholars claim that media are often born twice: the first time extending earlier practices (in this case photography, visual arts, etc.) and so configuring themselves not as brand-new media but on a continuum with old media. The second birth occurs when new media truly emerge through a process of self-consciousness (via its practitioners) and with a high degree of institutionalization: in doing so new media become autonomous and unrelated to old media (Gaudreault & Marion, 2002).

This idea has been further developed in other publications and the *two births* concept has been rechristened in various ways (Gaudreault & Marion, 2005). The first birth has been renamed *integrating birth* in reference to the fact that in early stages new media adapt to the existing media ecologies on a continuum with "older and better established generic and media practices" (idem, p. 12). Integration refers to the fact that new media do not emerge as a single medium but are rather marked out by a kind of *spontaneous intermediality* (on intermediality see also Box 5.1). New media are not simply integrated into the previous intermedia landscape but also borrow a range of "natures" or characteristics from other media not having yet acquired their own specific personalities. The second birth, rechristened *distinguishing birth* gives new media autonomous identities or "syntagma" or, in other words, specific and distinct natures or personalities. This process, which partially echoes the closure of flexibility in STS studies (see Chapter 1), brings with it another kind of intermediality referred to as *subjugated* or *negotiated*:

> This is the intermediality that is always present in it (the medium) but which it negotiates in its own fashion, in interaction with its own potential. This latter intermediality [. . .] could be compared with the intertextuality found in any process of cultural production. This *negotiated intermediality* is of particular importance in the contemporary media landscape, marked as it is by flux, contamination, interconnectedness and global Web. It is common knowledge that the

media today interpenetrate and combine to a high degree in such forms as hypertext and multimedia, not to mention the Internet.

(idem, p. 13)

The last step to a better understanding of the double birth model is applying it to the digital age–to paraphrase another paper published by Gaudreault and Marion (2013). Looking at the digital media landscape, and especially at digital cinema, the two scholars put forward the idea of a *third birth* because media are constantly changing and digitization is bringing back old forms of early cinema–especially a return to animation. More precisely, "it is necessary to argue for a pluralistic view of its birth/ emergence, one that will enable people to see the history of cinema as a succession of beginnings (in the plural) and a succession of deaths (in the plural)" (idem, p. 161). The third birth of cinema in the digital age is a de-institutionalization or post-institutionalization phase in which all the institutional constructions of its second birth are revised and transformed by digitalization.

The concept of double (and triple or multiple) birth can be applied to various media. We have explicitly used this model in the case of mobile phones but readers can also apply it to other digital media mentioned in this book and, in doing so, rethink a tension at the center of *A History of Digital Media*: change and continuity.

Further Reading

Gaudreault, A., & Marion, P. (2002). The Cinema as a model for the genealogy of media. *Convergence: The International Journal of Research into New Media Technologies, 8*(4), 12-18.

Gaudreault, A., & Marion, P. (2005). A Medium is always born twice. *Early Popular Visual Culture, 3*(1), 3-15.

Gaudreault, A., & Marion, P. (2013). Measuring the "double birth" model against the digital age. *Early Popular Visual Culture, 11*(2), 158-177.

4.2 Digital Rebirth and Growing up

Mobile telephone's second incarnation began at the end of the 1970s when the foundations for its popularization were laid and the first networks open to the public set up. Technically speaking, in 1947, Douglas H. Ring–an engineer at Bell Laboratories–came up with the idea of dividing portions of terrain into *cells* within which telephones communicated with a base station. This enabled Hertzian space to be used more efficiently by sub-dividing it up into sectors or cells—it is for this reason that mobile telephones are also known as cell phones. In the United States, this simple idea was put into practice only many years later partly as a result of the attitude to it of AT&T (the main United States telephone company) and FCC (the communication regulatory agency). On the one hand, AT&T hesitated to follow through on mobile telecommunications because of its leading position in landlines communication sector, another case of the so-called innovator's dilemma (see also Chapter 2 and Section 4.5 later in this chapter). On the other, the FCC long denied permits for the necessary experiment and these were granted only in the mid 1970s (Farley, 2005). This indecision effectively cancelled out all the technological advantages the United States had accumulated in previous decades and the first mobile phone system open to the public was actually launched in Japan in 1979 by Nippon Telegraph and Telephone, initially only in Tokyo but already, in 1984, with a first-generation analog network (1G) covering the whole country (on mobile communication in Japan, see Peil, 2011).

It was, however, in the 1980s that mobile telephones gained wider popularity initially in richer countries and with the wealthier classes with one notable exception: the United States (Agar, 2013, chap. 4). There were many reasons for this further US delay. To begin with, the 1980s was a challenging decade for AT&T when the company was accused of presiding over a trust. This turned into a refusal by national agencies to assign mobile telecommunications frequencies to the company and these were portioned out on a local basis to a number of regional operators, thus leading to fragmented networks with incompatible standards making it more difficult for callers to use their mobile phones when travelling through different states. A second factor was that AT&T had underestimated the potential of mobile telecommunications development (the same thing happened with the internet, see Chapter 3) and even when the firm had the right to enter regional phone markets it did not in fact apply for local mobile services (Murray, 2001). A further reason was the fact that early American mobile phone users, in contrast to Europeans, had to pay for both outgoing and incoming calls and were thus understandably cautious about handing out their phone numbers. According to some scholars, a fourth and interesting factor explaining limited initial mobile phone take-up in the United States was the unattractive design of the phones themselves. Motorola, the first company to gain a dominant position on the American market, made less attractive and larger phones than their European and Japanese competitors. A final distinguishing feature of the US situation (and one shared only partially by Japan) was competition to mobile phones from other mobile devices of the day. More than in any European country, in 1980s America, pagers and beepers, as well as CB radios, were very common. Pagers and beepers were not interactive telecommunications' devices, but they simply informed users that someone was searching for them and users had then to find a landline phone to call back. Despite this, these devices became very popular in the United States also because of TV programs in which they were regularly used by doctors and businessmen. Similarly, CB radios were an amateur radio legacy and they gained a certain popularity in the 1970s, as is reflected in a number of movies such as Sam Peckinpah's 1978 cult film *Convoy* where truck drivers created a sort of virtual community in movement based on these communication devices. In the United States pagers and CB radios met an initial demand for mobile communication from certain social and professional groups who later adopted mobile phones years later. Surprisingly, this demand for pagers was not completely replaced by the rise of mobile phones. For example, in the early 2010s Taiwanese elders still communicated through pagers because they are easier to use than smartphones and young subcultures used them as well to exchange "coded" messages. Let's take the screenshot of an ad, broadcasted in 2011 by the Taiwanese cable TV network CTi as historical source (see Figure 4.2) in which both dimensions are combined: specifically, the sequence of numbers 530 0358 (*wusanling lingsan wuba*) means in slang "I am thinking about you, are you thinking about me?" This distinctive but telling case can be interpreted in at least two different ways: on the one hand, the attempt to slow down digitization "progress" and "innovation" by older generations, bringing a widespread phenomena called digital disconnections, de-communication or digital detox (Kaun & Schwarzenegger, 2014); on the other, it is another example of reuse of old digital technologies, of rebirth of old users' practices and adaptation to a different (someone would claim more evolved) media ecology. Digital (and analog) media do not die often.

In sum, the concise analysis of the American situation shows that a technology's success in a specific cultural context is a matter of a series of interconnected factors that are political (the FCC's reluctance to assign frequencies and their fragmentation), economic (AT&T's short-sightedness), technical (competition from pagers and CB radios) and socio-cultural (the phones' attractiveness and the reluctance to share telephone numbers with others). New technology uptake and its consequences, therefore, is always a complex and multi-faceted phenomenon.

In Europe, the situation was a very different one where mobile telecommunications were launched by national governments over the course of the 1980s with varying degrees of success (Agar, 2013). The Thatcher government's privatization drive led to two permits being issued as early as 1982: one to British Telecom and the other to Racal (later renamed Vodafone) who set up the Cellnet network in 1985. In France, an ambitious project called Radiocom was launched in 1985 but its success was tempered by excessive military control, limited coverage and high costs. In Germany, Siemens set a new standard in 1986 with

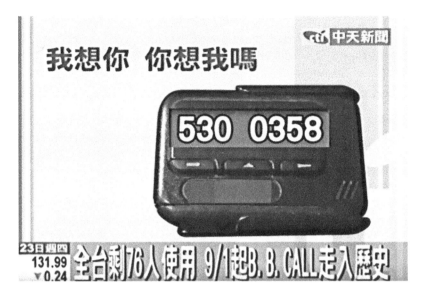
我想你 你想我嗎

530 0358

全台剩76人使用 9/1起B. B. CALL走入歷史

Figure 4.2 Screenshot of a TV commercial broadcasted in 2011 by the Taiwanese network CTi: the rebirth of pagers

virtually total country-wide coverage thanks to a personal card, which could be used in a range of telephones (a forerunner of modern SIM cards). A country with instantly high levels of mobile phone take-up was Italy, whose 1985 RTMS network was so successful that it was saturated by 1990 (Balbi, 2008).

The most interesting aspect of European mobile phone history in the 1980s was, however, the fragmentation and incompatibility of the various networks with governments setting up a grand total of *nine* alternative telephone systems, all of which were analog and all with different standards. In other words, a traveler in 1980s Europe wanting to use his or her mobile phone in a number of European countries had to buy a different phone for every country visited. An exception was Scandinavia where mobile phones were an instant success partly as a result of the early adoption of a standardized system—prompted by regional manufacturers such as Nokia and Ericsson and supported at political level—which led to the creation of the so-called Nordisk MobilTelefoni standard (in English Nordic Mobile Telephony, NMT). In the early 1980s, the governments of Denmark, Norway, Sweden and Finland decided to entrust the development of their mobile phone networks to a pool of engineers from the four different countries in order to ensure that the ether was shared out rationally. This group of experts came up with a roaming principle, in contrast to the *isolationist* policies of other European countries, in which mobile phones worked in any country adopting the NMT standard (Castells & Himanen, 2002, pp. 54-56).

The NMT was the forerunner of the GMS standard, which was set up in Stockholm in 1992, becoming the true key to the surprising success of European mobile telephones in the 1990s.

4.3 GSM: The European Digital-Bureaucratic Miracle

Jon Agar (2013, p. 57) has coined the term *bureaucratic miracle* for the adoption and dissemination of mobile telephones in Europe from December 1992 onwards when a number of nations adopted the Global System for Mobile Communications (GSM—previously, in French, Groupe Spécial Mobile) as their sole standard.

At least three factors prompted this convergence of interest and the adoption of a common system (Pelkmans, 2001). The first of these was in the realm of political economy and concerned the idea that GSM, a sort of European Union through communications, could act as a bridgehead and launching pad for proposed economic union and the creation of a common European market. The second was purely business related. Some of the larger European telephone companies and mobile phone manufacturers, in particular, lobbied for a single standard because they understood that it would give them global leadership in mobile communications. This did in fact generally occur and companies such as Finnish Nokia and Swedish Ericsson acquired a dominant share of the world market, which lasted for some time. The third and last factor behind this important decision was linked to GSM's technical and social advantages, some of which were borrowed from the Scandinavian NMT. Users could pass from one national network to another smoothly (this is the basis of what is still today called roaming). Frequencies and telephone signals were rationalized and qualitative improvements made. GSM also allowed SIM cards to be brought in enabling users' data to be collected and identified whatever the terminal used. Finally, GSM allowed mobile telephone communications to be digitized (Hillebrand, 2002).

GSM was in fact immediately linked to a new mobile standard—2G. In contrast to the first 1G analog networks, which we have looked at thus far, 2G was an integrated digital system, which was implemented for the first time in association with GSM by Finnish telephone company Nokia in 1991. The cell phone universe thus moved from analog to digital only in the early 1990s and, while 2G and GSM were actually distinct, they are often spoken of in the same breath precisely because they encouraged wholesale digitization of mobile services and increased their potential for exponential increase. The GSM system's success was rapid. When it was set up in December 1992, eight of the most important European countries (Germany, Denmark, Finland, France, Great Britain, Sweden, Portugal and Italy) immediately adopted it. By 1995, the whole of Europe had

Box 4.2 Documents

European Commission, *Reasons to Introduce a Pan-European Standard in Mobile Telephony* **(1987)**

Council Regulation 84/549/EEC (3) calls for the introduction of services on the basis of a common harmonized approach in the field of telecommunications; [. . .] the resources offered by modern tele-communications networks should be utilized to the full for the economic development of the Community; [. . .] mobile radio services are the only means of contacting users on the move and the most efficient means for those users to be connected to the public tele-communications networks; [. . .] the land-based mobile communications systems currently in use in the Community are largely incompatible and do not allow users on the move in vehicles, boats, trains or on foot throughout the Community, including inland or coastal waters to reap the benefits of European-wide services and European-wide markets; [. . .] the change-over to the second generation cellular digital mobile communications system will provide a unique opportunity to establish truly pan-European mobile communications; [. . .] the European Conference of Postal and Telecommunications administrations (CEPT) has set up a special Working Group, referred to as GSM (Groupe Spécial Mobile), for planning all system aspects of a second-generation cellular mobile radio infrastructure; [. . .] such a future system, offering both voice and data services, is to be based on digital technique, thereby facilitating compatibility with the general digital environment that will evolve with the coordinated introduction of the Integrated Services Digital Network (ISDN) in accordance with recommendation 86/659/EEC (4); [. . .] a coordinated policy for the introduction of a pan-European cellular digital mobile radio service will make possible the establishment of a European market in mobile and portable terminals which will be capable of creating, by virtue of its size, the necessary development conditions to enable undertakings established in Community countries to maintain and improve their presence on world markets; [. . .] the implementation of such a policy will lead to closer cooperation, at Community level, between the telecom-munications industry, on the one hand, and the telecommunications administrations and the recognized private operating agencies offering public mobile telecommunications services, hereinafter referred to as *telecommunications administrations* on the other; [. . .] the envisaged measures will allow the economic benefit and rapidly increasing market potential of public mobile communications to be fully realized in the Community.

Source: Council Recommendation of 25 June 1987 on the coordinated introduction of public pan-European cellular digital land-based mobile communications in the Community (31987H0371–87/371/EEC)

abandoned national standards in favor of GSM and by 1996, it was already in use in 103 countries worldwide.

The most revealing statistics on GSM's success and the extent to which it encouraged the popularization of mobile phones are those relating to the increase in mobile phone users that took place in the 1990s (see data appendix, Figure A.2 and Table A.4). In the West and certain areas of Asia, the 1990s was a decade of huge expansion in mobile phone use for a number of reasons. Economically speaking, mobile phone use was boosted by telecommunications sector privatization in Europe and some Asian countries in the 1980s and 1990s. This contributed to the setting up and growth of several telephone companies in Asia (in the 1990s the largest in terms of mobile phone users were Japan's NTT and publicly controlled China Telecom) and in Europe (Italian companies Tim and Omnitel Pronto Italia took a leading role, in third and eighth global positions respectively) (Goggin, 2011, chap. 2). These privatizations contributed to the popularization of mobile telephones because competing companies expanded their national networks and frequently engaged in price wars that worked to client advantage. Mobile telephone costs fell rapidly throughout the 1990s and, even more interestingly, new "pay as you go" cards enabled users to limit telephone costs and free themselves of traditional monthly phone bills allowing mobile use to be adapted to current financial resources.

Beside GSM and falling prices prompted by privatization, a third factor explaining the growth in mobile phone use in the 1990s was the technical, aesthetic and cultural transformation that took place in mobile devices. Until then—and returning to an issue already discussed in relation to radiotelephones—mobile phones weighed several kilos and had either to be installed in cars or, at a later date, carried in special over the shoulder bags.

Mobile phones started getting smaller and lighter once again from the early 1990s onwards when heavy, bulky telephones gradually gave way to small phones, which fitted into users' pockets with batteries that did not require recharging every few hours. In this period, it was once again Nokia that

Figure 4.3 Keanu Reeves performing as Neo with the symbolic presence of a Nokia mobile phone in *The Matrix* (1999) directed by Lana and Lilly Wachowsky

"reinvented" the mobile phone making a cult object out of it and, above all, making it user friendly for billions of users worldwide (Steinbock, 2001). One of the best-known models, and emblematic of the change in mobile phone culture and appearance, was Nokia 8110, which achieved great popularity also thanks to the use made of it in the famous 1999 science fiction film *The Matrix* (see Figure 4.3).

The 1990s and early noughties saw not only a quantitative increase in mobile phone use but also a horizontal expansion in its uses and the relevant social groups owning phones. Right up to the end of the 1980s mobile telephones were expensive and mainly used by the wealthiest classes of the population, a status symbol for powerful people or upwardly mobile young people working in finance for the most part. In this case, too, an interesting cultural portrayal is to be found in the film *Wall Street* (1987) in which unscrupulous broker Gordon Gekko manages his deals with the help of a Motorola (see Figure 4.4).

But an entirely different example also demonstrates the 1990s mobile phone's symbolic status as a powerful tool reserved for powerful people. In this decade in the Democratic Republic of Congo, under Mobuto's authoritarian regime, the majority of secret agents owned Motorola telephones, which they flaunted on the street partly as symbols of power because very few people in the country were then using this technology. Nevertheless, as a result, Congolese people were very cautious about talking in the presence of mobile telephones in order to avoid disclosing relevant information or simply in fear of negative consequences from the regime. In this case the mobile telephone was, on the one hand, a status symbol of power and repression and, on the

Figure 4.4 Michael Douglas performing as broker Gordon Gekko with his Motorola in a scene of *Wall Street* (1987) directed by Oliver Stone

other, a tool associated with autocracy with the proverb "*talking like a Motorola* (*Lingala, koloba lokoba Motorola*)" signalling "the undesired disclosure of information, or its unreflective transfer" (Pype, 2016, p. 641).

Over the course of the 1990s in many Western countries and the noughties in Asian, African and South American countries the situation changed rapidly. Mobile phones made their way into the pockets and hands of "ordinary" people living ordinary lives. Once again, however, national and cultural difference played a decisive role in new technology take-up rates. In Italy, for example, mobile phones were already everyday items as early as the first half of the 1990s thanks in part to the price policies adopted by its phone companies (Balbi, 2008). Research in France has shown that mobile phone users in the early 1990s were still using them almost exclusively for "serious", professional reasons and continued to prefer their home phones for personal and family matters thus keeping the two-call media strictly separate in usage terms (de Gourney et al., 1997).

4.4 A Concise History of SMS

Over the course of their history, mobile phones have acquired two further sensory dimensions and freed themselves of their exclusive reliance on hearing (and thus on speech) to embrace, first, sight and writing and then, via smart-phones in particular, the tactile dimension. The written dimension, however deeply influenced by orality in what Walter Ong (1982) would probably have called *secondary writing*, was brought to mobile phones via text messages.

There is nothing new in exchanging written messages from person-to-person. Paper letters have been sent and received for hundreds of years but, limited to the electric age, also wired telegraphy and wireless telegraphy/telephony can be considered media favoring the exchange of personal/private and short written communications—short because expensive. This brief text message idea was first mooted for mobile telephony at the beginning of the 1990s almost at the same time as the introduction of GSM (Taylor & Vincent, 2005). A number of technicians had, in fact, noted that every time a phone call was made a parallel and unused minute communication channel opened up. The idea was thus to fill this band space with brief messages whose features were, however, different from those that were popularized later. A first hypothesis involved the telephone companies sending messages to their own users, for example for network maintenance or device functioning notifications. A second option involved using text messages more or less in the same way as pagers with callers given the option of notifying a specific user they were trying to contact with a message sent via a switchboard request. Both options involved a one-way direction of communication from switchboard to users.

Mobile service providers, however, succeeded neither in identifying a promising business model nor an appropriate tariff for this service. And it was ultimately users themselves who came up with an original idea and began taking advantage of this channel to send brief messages to each other. It was a usage, and even a form of communication, which was profoundly different from that originally planned: horizontal, two-way, from one mobile phone (and thus individual) to another rather than between switchboard and user. Such messages could initially only be sent to compatible mobile phones managed by the same service provider. Then, from the mid 1990s onwards, such limitations were scrapped and text messages became one of mobile telecommunications' killer applications and a further factor in its 1990s' success. In the meantime, mobile phone companies had grasped the value of this new business and understood the profitability of a service that involved companies in no extra cost.

One of the best-known cases highlighting the connotations of text messages in contemporary culture relates to the Philippines (Rafael, 2003). Here text message services were launched in 1999 and quickly became a form of *collective obsession*, which, according to a number of researchers, played a part in the fall of the Joseph Estrada government in January 2001. Text messages were used to bring the extent of government corruption to public attention and hasten its fall by mobilizing mass protests. This explanation—which echoes the role played by the internet in the so-called Arab Spring in 2010–has determinist overtones. Nevertheless, it is interesting to note that this mythological power of mobile phones as an agent of change was so popular in the country that the young Filipinos who took part in the revolution in such huge numbers were significantly called *generation txt*.

This brief history of text messaging illustrates a crucial element in digital (and even analog) media histories: that media use is difficult to foresee. Social groups often use technologies for their own ends adding fresh layers of meaning to them. In this case, text message users widened its spectrum of uses in ways that were very different from those envisaged by telephone companies at the outset. The relationship between devices and users has been conceptually addressed in particular in the Actor Network Theory perspective, which intro-duced the concepts of *script* and *action program* to highlight the fact that technologies *configure* possible use patterns (see Chapter 1). Two of the main exponents of ANT, Latour and Akrich, have argued that objects contain a precise script, which is assigned to them in the process of creation by inventors and technicians. This script imposes a set of preferred functions on technologies that are, however, often modified by users who *de-script* and adapt these arte-facts to ends and purposes that are frequently different from those their inventors had in mind (Akrich, 1992; Akrich & Latour, 1992). In the case of mobile phones, text messages are certainly an excellent example of a *re-scripting* of a *program of action*, although Larissa Hjorth (2005) casts doubt on their revolutionary character, arguing that they combined new ideas with older ones inherited from past forms of communication such as postal services.

The technical and cultural form taken by text messaging is, however, an unstable one as is generally the case with all media and its symbolic meanings will change once again in the future. The centrality of text messaging, for example, would seem to be decreasing in contemporary smartphone era where alternative text services are changing their nature: apps such as WhatsApp, WeChat or Telegram are used to maintain constant, multimedia contact and combine text, sound and video. Chatrooms such as Facebook Messenger are directly linked to popular social network sites. Nevertheless, text messaging is not disappearing from users' experiences and habits. For example, young Danish people are still using them, but with a different symbolic status from the past: as compared to newer methods, text messaging is associated with stronger, more personal ties better suited to personal matters (Bertel & Ling, 2016). In other words, once again the recent history of text messaging shows that old digital mobile applications and practices do not die out or disappear on contact with newer ones but simply change, reconfigure and are re-domesticated.

4.5 A New Paradigm: 3G, Smartphones and Mobile Internet

If mobile phones had already moved a long way from the traditional telephone with text messaging, their definitive metamorphosis occurred with the launching of third generation mobile phone networks, namely 3G, and the shift from the idea of a telephone used in mobility to the smartphone, more similar to the concept of a mobile, connected computer.

The history of the so-called 3G has been separated from that of surfing the internet through mobile phones for a long time. The latter dates to the second half of the 1990s, when three mobile phone manufacturers and a new software company decided to launch a new standard for mobile digital communications. It was June 1997 when Ericsson, Motorola, Nokia and Unwired Planet (which was to deal with the software and, above all, to look into mobile surfing browsers) joined forces to set up the WAP standard enabling mobile phone users to access online contents and services from their phones (Sigurdson, 2001).

The companies launching WAP were convinced that it was poised to be as great a success as GSM while today it is generally seen as a glaring example of digital failure with many causes all related with user experience. First, services that could be accessed on it were limited because WAP had been designed as a sort of Web sub-group with users only able to access certain pages. Second, as the Ericsson manager responsible for the project later admitted, connecting to the Net was very time consuming and expensive also because the interface was difficult to use and user-friendliness did not improve even after prolonged practice. Third, WAP devices were conceived as an adapted form of traditional telephones, whereas it would ultimately prove necessary to invent new devices specifically designed for internet use (as in fact occurred with smartphones). Finally, due to the internet's gradual invasion of the home at the end of the 1990s with desktop computers and laptops, Web surfing standards were those offered by PCs and WAP was essentially a poorer and less attractive version.

WAP's failure was not a global phenomenon but primarily a Western one. In Japan, for example, with a XHTML standard that was better suited to internet use, WAP helped to popularize mobile communications themselves. Mobile phone internet network use in Japan—mainly for e-mail—even modified the public dimension and the popular image of mobile telecommunications. In fact, *ketai* ("mobile phone" in Japanese) went from being a technological device used almost exclusively within the country's youth sub-culture—and regarded with suspicion and apprehension as capable of subverting rigid pre-existing social hierarchies—to an object with such deep roots in Japanese society that it even triggered forms of "techno-nationalism" (Matsuda, 2005).

Box 4.3 Documents

Japan Ministry of Telecommunication, *Information and Communications in Japan* (2002)

This is an excerpt from a White Paper published by the Japanese Department of Public Management, Home Affairs, Posts and Telecommunications in 2002 describing Japan's progress in the mobile internet connection sector.

> Japan is by far the largest provider in the world of internet connection services via cell phones [...]. It has been a mere three years since the launch of the mobile internet in February 1999, and the number of subscribers has surpassed 50 million reaching 51.93 million as of the end of March 2002. In addition, Mobile Internet subscribers account for 75.1% of the total number of subscribers to cell phones, which is fairly high in comparison with the other major countries and regions. Furthermore, the Mobile Internet allows users to access diversified content, and the purposes for using the Mobile Internet include obtaining information services such as news and entertainment information, purchasing tickets, engaging in commercial transactions such as bank transactions, and downloading music for signaling an incoming call and stand-by screens. Designed to enhance the ability to express such content, advanced moving image services and navigation services have been offered. [...] In October 2001, full-scale service for 2GHzband third-generation mobile communications (hereinafter referred to as "IMT-2000") commenced in Japan, which was the first of its kind in the world. [...] With respect to the desired functions and services for the third-generation cell phone, more than half the people surveyed would like to see a fast communication speed, and one-third would like to see a videophone function. Also, with cell phones most people would like to have a high-speed, large-capacity and easy to utilize communication usage environment, suggesting that there are high expectations for the further development of cell phones. [...] with respect to the use of Internet via cell phones, most users were pleased with the freedom from time and spatial constraints, which is a unique feature provided by the cell phone. [...] While the United States has been the leader in Internet-related technology developments, the trend towards ubiquitous network, which will broaden the demographics of Internet users, is a promising one for Japan, which will be able to make its mark in the world by leading in areas that will grow

more important: mobile communications, information appliances, human interface technology.

Source: Ministry of Public Management, Home Affairs, Posts and Telecommunications, (2012) *Information and Communications in Japan*, White Paper, Tokyo

As mentioned, what is today considered the essence of 3G—surfing the internet on mobile phones—was not even on the cards initially. The concept of a third-generation network emerged in the ITU fold in 1992 when 2G was still at its inception. 3G was envisaged as having two main functions, which have still not come to fruition: first, setting up a standard intended to be adopted the world over and to lead to universal roaming and, second, giving individual users access to a single, personal number for their mobile phones, landlines and work numbers with the so-called PCS (Green & Haddon, 2009, pp. 22-23). The concept of potentially integrating mobile telecommunications and internet was not even mooted because the latter was not then yet popular and not seen as likely to be a key media in the future.

Many countries only began allocating airwaves for 3G from 1999 to 2001, assigning frequencies and concessions to private companies. The first services were launched in Japan and South Korea, which were once again in the noughties, together with Italy, the quickest to adopt the new standard (Srivastava, 2008, p. 20). Corporate history provides useful information for an evaluation of the "whos" and "hows" of this process. It was, in particular, Hong Kong-based company Hutchison Whampoa, better known in various countries simply as "3", that adopted an aggressive license acquisition policy especially in Europe and some Pacific Rim countries. Hutchison Whampoa's policy was also dictated by the fact that, unlike its competitors, it had no privately owned 2G network or interest in defending the status quo and exploiting existing structures and thus invested strongly in 3G (Goggin, 2011, chap. 2). This is a further example of the *innovator's dilemma* referred to in Chapter 2 with reference to computers. In telecommunications, too, in fact, companies that invest to the greatest extent in launching new technologies—and especially in network creation—are then reluctant to invest additional sums, fearing that old and new infrastructures could be in competition. Furthermore, in the early years of its market presence, even Hutchison Whampoa did not view mobile internet as the 3G's killer application but concentrated on promoting video calling (with limited success as had already, in fact, been the case with landline video phones, see Lipartito, 2003) and other services such as mobile TV (see Chapter 5).

Mobile telephones and the internet started to converge properly in the second half of the noughties. At that time, a base infrastructure that could support the exchange of huge quantities of data had developed and the Web had become a mass phenomenon, which was central to the daily lives of billions of people. The third key towards the convergence was the popularization of new devices (the so-called smartphones) that made internet access the fulcrum of mobile telecommunications. Smartphones are radically different from first generation mobile phones and are more like computers than telephones and it is thus not surprising that, like Kodak in the history of photography (Chapter 5), traditional companies producing mobile phones 1.0 were not able to maintain their dominance on the mobile handset market. Nokia, for example, was soon overtaken by other manufacturers because its leadership was not capable of strategic change and did not fully understand the new telephone eco-system's increasingly internet focused orientation (Bouwman et al., 2014). At the same time, companies investing and producing in other sectors gained an understanding of the new market potential: in 2003 Canadian company BlackBerry, a pager producer in the 1990s, launched its first, popular model that had a miniature QWERTY keyboard and was something of a telephone-computer hybrid in appearance. However, the appeal of devices like BlackBerry, and also hand-held devices like Palm Pilot, was mainly business and corporate with firms buying them as benefits for their employees (see Figure 4.5).

It was not until the second half of the noughties that mobile phones with online access potential became gadgets attracting ordinary users, and the younger generation in particular, and taking the name "smartphone". Once again Apple played a pivotal role in this popularization process with the iPhone: this smartphone was important not only in terms of technical innovation but also for the cultural and symbolic influence it exerted on fashion and lifestyle choices. The first iPhone model in 2007 was indeed ergonomically innovative—and ergonomics have played an important role throughout the whole of mobile phone history. For example, a large touch screen with few other keys was an important shift triggering a reshaping process in the media universe as a whole in which touch today plays a central role in user-device interaction. Furthermore, the iPhone has acted as a trailblazer for a whole new mobile phone concept whose logic is closer to that of the PC and in which flexible operating systems can use programs made by other companies for a range of functions—note that by 2017 the grand total of applications available on the Apple platform to personalize mobile phones are more than 2 million. Finally, Apple has proved capable of charging its smartphones with symbolic meanings, which have transformed them into one of the most attractive, desirable consumer products of the moment, a fashion and *mythical icon* that has revolutionized

Figure 4.5 The CEO and founder of Capital Management Group, an investment bank in the US, promoting the use of the BlackBerry in his company in 2006

phones themselves (Magaudda, 2015; see also Box 4.4 and the conclusion). Thanks also to its consumer appeal, the iPhone has contributed not simply to popularizing smartphones in social groups previously not already "enrolled" (thus contributing to changing the classic communication technology take-up

Box 4.4 Documents

Steve Jobs, *The Presentation of the iPhone* (2007)

This is a short extract from the transcript of Steve Jobs' keynote speech at MacWorld 2007, where he introduced the iPhone and presented Apple as the most "revolutionary" company in digital media history.

> This is a day I've been looking forward to for two and a half years. Every once in a while, a revolutionary product comes along that changes everything. And Apple has been—well, first of all, one's very fortunate if you get to work on just one of these in your career. Apple's been very fortunate. It's been able to introduce a few of these into the world.
>
> In 1984, we introduced the Macintosh. It didn't just change Apple, it changed the whole computer industry. In 2001, we introduced the first iPod, and . . . it didn't just . . . it didn't just change the way we all listen to music, it changed the entire music industry. Well, today, we're introducing three revolutionary products of this class.
>
> The first one: is a widescreen iPod with touch controls. The second: is a revolutionary mobile phone. And the third is a breakthrough Internet communications device. So, three things: a widescreen iPod with touch controls; a revolutionary mobile phone; and a break-through Internet communications device. An iPod, a phone, and an Internet communicator. An iPod, a phone . . . are you getting it? These are not three separate devices, this is one device, and we are calling it iPhone.
>
> Today, Apple is going to reinvent the phone, and here it is.

curve and making consumers who are usually non-technological into *early adopters*, see Carey & Elton, 2010), but also to making the huge sums required for the latest models more socially acceptable.

Apple's symbolic importance notwithstanding, in recent years, the geography of the smartphone production and market has clearly shifted towards the Far East, making Korean and Chinese firms, in particular, into crucial sector players. Korean Samsung soon became world market leader selling around 25% of the world's smartphones but Chinese companies such as Huawei, Oppo and Xiaomi have also become very important players, taking over from European and US firms such as Motorola and Nokia. Focusing on China, an interesting aspect to the evolution of the Chinese mobile phone industry has been a shift from a *shanzhai* vision (making copies of well-known mobile phones produced in Western countries for the Chinese market) to national companies exporting products to the West as well (Shin-Horng Chen & Pei-Chang Wen, 2016). So, it is not surprising that, according to the market research firm Gartner, China overtook the United States to become the world's largest global smartphone market (in terms of shipments) in 2012 with 208 million units shipped.

Even if futurologist newspapers and magazines report frequently on the end or the death of smartphones (as any other previous medium, at its peak there are rumors of death), smartphones are still icons of modernity not only for their seductive design or market importance but especially for their ability to perform very different functions from straightforward phone calls—a cursory list includes computers, cameras and photo albums, watches, address books, diaries, radios, TVs, sound recorders and reproducers, Web browsers, note-books and devices with which to interact with TV (think of tele voting). This is mainly the result of the availability of operating systems. Until the mid noughties, the mobile phone giants concentrated their attention primarily on hardware innovation. Then in the last decade two IT companies new to the telephone sector developed their own operating systems thereby boosting the smartphone market. In 2007, Apple introduced the iOS operating system designed exclusively for Apple iPhones while, that same year, Google began making its Android system, a Linux-based software that on the contrary was designed for any mobile telephone manufacturers (Apple excluded). These alternative strategies designed to dominate the mobile operating system sector largely resemble what we have already observed in the history of computers (see Chapter 2): in the late 1970s and early 1980s, Apple had already adopted a policy based on close and exclusive software-hardware integration while Microsoft's strategy was similar to that used by Google with smartphones, aiming to sell its software to any computer producers and thus become market leader. On the other hand, Google's strategy differed from Microsoft's too: while Microsoft has often fought to protect its computer software and make users pay for it, Google apparently decided to embrace an open software basis for its operating system. This must not be misunderstood: as media scholar Gerard Goggin (2012) has noted, Google was not supporting the so-called open software movement but kept the open source concept under strict corporate control within a traditional corporate strategy.

Within a very short space of time not only did these two operating systems establish an oligopoly in the global market (in 2016, for example, Android's 86.2% and iOS's 12.9% accounted for 99.1% of the worldwide smartphone market, while ten years before both platforms didn't even exist and Symbian and Rim were the sector leaders; source: Gartner) but a whole new mobile telephone business has emerged as a result. Both Apple and Google have, in fact, developed their own applications and contents while at the same time controlling the distribution of apps produced by other small and big firms—both free and at a cost. The multiplication of available software apps as well as the integration of further technologies into telephones (such as Wi-Fi, Bluetooth, GPS and their potential use as routers for computers) has enabled further internet, computer and smartphone integration to take place. There is nothing accidental about the fact that smartphones have become all-important internet access devices in recent years.

In sum, what we have referred to as a shift in the mobile telephony paradigm from 1.0 to 2.0 is, as we have seen in various parts of this book, a complex *socio-technical network* including people and institutions, technologies and cultural visions. Different and originally unrelated ideas have slowly converged: think of linking the internet with mobile phones (a partially failed attempt with WAP and then a successful one); the changing image of 3G networks carrying data; new devices like smartphones; operating system companies (the most powerful of these involved in the internet sector) but also new everyday practices like surfing the internet continuously. All these aspects have changed and are still changing mobile phone history, integrating internet and computer logics into the old phone paradigm—a phenomenon we refer to as a *digital media pattern* in the next chapter. This tendency is apparently becoming more and more important for the emergence of other new mobile standards: 4G and 5G. If the main aim of 4G has been to increase speed, interconnectivity and user data exchange (growing digital communication flows require new and more broadband wireless networks), 5G is considered the new standard capable of enhancing the so-called "internet of things". Experts claim that the great majority of future mobile digital communication flows will not be between humans but between machines: connected homes will connect up washing machines, fridges and home computers with our smartphones continually, self-driving cars will communicate with satellites and GPS constantly in an interconnected environment and so on. But, as we are learning from past examples, the characteristics and services offered by new generations of mobile telephone—assuming that this name survives into the future—are difficult to forecast. The only certain fact is that the way in which politicians, telephone operators and technicians imagine the future of communications today will have to take account of the cultural contexts, which will emerge as a result of future unexpected user re-workings. As the history of 3G—and that of mobile internet in general—reminds us, the way we imagine the future of mobile telecommunications and of communication itself is often very different from what really happens. 4G and 5G will probably follow this unwritten rule of media history.

4.6 The Global Mobile Phone *Fever*

Mobile telephones are one of the most successful means of communication in media history. A world population of around 7 billion was using around 7 billion mobile phones in 2015 (see data appendix, Table A.2), an average of one per person. Even more interesting is the fact that this popularization of mobile telecommunications has taken place at great speed. After their (re)introduction in the 1990s, mobile phones' massive take-up occurred in the space of just a couple of decades even in continents such as Africa, Latin America and some areas of Asia, where communication devices and media had low take-up rates previously. Another point to note here is the fact that while internet and mobile phone use grew in parallel up to the end of the 1990s, from the year 2000 onwards a clear divide in popularization of the two media has occurred (Srivastava, 2008, pp. 15-16).

On the difference between internet and mobile phones' penetrations, it should also be remembered that mobile phones require fewer skills than surfing the internet. The internet requires users to at least know how to handle a computer, have access to a telephone or a data network and possess the necessary intellectual resources to search for information. Mobile phones, on the other hand, are much simpler to use, cheaper to buy and use and, last but not least, they are oral media in which even writing is speech influenced and thus accessible to the illiterate and semi-literate. Recently, the convergence between the two media, or better the possibility to surf the Web through smartphones, has also boomed internet's penetration worldwide even if digital divide is still a relevant concept (see especially Box 3.4). "Digital divide" has been coined to highlight the disparity of access and dissemination that digital media apparently cause but it has been applied almost exclusively to internet use. Although they are digital devices, mobile phones have been given limited consideration in the digital divide debate perhaps also because they may be capable of controverting, or at least limiting, the relevance of alarmist views on the subject.

Mobiles probably owe their success to their ability to resolve some of the historical and long-lasting limitations of prior forms of telecommunications. For example, world regions that were not previously covered by telephone and telegraph networks—either because costs were prohibitive or for geological and climate related reasons—have been made phone accessible. This process is clear especially in the so-called "Global South", meaning Asia, South America and Africa. These are parts of the globe where a lack of infrastructure and landline networks is a chronic problem and this has meant that an unsatisfied demand for long distance communications had been decades in the growing (Castells, Fernandz-Ardevol, Qiu, & Sey, 2007, chap. 1). In many of these regions mobile phone networks were thus the first available telecommunications and, in other cases, newly established landline networks slowed down as a result of the development of mobile, as the case of Jamaica shows (Horst & Miller, 2006). New technology has been a success in terms both of lower costs for users and better Wi-Fi network coverage, ease of use and the adaptability of mobile phones to profoundly different social situations. Some research has shown, for example, that the mobile phone aural dimension fits well into the oral nature of African countries such as Burkina Faso, for example (Hahn & Kibora, 2008).

A glance at the number of mobile phone users per head of the population rankings shows that a number of countries that played a secondary role in the global media market in the past are now in the avant-garde: the so-called BRICS countries (Brazil, Russia, India, China and South Africa) account for more or less half of world mobile telephone subscribers and other countries such as Indonesia, Nigeria, Pakistan and Bangladesh are among the most important in worldwide user terms. In the last year, Africa and especially Asia have boomed and are now the most important for mobile telephony worldwide (see data appendix, Table A.5 and Figure A.2 and also Figure 4.6 on the next page).

This is also because, compared to other media and prior forms of telecommunications, mobile telephones were instantly viewed as individual and private. With the exception of a few cases, which we will deal with later, each individual has his or her *own* mobile phone and, in certain countries, even more than one per person resulting from the growing habit of owing multiple Sim cards (as show in Table A.5 in the data appendix).

Many cases of mobile "fever" have attracted scholarly attention but we will focus here on two of them. The first is India where mobile phones went from a very low take-up rate to over 80% coverage in the first two decades of the 2000s. This process was almost certainly dictated by specific strategic choices made by governments, telephone companies and manufacturers. Vodafone, for example, has ten times more subscribers in India than in its homeland, the United Kingdom, and mobile phone manufacturers who have now saturated Western markets have been able to offer Indian clients ultra-low cost mobile phones (Agar, 2013, chap. 12). The cultural implications are even more interesting. Doron and Jeffrey (2013) have argued that mobile telecommunications have brought radical changes to Indian society in terms of social control, personal connectivity and mass consumption. In a society with still rigid caste divisions and hierarchies, mobile phones have increased contact between the sexes and social classes, democratized access to information, created new forms of terrorism and made access to previously forbidden content such as pornography possible. Nevertheless, the mobile phone is not necessarily a breakthrough or a revolutionary tool. In India mobile networks and devices, for example, continue to coexist with poverty and extreme social inequality. Mobile telephones are

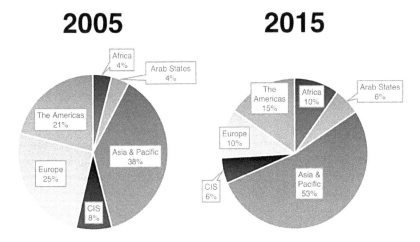

Figure 4.6 Percentage of mobile cellular subscriptions across six world regions, 2005 and 2015

Source: authors' elaboration on ITU data

more common than bathrooms in homes (in 2013, around 50% of the Indian population had a bathroom while more than 70% had a mobile phone), for example. On the one hand, the Indian example shows that digital media are not only metaphors of technological and social progress but can also be indicators of the contradictions and ambiguities inherent in globalization processes. On the other, as other researchers in the so-called global South have shown, the mobile phone has rearranged rather than revolutionizing power hierarchies, gender relationships, social networks and urban-rural relationships (Ling & Horst, 2011). These social structures are deep and stable and digital media can hardly be expected to overturn them.

A second frequently studied case is actually an entire continent: Africa. Although disparities between nations are still relevant, compared to internet and computers, mobile telephones have spread slowly but surely through the African continent (Alzouma, 2008; de Bruijn, Nyamnioh, & Brinkman, 2009). This has occurred despite the fact that the costs involved in mobile phone use are a problem for many Africans as the name given it in Nigeria *"ok una iri ego"* namely "the fire that burns money" shows. African users have, however, attempted to limit costs by using mobile phones in innovative ways. Sharing a phone with other people or even with an entire village, as in the case of Gade Kébé in Senegal (Tall, 2003)–these are cases where mobile phones are no longer individual but rather collective communication media. Making thorough use of telephone rings with a clear language known to users. Buying old and second-hand telephones from Europe, the United States and Asia. Using text messaging extensively in everyday life, as well as on special occasions like wedding invitations, death announcements or simple greetings (see Chéneau-Loquay, 2010 for an interesting overview of the "tactics" used in various African countries to reduce mobile telephone costs). Expensiveness is not the only "problem" experienced by mobile telephone users in Africa. Another relevant issue is cellular signal weakness and, again, African solutions to these problems are extremely interesting. For example, in Santidougou, a village in Burkina Faso, a bush nurse has been nominated to send messages for the whole village after he found a tree top from which he has been able to send and receive text messages—once a day, at 7 am, before starting work, he climbs the tree and sends or receives messages from all his friends and villagers (Kibora, 2009). This funny episode shows that mobile telephones can be used in alternative ways: in this case, users have access to mobile communications only once a day and so communication rules obviously need to be re-negotiated. We tend to think that mobile telephones have radically changed the speed of our interactions, making it perpetual and obsessive, but there are case studies showing the contrary. Once again digital media have not had uniform consequences for different societies and cultures but they are constantly re-used and re-shaped by people in specific contexts.

The most interesting alternative use of telephones in Africa is, however, M-Pesa (M for mobile and *pesa* meaning money in Swahili). Essentially more and more people use mobile phones as a sort of electronic wallet as, in some African countries, small amounts of money can be credited to mobile phones and then be spent on micro-transactions and everyday purchases such as food, medicine and household items. Interestingly, a number of attempts to popularize electronic cash mobile phone use have also been made in the West (and a revival is currently underway) but the system became very popular only in Africa where cash machines can be difficult to access since banks are few and far between in many rural areas. M-Pesa resolves such problems. Money can be transferred with a text message and payments are cash free as many shop owners also have mobile devices receiving money transfers. After several years of experiments, a microcredit project of this sort was launched in 2007 and was particularly successful in Kenya where an associated socio-cultural problem also emerged. As cash transfers are usually made from mobile phones belonging to men working in cities to those of women living in rural villages, wives are concerned that M-Pesa will make it less necessary for men to return to villages with cash and thus reduce their visits home. The authors of this research (Morawczynski & Pickens, 2009) have shown that in such cases the function of mobile phones is the opposite of what is generally considered to be their "natural" attitude, reducing rather than increasing social contact.

While mobile phones have spread more widely and uniformly worldwide than any other medium in history, this does not mean that inequalities and imbalances have disappeared. There are still vast swathes of the planet that are not covered by mobile phone networks, such as some uninhabited areas (for example the Amazon, the Sahara, some regions in Asia and Australia), the great oceans, the skies over a certain altitude and even regions of some Western countries where governments or telephone companies have not supplied uniform coverage to the whole population.

To this must be added a number of places where mobile phones are banned or have to be used in silent or alternative modes in part still today for security or more often social reasons: think about planes, quiet cars in trains, theatres, libraries, hospitals, special restaurants and many others.

Finally it is important to remember that there is nothing mandatory or irresistible about mobile telecommunications, like all digital media, and potential users choose *not* to buy them because they think they are a nuisance or would disturb their privacy, because they are too difficult for them (as we mentioned also in the case of pagers), because they belong to religious groups which strictly limit use, because can use other people's phones, or again are not interested in new technology or cannot afford one (an interesting case of impoverishment and mass abandonment of mobile phones is Mexico, see Mariscal & Bonina, 2008). Resisting mobile communications means also resisting smartphones and, more in general, the integration of mobile phones and the internet. Looking at statistics about the spread of smartphones, a divide between rich and poor countries, but also young and old people, is re-emerging. Smartphones have some weaknesses compared to old mobile phones. First, the great success of the mobile phone 1.0 dealt also with its user-friendliness and the mobile phone 2.0 (not by chance, renamed *smart*phone) introduces a degree of complexity in approaching and using the new technology. Second, the batteries run out fast and need to be recharged quickly: this is simply impossible in some African regions where the electric network is difficult to access. Finally, children or aged people need strong, functions-limited and inexpensive phones, while smartphones have opposite characters. These are all reasons explaining why some people refuse smartphones and a market for *not-smart* phones is reemerging: Nokia, Microsoft, Samsung and Doro are still producing low-tech mobile phones (Thomas, 2016).

The global perspective adopted in this section, and in the book as a whole, is of particular relevance to mobile phones and there is even an academic debate around the ability of mobile phones to represent globalization phenomena. Certain scholars (Katz & Aakhus, 2002) see almost universal cell phone take-up as an example of the globalization and standardization processes underway in contemporary society. In this respect, mobile phones seem, in fact, to have been taken on board, and favored social phenomena in similar ways in very different parts of the world with extremely diverse cultures. Other scholars (Geser, 2004), by contrast, have pointed out that the global dissemination of mobile phones has brought out great diversification of usage between various segments of populations and cultures with local customs, which are tolerated only in specific contexts. Both these approaches are valid to some extent and we have tried to throw light on this debate in our analysis of the various case studies cited in this chapter.

4.7 Sociocultural Implications of Mobile Connectivity

More than any other digital media analyzed in this book, the omnipresence of mobile phones and the forms of "dependence" that appear to come with them, have prompted a great deal of research aimed at assessing their impact on contemporary societies and cultures (for example see Katz, 2006). A thorough-going review of this work would be a challenging task but Green and Haddon (2009, pp. 11-13) have identified some of the main long-term trends on this subject.

First, the ability of the mobile phone to subvert and juxtapose public and private space attracted scholarly attention right from the start. Mobile phones have presided over the downfall of a rigid distinction between work and leisure time allowing us to remain connected even during our free time and keep up with our private lives during working hours. To an even greater extent mobile phones have led to subjects once regarded as private *par excellence* or strictly kept to the privacy of our own homes being aired in public places such as streets and public transport—this has something to do with the concept of *mobile privatization* and *privatized mobility* (see Box 4.5). Conducting our private lives in public has required the development of new codes of good manners for both those using their phones and those forced to listen to them.

A second theme linked to mobile telecommunications, and one which has been examined in depth in sociological research, is individuals' ability to safeguard their privacy in the age of mobile phones. One of the greatest risks in being constantly contactable is in fact to our privacy, our inability to find a foothold in this new open-ended time and space. As well as the time issue, management of space has also been the subject of sociological research, which has looked in particular at *where* mobiles are used.

Another frequent subject of study, above all in relation to massive youth mobile phone use from the late 1990s onwards, has been the evolution of relationships between adults and the young, parents and children and also within young groups of peers. Sociology has been joined in this by other academic disciplines such as pedagogy, psychology and even linguistics—which has

Box 4.5 In-depth Theory

Mobile Privatization

Socially, this complex is characterized by the two apparently para-
doxical yet deeply connected tendencies of modern urban industrial
living: on the one hand mobility, on the other hand the more apparently
self-sufficient family home. The earlier period of public technology,
best exemplified by the railways and city lighting, was replaced by a
kind of technology for which no satisfactory name has yet been found;
that which served an at once mobile and home-centered way of living:
a form of *mobile privatization*. [. . .] The contradictory pressures of this
phase of industrial capitalist society were indeed resolved, at a certain
level, by the institution of broadcasting. [. . .] Yet this privatization,
which was at once an effective achievement and a defensive response,
carried, as a consequence, an imperative need for new kinds of contact.
The new homes might appear private and "self-sufficient" but could
be maintained only by regular funding and supply from external
sources, and these, over a range from employment and prices to
depressions and wars, had a decisive and often a disrupting influence
on what was nevertheless seen as a separable "family" This relationship created both the need and the form of a new kind of "communication": news from "outside", from otherwise inaccessible sources. [. . .]
The new "consumer" technology which reached its first decisive stage
in the 1920s served this complex of needs within just these limits and
pressures. There were immediate improvements of the condition and
efficiency of the privatized home; there were new facilities, in private
transport, for expeditions from the home; and then, in radio, there was
a facility for a new kind of social input—news and entertainment
brought into the home.

(Williams, 1974, pp. 26–27)

Raymond Williams coined the term *mobile privatization* in the 1970s
with special reference to radio and TV. He identified two conflicting tendencies in nineteenth- and twentieth-century urban and industrial societies:
on the one hand the desire and opportunity for mobility (now intensified
by mass transport systems and mobile media such as cell phones) and, on
the other, the home's progressive transformation into a self-sufficient
consumption system following the constant process of privatization of
everyday life centered in households. These trends are in apparent contra-
diction: mobility implies movement, travel, leaving the domestic sphere while

family life would seem to embody stasis, peace and quiet, the convenience of home relax. For Williams, this tension was broken down by twentieth-century broadcasting as a communication technology suited to a mobile lifestyle and, at the same time, to the home. Broadcasting is movement, however virtual, because radio and TV programs enable us to "travel", visit places we have never seen, come into contact with cultures that are very different from ours. At the same time, however, this virtual movement takes place in the comfort of our own homes without us needing to move. It is mobility itself that is integrated into and brought within the home.

Williams' ideas have been re-worked over recent decades by a great many writers and adapted to the new means of communication that are gradually emerging. One of the best known of these re-workings is probably that of Lynn Spiegel (2001) who, in a study on portable TV (see also Chapter 5), coined the expression *privatized mobility*. Essentially, if traditional TV, as William argued, promised to bring the outside world into the home, portable TV, on the other hand, brought the inside world outside, i.e. it brought aspects of private life into the public domain.

This aspect is naturally linked not only or even mainly to portable TV but, in the digital world, to all the mobile devices that have appeared in recent decades. To cite just three examples: portable computers (see Chapter 2), portable music players (see Chapter 5) and, naturally, mobile telephones (the subject of this chapter). It is perhaps mobile phones which, more than any other, have reconfigured the public-private threshold, as we have seen, allowing people to take their private worlds to the public domain and so eroding the spaces between home and work and the differences between movement and stasis. As Stephen Groening has, in fact, argued, the mobile phone

> allows its users to carry the home with them, even into the workplace, creating an uninterrupted path of mobile private space throughout the day, a withdrawal into interiority unsullied by social obligations, even while commuting. Cell phones link users to these stationary private interior spaces such as the home and the workplace. Additionally, with its capacity to take and store digital images, phone numbers, addresses and other personal information such as birthdays, cellphones supply mobile users with an approximation of the comforts of home. [. . .] Likewise, e-mail, instant messaging, clock and calendar functions turn cellphones into a portable facsimile of the workplace. Company-issued cellular phones, especially, strengthen worker to workplace obligations

even when employees are physically absent. Indeed, cellphones can remove the boundaries between workplace and home.

(2010, p. 1335)

But there is a further aspect to consider in the 2.0 version of mobile privatization or privatized mobility: the increasingly important bond between mobile phones and self-representation platforms (better known as social network sites). Billions of people today have private Facebook, WeChat, Snapchat, etc. profiles and thus manage—more or less con-sciously—their own images and private spheres in public. The lion's share of users, moreover, access and check their profiles and those of their "friends" by means of mobile devices, especially mobile phones, several times a day. This allows people to revise and adjust their images on the move and practically constantly. This can be considered a *new form of mobile privatization* played out for the most part in public, which is today becoming almost second nature in the digital society. It is a different phenomenon from that identified by Williams in relation to broadcasting but one which once again involves the media (in this case digital), the public and private spheres.

Further Reading

Groening, S. (2010). From "a box in the theater of the world" to "the world as your living room": Cellular phones, television and mobile privatization. *New Media & Society, 12*(8), 1331-1347.

Spiegel, L. (2001). Portable TV: Studies in Domestic Travel Space. In L. Spiegel (Ed.), *Welcome to the Dreamhouse: Popular Media in Postwar Suburbs* (pp. 60-106). Durham, NC: Duke University Press.

Williams, R. (1974). *Television: Technology and Cultural Form*. London: Fontana.

analyzed new languages and the way they evolve via structure analysis and text message content.

Additional research has concentrated on similarities and, to an even greater extent, differences between landlines and mobile phones in terms of identity and attempted to pinpoint what it assumes are the differences between the two media. We examined this debate in the first section of this chapter.

Finally, even biomedical sciences have examined the potential risks to our health of electromagnetic waves and mobile phones themselves. This kind of research has often found space in alarmist press articles but the jury is still out on this issue. And the same is true of much of the sociological research mentioned previously with mobile phones seen by some as a medium that reduces face-to-face contact and, by others, as encouraging social contact, invading our privacy or combating loneliness, freeing women from rigid hierarchies in certain cultures or simply perpetuating them, as a democratic medium or a means of social control. Generally speaking these are the very same ambivalent results ("Wherever we look, the telephone seems have effects in *diametrically opposite directions*") as the research done by Ithiel de Sola Pool (1977, p. 4) on the social role of landline telephones showed some decades ago— yet another similarity between the old analog phones and new digital mobile phones with which this chapter began.

LEARNING MATERIALS

Key Points to Focus On:

- The mobile telephone's late-nineteenth-century roots: landline telephone and wireless telegraph/telephone.
- The *first birth*: radiotelephony in the early twentieth century.
- The *second birth*: mobile phones in the 1970s and the 1980s.
- The mobile phone take-up time lag in the US.
- Institutional support for GSM in the EU.
- From analog mobile phones to digital GSM.
- The unexpected popularity of text messaging and its apparent decline.
- Convergence with the internet: the failure of WAP and the rise of 3G networks.
- The iPhone and the shift from the mobile phone to the smartphone.
- Apps and OS as smartphones' distinctive features.
- Appropriations of the mobile phone in the global south.
- The M-PESA service in Africa.
- Wide ranging social consequences of smartphones.

Some Questions to Answer

- How does early-twentieth-century radiotelephony differ from what we call mobile telecommunications today? What similarities are there?
- Early mobile phone take-up in the US was delayed by several factors: please list them.
- Which factors contributed to the European *digital-bureaucratic miracle* in mobile phone take-up in the EU?

- Why did text messaging become so popular?
- What was different about iPhone take-up to that of earlier mobile phones for accessing the internet?
- Identify and describe an alternative use of mobile networks that has occurred in non-Western countries. What is unusual about this kind of use?

A Text to Read and Discuss

Read the following blog post in Web magazine Slate.com about mobile phone use by movie character Gordon Gekko in *Wall Street* (1987): www.slate.com/blogs/browbeat/2010/09/23/gordon_gekko_s_cell_phone.html

How do you think the way this object was presented in the movie contributed to culturally contextualizing this technical device?

A Few Books for Further Study

Agar, J. (2013). *Constant Touch: A Global History of the Mobile Phone*. London: Icon.

de Bruijn, M., Nyamnjoh, F., & Brinkman, I. (Eds.). (2009). *Mobile Phones: The New Talking Drums of Everyday Africa*. Bamenda, Cameroon: Langaa; Leiden, the Netherlands: African Studies Centre.

Doron, A., & Jeffrey, R. (2013). *The Great Indian Phone Book: How the Cheap Cell Phone Changes Business, Politics, and Daily Life*. Cambridge, MA: Harvard University Press.

Goggin, G. (2006). *Cell Phone Culture. Mobile Technology in Everyday Life*. London: Routledge.

Ling, R. (2004). *The Mobile Connection. The Cell Phone's Impact on Society*. San Francisco, CA: Morgan Kaufmann.

----

5 The Digitization of Analog Media

5.1 Intermediality and the Digital Media Pattern

Up to this point in the book we have retraced the evolution of three specific media in the digital universe: the computer, the internet and the mobile phone. The intention of this chapter, by contrast, is to supply a panorama of the consequences of digitization in six of the main communication and contemporary culture sectors: music, publishing, cinema and video, photography, TV and radio. The objectives of this chapter are two-fold: first, highlighting specific *intermedia trajectories*, to gain an understanding of the consequences of digital technologies in a range of media sectors; and, second, to analyze to what extent digitization has represented, as we are frequently led to believe, a "disruptive revolution" or rather continuity with the analog past.

The term *intermedia*, which we will use in this chapter, enables us to highlight the fact that devices, markets, aesthetics and media practices previously differentiated in specific media sectors (such as TV, music or printed books) have interwoven in the digitization process. If we can think of analog media as single media, all interrelated and integrated but still recognizable in their differences, digital media can be better represented as a unique and stratified *digital media pattern* made up of a set of interlaced devices, markets, aesthetics and practices woven together—a textile metaphor underlining the fact that today's digital media are an interwoven environment where the original elements are still recognizable but constitute now a new and distinctive object. We are thus not talking about the "old" concept of media convergence, according to which we will all, in the future, use a single media for everything we do. Rather what we are witnessing is the interweaving of single media in very much the same way as the wool used to make a jumper is interwoven: we know each piece of yarn is separate, especially when one of them unravels, but all these yarns knitted together make up something more and different from the simple sum of their individual yarns. This effectively did not occur with the traditional analog

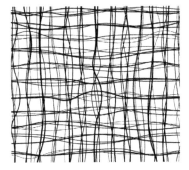

Single analogue media   Digital media pattern

Figure 5.1 From single analog media to a digital media pattern

Source: authors' artwork

media, where each single medium was generally separate both in terms of individual user experience and its reference economic sector: using the knitwear metaphor once again, analog media remained different and unique balls of wool (see Figure 5.1).

An example of the intermedia dimension that makes up this interwoven pattern of different media, is a specific media practice such as watching a TV series on Netflix on a tablet, perhaps recommended by one of our Facebook contacts. In this case, what media are we referring to? Internet? Telephone? TV? Cinema? Social network site? Rather than a single medium what we are looking at here is a pattern made up of different media interwoven together to the extent that it is increasingly difficult to establish the dominant element within it. The transformations occurred in the audio-visual world are undoubtedly an excellent example of digitization's intermedia trajectory: contents that remained linked prevalently to cinema or TV for decades began to interlock in ever-more profound ways with other media devices, markets and languages. In this and other cases, which we will observe in this chapter, digitization has not simply been a process of technological translation from analog to digital but has rather generated a mixing up of the technical, social and cultural elements of traditional analog media. We will summarize this mixing up process in the idea of *intermediality* (see Box 5.1).

Naturally the goal of this chapter is not to offer a thoroughgoing and complete analysis of *all* the intermedia transformations at the heart of the digitization process (this would probably require an entire book or even individual books for each media sector considered). Our goal is much more modest but at the same time more specific: highlighting the fact that the digitization process has not simply been a matter of individual media sector transformation

Box 5.1 In-depth Theory

Intermediality

In this book and this chapter in particular, we adopt the term *intermediality* to describe a fundamentally important media change under the promptings of digital innovation. The purpose of this term is to highlight the fact that devices, markets, aesthetics and media uses previously differentiated in specific media sectors have begun to interweave and increasingly depend on one another. The aim is thus to underline the interconnectedness of contemporary digital media.

The intermedia concept is not a new one and was *not* coined for digital media. It was used for the first time by critic and artist (member of the Fluxus collective) Dick Higgins (1966/2001) to describe a growing tendency in avant-garde art work to develop artistic dialogues on hybrid terrain and no longer remain confined by a single lexicon, be it painting, theatre or cinema. Born in the world of art and literary criticism, then, the inter-mediality concept is increasingly used in communication studies, especially together with the dissemination of digital media. It was initially used to critique the concept of *media convergence*, namely the idea that all the "old" media are converging towards a new single communication channel (Storsul & Stuedahl, 2007). In this respect, as Juha Herkman has observed, "one of the most critical observations is perhaps the empirical fact that, instead of coalescing, as the term convergence suggests, there is nowadays more variation in communication and media technologies, gadgets, devices, formats and standards than ever before" (2012, p. 11).

In contrast to the idea of media convergence, then, intermediality offers a less linear explanation of what has been happening to digital media in recent years. In the first place, it avoids describing the digital media trajectory in terms of a one-way process, with a specific final destination but rather highlights the diverse outcomes and rhythms of this trans-formation. Furthermore, it does not cancel out the differences between the various media but rather helps to identify the reciprocal influences to which these are subject, as well as the continuities with the past and their constant reconfiguration. The intention of the intermedia concept is thus to underline that all media reciprocally cross fertilize and co-evolve at a specific historic juncture and consequently that analog and digital communication media must be studied together and in their inter-actions. As we also underlined in the first chapter, digital media cannot be studied in isolation and their economic, technical, socio-cultural and even anthropological dimensions can only emerge in the context of the media *systems*, *ecologies* or *repertoires* of which they are an integral part.

Intermediality is certainly not the only concept used to understand a phenomenon as complex and multi-faceted as the intersected evolution of digital media. For example, Marshall McLuhan used the term *media ecology* to highlight the fact that the media must be understood in an integrated way. McLuhan himself argued that media ecology

> means arranging various media to help each other so they won't cancel each other out, to buttress one medium with another. You might say, for example, that radio is a bigger help to literacy than television, but television might be a very wonderful aid to teaching languages.
>
> (2004, p. 271)

In the mid 1990s both Danish Hans Fredrik Dahl and Italian Peppino Ortoleva defined the interweaving of the various media in a similar way using the expression *media system*. Dahl underlined that

> by "the media" in the collective sense I take it that we mean both a structure and a system: an entity composed of single parts (news-papers, radio, TV) distinguished by their characteristic relations and positions, and at the same time determined by their interdependence and reciprocality mediated by some sort of a cohesive power. [. . .] When "the media" are considered as a whole, it is—we may assume—because each of its entities is taken to play a particular role in ful-filling a common informational, entertaining or otherwise cultural purpose.
>
> (1994, p. 554)

Italian media historian Ortoleva similarly identified

> the need to retrace the plurality of forms of communication to a unitary and coherent framework. Speaking of a system in fact involves identifying an interdependence and complementarity relationship between the various media used for the exchange of messages, an awareness that the evolution of any single medium cannot be understood on the basis of its supposed technical 'nature' or cultural 'specifics' but only by taking account of the influence that each of the existing media has on the development and transformation of the others.
>
> (1995, p. 27)

The expression *media system*, incidentally thanks to the work of another Italian scholar (Hallin & Mancini, 2004), has, however, taken on a further meaning in international research relating to national and regional characteristics a single "media system" has and which in general differ from those of other nations or regions. Compared to the original idea this media system concept does not underline the inter-dependencies, inter-connections and precisely the intermediality that is triggered *among* the media, but it focuses mainly on the political and cultural characteristics of the media.

More recently, a notion adopted to grasp the interweaving of media consumption, deriving from a German language theory tradition, has been that of "media repertoires". The intention of the *media repertoires* concept is to describe the fact that individuals are not users of single media but rather build their own consumption environments made up of a repertoire of different media, channels and tools on which to draw as needed (Van Rees & Van Eijck, 2003; Taneja, Webster, Malthouse, & Ksiazek, 2012). The study of media repertoires developed also because media use is increasingly "cross-media" or "cross platform" in style, namely contents increasingly circulate by means of different platforms and individuals consume them by means of different media (Kim, 2016; Hasebrink & Hepp, 2017).

These perspectives reflect the theoretical approach centred on *media practices* and put forward by media sociologist Nick Couldry (2012). According to Couldry, the task of communication scholars is no longer to focus on the characteristics of single media, media institutions, texts or specific media activities but rather on media practices, how they evolve and intersect, whatever the actual device, platform or media used and when.

Further Reading

Couldry, N. (2012). *Media, Society, World. Social Theory and Digital Media Practice.* Cambridge: Polity Press.

Herkman, J., Hujanen, T., & Oinonen, P. (Eds.). (2012). *Intermediality and Media Change.* Tampere, Finland: Tampere University Press.

Storsul, T., & Stuedahl, D. (Eds.). (2007). *Ambivalence Towards Convergence: Digitalization and Media Change.* Göteborg, Sweden: Nordicom.

but, also and primarily, of a systematic intermediality trend interweaving previously separate media. As we will see, the consequences of the digitization process have not been homogeneous and coherent across all sectors and have led to more or less profound changes with diverse rhythms and implications in different regions of the globe. In some cases, the significance of this intermedia trend has been such as to make it almost impossible to distinguish the contours of each individual media sector clearly. In other cases, models shaped over the decades around specific analog media have remained visible and central to the functioning of certain media sectors: coming back to our textile metaphor, some sweaters have a very fine weave while others are tacked together in a looser knit.

Together with intermediality, in this chapter we will also encounter a constant tension between the two logics we have already referred to (see Chapter 1), which help us to make sense of the multiplicity of changes media have undergone with digitization.

The first can be christened *logic of continuity* and highlights the stability of the transition from analog to digital focusing on the tendency to preserve existing production models, consumption habits and cultural media formats. As science and technology studies and the path dependency tradition have highlighted, the networks, infrastructure and technological devices "incorporate" existing models and habits and thus contribute, in a certain sense, to stabilizing the potential of digital innovation in conservative directions. For example, in the history of the computer we observed that this was initially used to substitute pre-existing machines such as calculators and typewriters rather than responding to entirely new social demands (see Chapter 2). Highlighting the continuity trends within the digitization process helps us to cut the myth of the presumed "disruptive revolution" of digital media, in the sense that in many cases changes remained bound to distribution and consumption models developed in the analog era (see again Chapter 1).

A second recurring logic in our tale tends, by contrast, to highlight the tendency to a reconfiguration of cultural forms, markets assets and consumption practices triggered by digitization, which we'll call the *logic of change*. In Chapter 3 on the internet, for example, we have underlined that the internet has changed many times along its history from a military to an academic net, from a counter-cultural to a public service, from a commercial to a "social" environment. History can easily grasp this logic of change because it observes phenomena through time and so in movement.

As we will examine in greater depth here, these two apparently juxtaposed logics—change and continuity—are not alternative but represent two sides of the same coin: computers have changed a lot from calculators and typewriters and, at the same time, every internet "era" has left to subsequent and contemporary internet many inheritances and forms of continuity. Continuity and change are thus complementary tendencies, which interweave differently with the digitization process in the six sectors we will now begin to analyze: music, publishing, cinema, photography, TV and radio.

5.2 Music

Music was probably the earliest analog media sector to experience the consequences of the digitization process and the one that underwent the most rapid
changes. For example, while MP3 format music began to be sold only from 2003
onwards, in the largest world music market (the USA) revenues from digital
music sales had already, in 2011, overtaken traditional physical format music
sales (Source: RIAA). In contrast to other sectors with traditionally similar
industrial frameworks (for example book publishing or cinema), music consumption moved to "liquid" supports very rapidly thus becoming a case of sudden
digitization generated change, with profound consequences for listeners' habits,
industry assets and the way music circulate globally. The rapidity and scope of
these consequences are the reasons this chapter on the digitization of analog
media starts with music.

   While today what is generally meant by *digital music* is music in compressed
form (commonly called MP3) circulating on the internet or via streaming
services, in actual fact the history of music digitization started well before the
onset of file sharing, iPods and Spotify. It was, in fact, in 1979 that the first
Compact disc (CD) player–a music reproduction system based on laser technology capable of reading optical discs containing audio signals codified into
digital format–was made. CDs could hold 650 MBs (i.e. around 74 minutes of
music) of data in their initial form, promised consumers higher audio quality than
analog supports could deliver and, above all, guaranteed this quality practically
forever. While records on analog supports like vinyl deteriorated every time a
needle was placed on them, CDs were at least initially free of wear and tear
issues (Immick, 1998; Millard, 2005).

   The most interesting fact, however, is that while CDs were based on a digital
code, they did not actually contribute to the emergence of a new and disruptive
model, but followed a conventional pattern common in the entertainment
industry. In their first decade, then, CDs fully embodied the analog to digital
continuity logic. While they were based on digital technologies, CDs replicated
the production, distribution and consumption dynamics that had characterized
the record industry since the invention of the phonograph in the late nineteenth
century. Indeed, from a technical and economic point of view, CDs were the
product of a joint effort by two multinationals, Sony and Philips, who had been
benchmarks in music hardware manufacture and contents' creation and
distribution for decades. These large firms aimed, on one hand, to sell reproducing devices (gramophones, turntables, cassette players)–generally expensive
and designed to last–and on the other, at the mass dissemination of physical
copies of contents (phonograph cylinders, records, music tapes), which were
cheap and frequently purchased. From a distribution point of view, too, CDs

continued earlier practices and were sold in dedicated physical shops just as had been the case previously for records and tapes. From a consumer perspective, finally, following in the footsteps of the turntable, in the first half of the 1980s CDs initially targeted a medium-high segment of the music market made up of Hi-Fi enthusiasts and classical music lovers mainly. It was only in the early 1990s that CDs emerged as the most popular musical support across all listening categories, including teenagers and youths.

However, this consolidated model hit hard times verging on sudden collapse in the early years of the new millennium when it was confronted with a new paradigm also based on digital but with radically different implications. This new digital music paradigm was mainly embodied in three elements: the compressed MP3 digital format, the iPod or, more generally, MP3 players and internet-based tools for the online exchange of music contents, such as file sharing platforms.

The success of compressed digital music and its explosive consequences for the music industry and its consumers originated with the specific innovation trajectory of the MP3 music format. Media historian Jonathan Sterne (2012) has retraced the history of the MP3 over the long term and, thanks to what Sterne himself baptizes *format theory*, he has been able to focus simultaneous attention to "smaller registers like software, operating standards, and codes, as well as larger registers like infrastructures, international corporate consortia, and whole technical systems" (Sterne, 2012, p. 11). The results of this study can be considered an example of a new wave of communication history able to expand the historical reconstruction through the creative use of theories and critical standings, as we mentioned in Chapter 1.

The long-term history of MP3 originated from the developments of psychoacoustics and the business models adopted in the 1920s and 1930s by Bell Laboratories, which were the first to explore the innovative idea of *compressing* the human voice through telephone lines. In other words, this sound technology, which has significantly contributed to reconfigure the creative world of music, has been in origin triggered by capitalistic pressures aimed at optimizing the business of *telephonic* communications—another case where key technologies in a specific media sector were implemented in another and apparently unrelated one, demonstrating the relevance of a broad intermedia perspective.

While some other ideas contributing to the creation of MP3s can be traced back as far as the 1970s (in particular wired broadcasting, a radio broadcasting system that used telephones lines to transmit music), it was only at the end of the 1980s that algorithms capable of compressing sound to broadcast it easily in digital format were experimented with. The MP3 creation process went live when the MPEG, a working group within the International Organization for

Standardization (ISO), began to draw up the technical standards required for the dissemination of contents both for the digital radios and TVs of the future and for CD-ROM video contents (Chiariglione & Magaudda, 2012). A considerable part of the subsequent work contributing to the MP3 format was the outcome of public funds guaranteed by the European Community originally set aside to support digital broadcasting (see the section about the digitization of radio later in this chapter). In 1992, the final tests to select the best audio compression algorithm were completed and the audio MP3 standard format was officially released in 1995 (Sterne, 2012, p. 129 and subsequent).

Hence, in contrast to CDs and all the music supports preceding them, the MP3 was a technology that did not emerge as the outcome of business strategies by the major record companies but was rather the result of a complex negotiating process involving actors which, for the most part, had nothing to do with music sales. Indeed, MP3s were not initially designed to be the most common music format but rather to respond to the needs of the audio broadcasting and the ICT industries: the former sector required a standard for distance transmissions to apply to digital radio, while the latter was in search of an audio format capable of functioning on all types of machines, from computers to portable devices (Sterne, 2012). From this moment on, then, the music sector became increasingly intermedial, i.e. progressively less bound to the logics and interests of conventional music record companies and, by contrast, influenced by the drives and demands of industries, producers and technologies of other media sectors. It was precisely other media sectors that pushed musical technological development into unexpected directions: the new format's ease of circulation and versatility of use juxtaposed to the closed nature and need for copy-right protection typical of the traditional music industry encouraged the creation of a "viral" type digital format, which was difficult to control and well-suited to the diverse types of digital media: the MP3, abbreviation of MPEG Audio Layer III.

As the new format had not been thought up by, or even received the initial backing of, the major record companies, in its first years MP3s were not taken up by the music industry, also because they were raking in the profits of the CD's success at the time. On the contrary, the adoption of MP3 originated as a bottom-up process enacted, above all, by amateur projects and also thanks to emerging online services seeking visibility on the fast-growing WWW. For example, in 1997 a Stanford student made his music collection freely available on the Web in MP3 format and the success of this led to his university's server crashing (Alderman, 2001, p. 30). New websites with no links to the music industry whatsoever began using this format: MP3.com, another 1997 site, is a case in point as it acquired visibility among internet start-ups offering mainly MP3 music from independent labels not linked to the main record companies.

The music industry thus began to take note of MP3s but for the most part decided not to take them up, seeing them as an easy-to-transmit format, which could potentially encourage piracy. It was for this reason that the music industry initially took the MP3 format hostage, refusing to sell audio players capable of reproducing the format, for example, and later attempted to find copyright defence mechanisms and new commercial models (Gillespie, 2007).

From 1999 onwards, the fate of the MP3 format changed radically partly because of high speed internet connections, which were becoming the standard in the majority of developed countries' households. A central event in the history of the MP3 was the creation of Napster in 1999, the first file sharing software, once again the non-profit brainchild of an American university student only just over 20 years of age. Although the first version of Napster was short-lived (the service was closed down for copyright violations just a year and a half after its foundation but re-opened subsequently in an alternative form), its cultural impact was huge. Napster ushered in a new user-based file exchange called *peer-to-peer*, which was doomed to become a model of circulation for the majority of Web contents over the subsequent decade. It was precisely this idea that set the foundations for the breakup of the analog-digital continuum: not only were peer-to-peer systems partially disconnected from the need for physical supports, which had been a determinant characteristic of the music industry since the days of phonograph cylinders, but above all they overcame the established distribution model linked to physical shops, as Napster users could download music files from the comfort of their own homes on their personal computers (Allen-Robertson, 2013). Moreover, the vast journalistic coverage of the judicial vicissitudes that led to Napster being closed down for copyright violations in 2001 transformed the MP3 digital format from a niche interest of Web experts to a wide reaching social and cultural phenomenon especially among the young and teenagers (Marshall, 2005).

The second element with a determinant effect on the popularisation of MP3 digital music was the success of the iPod, released onto the market in 2001 by Apple, a company that had not, to date, taken any interest in music. While certain portable MP3 players had been available on the market since 1998, and thus pre-dated iPods, these were impracticable for the most part because their storage memories were too small (initially 32 MB, enough for just six songs). iPods were the first MP3 players capable of storing a thousand songs, which could be managed on a user-friendly interface and common-sense synchronisation system. It was also for these reasons that the iPod succeeded in becoming the most popular portable music player, accounting for 70% of the US market and becoming a cultural "icon" not just among teenagers, but also heads of state such as US President George W. Bush who, in 2005, made public his iPod playlist (prevalently deeply American and rock music based) in order to improve his awkward political image (Jordan, 2013).

The buyers of the first portable music players such as iPods found themselves, however, in an entirely novel situation in the history of recorded music: they were effectively buying music reproducers without an official (and legal) sales channel having been set up for the distribution of songs. To resolve this problem, in 2003 Apple created the iTunes Store, a digital platform initially designed to sell digital music online with the objective of shoring up iPod player sales. It was a sales formula that marketed songs for 99 cents each and turned out to be such a huge success that just five years later the iTunes Store became the number one music shop by turnover in the US, making Apple into the world's primary musical distributor.

Apple's two-fold success in the music industry with iPods and the iTunes Store is a sign of the radical changes that occurred in both recorded music industry and listeners' consumption practices. In fact, in just over five years, the major record companies lost control over the two strategic sectors they had managed for at least a century: hardware manufacture and contents distribution. In the former sector, at least since the early 1980s, Sony in particular had played a leading role first with tape Walkmans and then with Discmans. Distribution was effectively the true power lever with which major record companies had controlled the market and safeguarded their own positions from the emergence of new independent labels (Hesmondhalgh, 1997). In the space of just a few years, music digitization based on MP3 files catapulted Apple to new market benchmark status.

With the success of the MP3 format and the online sharing of music files, digital music circulation began to take radically different directions from past record and CD-based trajectories. From the late 1990s onwards, compressed digital music circulated via at least four channels. In the first half of the noughties digital music sales followed a commercial pattern which in part resembled that of traditional physical music: consumers bought songs or whole albums in MP3 format in a virtual shop, in the vast majority of cases through the already mentioned Apple's iTunes store. As we saw, this model eliminated the physical component of the shop and allowed contents to be downloaded at home, but it also retained the logic of *buying* music in specific (even if virtual) places.

A second model especially influential in digital music circulation was based on file sharing software and peer-to-peer systems, which were a direct follow-on from Napster and frequently based on breaking copyright laws and alleged piracy. While certain figures are hard to come by, the popularity of this type of sharing platforms culminated in around 2005 with 20% of music in America circulating by means of it. While the USA saw a flourishing legal market spring up around digital music, in other countries legally purchased music accounted for only a small proportion of the total: the most extreme example was China, where digital music piracy rates reached a total of over 90% (Liu, 2010) as a result of a combination of political, economic, cultural and social influences, including a diverse conception of copyright (Priest, 2014; Ren, 2016). In several countries, music file sharing has diminished in recent years, both as a result of controls over illegal sharing and following on from the popularisation of a further two music circulation models, the third and fourth in our list.

The third model consists of platforms such as YouTube, which make music videos uploaded by users or musicians and recording studios themselves available, frequently linked to brief advertising commercials. In 2010, around 30% of total YouTube viewings were music videos and, by 2017, 66 out of 70 of the most frequently viewed videos ever were musical. In the wake of this success, in 2009 traditional record companies (like Sony and Universal) attempted to win back part of their control over digital musical circulation on the Web in partnership with YouTube creating Vevo, a new music video platform. Vevo's aim has been to allow big records companies to regain control over the music distribution, for example through the Vevo Certified Award, a prize that goes to songs achieving 100 million official viewings, mirroring the pre-digital streaming Gold Album model, set up in 1958 for records selling at least 500,000 copies. While the Vevo Award is a new idea launched in 2012, it really looks like a reworking of earlier well-known mechanisms revolving around the role of prizes in the processes of *artistic consecration* (English, 2005) which came to the fore in the golden age of the analog cultural industry history.

Box 5.2 In-depth Theory

The Globalization of K-pop

The profound transformation of music circulation generated by digital technologies has prompted a series of changes to pop music aesthetics and the way global music consumption works. An especially emblematic case is the global success of K-pop, a specific genre of South Korean pop music. K-pop is linked to an early 1990s Korean-born music genre, which at the time did not achieve vast international visibility until *Gangnam Style* by Korean musician Psy became the first video ever to achieve more than 1 billion viewings on YouTube in 2013 (reaching almost 3 billion in 2017).

This event exemplifies some of the transformations that have taken place in the relationship between digital technologies and global music circulation. Before then, it was virtually unheard of for a song from an Oriental country to reach the highest levels of the global pop music market, which has been historically dominated by English language or European music. A first interesting aspect of Gangnam Style's success and that of many other K-pop bands clearly relates to the transformation that has taken place in music's global level distribution processes: thanks to online streaming platforms, music no longer needs to pass through what cultural industry scholars have referred to as national *gatekeepers* (Hirsh, 1972), such as local branches of multinationals, local language TV channels or specialised shops, to achieve international success.

The music circulating over the internet does, however, need to adapt to the cultural formats specific to a new type of distribution infrastructure. A song like *Gangnam Style* is especially well-suited to YouTube and social media logics, as Lee and Kuwahara (2014) have noted. Indeed, this song has lended itself to a great many parodies, memes and re-workings, which have effectively been crucial to widening its global appeal.

Moreover, K-pop's success is based not only on new digital streaming services but also on a change that has taken place on the production level. In fact, as Ingyu Oh (2013) has observed, K-pop's greatest successes have not been simply a matter of musicians and producers based in Korea but are the outcome of a flexible, delocalized production network combining melodies produced in Switzerland, lyrics written in the UK and electronic rhythms conceived in the USA with a shared South Korean identity paradigm. Thus we can see that behind the international success of an apparently local music genre lies a complex global socio-technical network.

Further Reading

Kuwahara, Y. (Ed.). (2014). *Korean Popular Culture in Global Context*. London: Palgrave.

Oh, I. (2013). The globalization of K-pop: Korea's place in the global music industry. *Korea Observer, 44*(3), 389–409.

A fourth and more recent digital music circulation model is centered around music streaming services, supported financially by forms of subscription and to some extent advertising. This is the case of musical services offered, for example, by Pandora, set up in 2005, and to an even greater extent Spotify, founded in 2006 and launched initially in several European countries in 2008, which has become the most popular music platform in the space of just a few years. Subscription streaming is a good example of intermediality as it combines radio broadcasting, informatics data and file sharing with practices linked to social network sites and the constant connection experience ensured by smartphones. This circulation model, which seems to have made the need to own music files obsolete, is a tangible example of cloud computing (Morris, 2011) and makes evident the convergence between methods typical of the world of music with parallel trends in the use of the internet, especially, in its "social" influence (see Chapter 3). Nevertheless, the industrial consequences of streaming services still remain controversial: if, on the one hand, this new method has revived hopes of building a paying consumer market for digital music; on the other, a range of analyses have shown that Spotify actually contributed to diminishing downloads and encouraging piracy (Wikström, 2013; Aguiar & Waldfogel, 2015). Furthermore, the revenue model embodied by music streaming services has still to completely prove to be really viable and rewarding: ten years on from Spotify's launch, while its revenues are continuing to mount up consistently (from $1 billion in 2014 to 2.9 in 2016), so are its losses (increased from 165 million in 2014 to 539 in 2016), revealing the difficulties to establish an effective economic model for digital streaming music services.

Overall, then, the guiding forces behind music's digitization and dematerialization processes have been intermedial: music media have interacted and intermingled with drives from other media sectors and actors, which had no apparent links with the music world. For example, the outcome for music production has been a fragmentation of players and activities to the extent that it is difficult to speak of a single music industry today and the current situation can be best described as "many industries with many relationships to music" (Sterne, 2014).

The tension between continuity and change in the development of digital music is now highly evident. On the one hand, it is clear that digitization has not in itself prompted paradigmatic change, as the fact that the advent of CDs ushered in surprisingly little change in production and consumption patterns characteristic of the analog era proves. By contrast, the integration into the music sector of elements characteristic of other digital media via the MP3 standard, file sharing and streaming has led to the emergence of new music circulation paradigms and, ultimately, a radical break with the past.

But a further surprising continuity element in the music world should also be highlighted. The digitization process has not completely replaced old formats with new ones leading to the "death" of analog technologies. Quite the contrary, in the digital era we have witnessed the survival of certain old analog supports such as audio tapes, which have been used for a number of years in music sub-cultures such as hip-hop in the San Francisco's Bay area (Harrison, 2006) and have also resisted replacement in a large, modernizing country such as India (Manuel, 2014). The most visible example of the survival of analog formats in music, however, has been the resurgence of LP records (Bartmanski &

Woodward, 2015). Gradually forgotten over the 1990s, in the digital music era record albums have been seen by musicians and music lovers—in particular by independent rock and electronic music—as embodying cultural meanings and alternative listening practices contrasting with those associated with the "liquidity" of digital music (Davis, 2007; Magaudda, 2011; 2012). Remaining a niche phenomenon, in recent years vinyl records sales in the US went from around 1 million in 2007 to nearly 17 million in 2016 (RIAA data), mostly sold via small physical independent shops, which have come to symbolize, together with records themselves, an alternative to the consumer models subsumed by the digital music industries. The case of the rebirth of vinyl records provides further illustration of the way in which apparently obsolescent analog devices and new digital media can coexist in an increasingly complex and stratified (analog and digital) media pattern.

5.3 Publishing: Books and Newsmaking

Publishing is one of the longest-lived media sectors and has remained relatively stable over the course of more than five centuries of history. From the invention of the printing press in ancient China and post-medieval Europe, first books and then magazines and newspapers have been crucial in modern media ecologies, playing a central role from the seventeenth century onwards in the building of the Enlightenment and of modern science (Eisenstein, 1979), of the "public sphere" in Western democracy (Habermas, 1962/1989) and, from the latter half of the nineteenth century, of industrial and mass societies. This longevity notwithstanding, digitization has generated significant consequences for the publishing sector too: first with the creation of new text writing and printing methods and then, in a second phase, new digital devices, platforms and textual styles have shaken up the whole written word media environment. At the same time, having remained for centuries a matter of printed paper, in recent years reading practices have also begun to encompass digital supports thus reviving forecasts of the abandonment of paper, which have recurred over the course of history and found new, vociferous supporters in the digital age (Coit Murphy, 2003). There is, thus, no doubt that digitization has had powerful consequences in the last half century of reading and writing history. Four phases are identifiable in the digitization of publishing.

The first of these phases took place from the 1960s to the end of the 1970s and saw the dissemination of the first computers capable of managing text writing and storage work above all in the context of large firms and newspaper printing houses. In a second phase—from the late 1970s to the early 1990s—accessible word processing as the first PCs attracted a growing number of non-professional users. The third phase, stretching from the early 1990s to the latter half of the noughties, was characterized by the integration of writing and reading with the internet, generating new forms of written text circulation but only directly affecting traditional publishing forms such as newspapers and books. From the first half of the noughties onwards, finally, a new phase can be identified that is still fully under way and is more clearly intermedia in nature with consequences which remain contradictory and partial, still. This phase has seen attempts to leave behind printed paper as the main reading support and replace it with digital devices such as tablets, ebooks and smartphones with still mixed results. Let us now take a closer look at some of the features of these four phases in the digitization of publishing.

As we have seen, the initial steps in publishing digitization were contemporary to the advent of the first computers, as writing was one of the main sectors of application of computers in offices and other business sectors. Right from the mainframe era, IBM developed digital writing systems for offices, which competed with typewriters and professional typists, with the latter consisting in the 1930s of a workforce which was 95% female (Wershler-Henry, 2005, p. 86). The advent of the digital elaboration of texts took place one small step at a time. In the 1960s, the first computers for the exclusive purpose of writing made their appearance. The first text file storage systems were developed in the 1970s once again for the use of large offices, which were now able to store and access large quantities of texts on magnetic supports thus simplifying research and filing work hugely. These large and expensive systems spread exclusively in the office and business worlds and contributed to changing the work lives not only of secretaries and filing departments but business organization as a whole as well.

The dissemination of personal computers from the latter half of the 1970s onwards contributed to launching a second phase, when digital writing began to emerge from offices and take its place in other social contexts and the home in particular. Together with the first personal computers, writing software began to spread, too, and was soon an important part of the success story of the PC's shift to the non-professional-home context (see Chapter 2). In a period when the usefulness of PCs for home users was still not entirely clear, word processing programs were a hint of a tangible function for these new machines, i.e. letter and text writing done on traditional typewriters or even by hand for decades. The first word processing program for personal computers, called Electric Pencil, was released in 1976 and was the harbinger of a long series of other word processing software (Bergin, 2006). As we saw in Chapter 2, Microsoft also developed a word processing system, simply called Word, whose first version was launched in 1983 but became a standard program on all personal computers only in the late 1980s, following on from the dissemination of a new version optimized for the Windows operating system.

Word processing was not the only way that personal computers modified writing and publishing work. From the mid 1980s onwards the first graphic page layout software emerged–e.g. PageMaker and QuarkXpress–which enabled page layouts to be created with PCs and without the help of professional machinery. In 1993, the PDF format was created, which subsequently became the electronic reference standard for many digital publishing sectors (from academic work to digital versions of daily newspapers). In brief, in this second phase, all work linked to text creation and processing could be managed by PCs, which could also, from the late 1980s onwards, be linked up to relatively affordable printers, the availability of which completed the digital independent creation and printing chain for non-professionals.

The third phase in printing digitization began in the mid 1990s with the popularization of the internet (see Chapter 3). In contrast to the logic of continuity of earlier phases, when digital elements were integrated into writing, printing and reading practices without revolutionizing them, in this third period the potential for circulating and reading written texts via the internet opened a new era of publishing. In actual fact, the first attempts to use the internet to disseminate written texts dated at least as far back as 1971, when Michael Hart launched the still active Gutenberg project using access to one of the earliest ARPANET network nodes (Lebert, 2009). Hart's intention was to create a sort of virtual public library and he thus began digitizing and sharing classic texts not covered by copyright law on the network, beginning with the American Declaration of Independence. More generally speaking, as we saw in Chapter 3, the sharing of written texts was the basis of the very idea of the World Wide Web, which emerged at the beginning of the 1990s.

These precedents notwithstanding, however, it was only from the late 1990s onwards, as the internet progressively made its way into the home, that writing and reading began to be transformed in a significant way and this for at least two reasons. On the one hand, the potential for free and immediate publication on the web, in blogs for example, transformed ordinary readers into *potential* written text producers. On the other, the new logical form of writing based on the HTML language made possible a different non-linear reading method thanks to the use of links creating so-called hypertext (Landow, 1991). Hyper-text differs from the classic texts in three fundamental ways: it has no pre-defined linear sequence but users decide how to combine elements and build a personalized reading trajectory; it has no pre-defined beginning and end but rather, in theory, is made up of an unlimited number of links; finally, it is never the same twice–like a book that remains unchanged over time–but part of the constant change, which is such a feature of the internet's magma (Bolter, 1991). Thus, hypertext constituted a clear break with traditional texts, although certain scholars have argued that the two forms always co-existed also in the pre-digital analog world.

Thus, at the end of the 1990s, reading and writing hypertexts turned into common practices on the Web, thanks to free-to-use platforms for non-expert users who wanted to reach out to others with their writings, in blogs for example. If the first blogs served above all as "filters" with which to organize other Web contents, in the space of just a few years users began to exploit the flexibility of this format mainly in three directions: online diaries, personal publishing journals and Weblogs (Siles, 2011). Furthermore, the strictly textual nature of the early content offered by the World Wide Web led to the creation of various and innovative forms of text ranging from personal diaries published online in blogs, via shared writing experiments on the Web, to the most recent creation of texts and novels in social network sites, as in the case of the so-called micro-blogging format.

Despite these innovations in written text production and reading opportunities, in this third phase of publishing, digitization only partially challenged the central role of traditional paper supports: books, newspapers and periodicals continued to be printed and read mainly in paper form, thus highlighting the survival of paper publishing ensured both by the existence of a large scale publishing infrastructure (including publishers, authors, distribution networks, print houses, kiosks, etc.) and by the social practices of readers—reading newspapers at home, on the metro or at work.

A characteristic trait of the fourth and last phase, which is still under way, is precisely the attempt to go beyond, or at least partially replace, traditional paper supports in favor of a convergence between digital devices and the internet. However, the consequences of digitization still remain uncertain as different outcomes in diverse publishing sub-sectors with huge variation between the different regions of the world is visible. We can examine these uncertain outcomes by looking more specifically at books and periodicals publishing sub-sectors.

This last phase has seen an attempt to transform social reading practices in two different ways: on the one hand with digital devices capable of effectively replacing paper and, on the other, with the evolution of a digital infrastructure capable of integrating all the various consumer reading phases starting with purchases. The idea of replacing paper books and periodicals with an electronic equivalent has a long history. If we limit ourselves to the digital era, in the mid 1970s at the Xerox Palo Alto Research Center (PARC) scientist Alan Kay envisioned the Dynabook, an electronic prototype designed to be an educational tool for drawing and composing music (Manley & Holley, 2012; see also Box 5.3). Kay's vision was not simply that of creating a sort of electronic book, but

Box 5.3 Documents

Alan Kay and Adele Goldberg, *The Dynabook* (1977)

Imagine having your own self-contained knowledge manipulator in a portable package the size and shape of an ordinary notebook. Suppose it had enough power to outrace your senses of sight and hearing, enough capacity to store for later retrieval thousands of page-equivalents of reference materials, poems, letters, recipes, records, drawings, animations, musical scores, waveforms, dynamic simulations, and anything else you would like to remember and change.

We envision a device as small and portable as possible which could both take in and give out information in quantities approaching that of human sensory systems. Visual output should be, at the least, of higher quality than what can be obtained from newsprint. Audio output should adhere to similar high-fidelity standards.

There should be no discernible pause between cause and effect. One of the metaphors we used when designing such a system was that of a musical instrument, such as a flute, which is owned by its user and responds instantly and consistently to its owner's wishes. Imagine the absurdity of a one-second delay between blowing a note and hearing it!

These "civilized" desires for flexibility, resolution, and response lead to the conclusion that a user of a dynamic personal medium needs several hundred times as much power as the average adult now typically enjoys from timeshared computing. This means that we should either build a new resource several hundred times the capacity of current machines and share it (very difficult and expensive), or we should investigate the possibility of giving each person his own powerful machine. We chose the second approach. [. . .]

What would happen in a world in which everyone had a Dynabook? If such a machine were designed in a way that any owner could mold and channel its power to his own needs, then a new kind of medium would have been created: a metamedium, whose content would be a wide range of already-existing and not-yet-invented media.

Source: Kay, A., & Goldberg, A. (1977). Personal dynamic media. *Computer, 10*(3), 31–41

Figure 5.2 The original prototype of the Dynabook, designed by Alan Kay
Source: photo and courtesy of Marcin Wichary

a general-purpose device that could be used both by businessmen, ordinary people and even children for a wide set of activities, including art and poetry (Kay & Goldberg, 1977).

In the 1990s, a few devices were released into the market, but they quickly failed. In the early 1990s, the Data Discman was introduced by Sony: it was a portable reader capable of searching text strings within an archive stored in its memory that, as the name suggests, was also an attempt to follow in the successful wake of the analog Walkman in the music sphere. Perhaps the first device explicitly aiming to replace paper books was the Cybook, which came out with limited success in France in 1998 and soon disappeared. Another notable attempt was the Rocket eBook, released again in 1998 by a Californian company that also established a deal with the Barnes and Noble bookstore chain to sell both its readers and compatible ebooks, but the device was retired from the market in 2003 (Manley & Holley, 2012). These early failed attempts reflected a range of problems, including the initial technical limitations of these devices: they could store just a limited number of books, could not download books directly from the internet and had a liquid crystal screen way less comfortable than contemporary electronic ink ones.

Above all, these early attempts to establish digital reading devices lacked a complete *infrastructure* integrating in an effective way physical readers, digital formats, online selling platforms and contents distribution networks. Indeed, true competition with the paper versions of books and newspapers really only occurred in the latter half of the noughties with investments by large internet firms to develop an integrated ebook distribution infrastructure. For example, Kindle, launched in 2007 by Amazon, owed its success especially to the fact that it was an integral part of a wider ebook digital infrastructure. Amazon is, in fact, paper book sales leader (in 2015 it controlled around 40% of the whole US market), producer of the most commonly used digital reading device (Kindle) and finally, distributor, via its online platform, of ebooks encoded with a specific standard, readable only with its own device, Kindle. It is precisely this integration between online platform, physical devices and codification systems (and thus contents protection) that enabled Amazon to become the main player in the ebook sector whose sales on the American site overtook paper book sales in 2011.

The second device that played a major role in book digitization, was Apple's iPad tablet, introduced in 2010. Not only have iPads, like Kindles, benefited from a tried and tested integrated distribution platform (in this case the iTunes Store) but they have also been favored by the fashion trend generated around Apple products and the iPhone in particular, which was launched just three years earlier. It is thus not a coincidence that the ebook market developed quickly as a highly concentrated one, especially in the United States, where in 2009 90% of the sector was already controlled by Amazon and Apple together with the Barnes and Noble chain, which built its digital book infrastructure around the Nook reader in 2009.

Globally speaking, however, the penetration of electronic publications has remained very small. A range of statistics show admittedly contrasting figures indicating that the ebook market still accounts for a small percentage of total sales. A 2013 International Confederation of Societies of Authors and Composers (CISAC) report estimated that, of the various digital cultural industries, books had seen very limited development, as digital sales accounted for around 7% of the digital market at global level (UNESCO, EY and CISAC, 2015, p. 24). The impact of digital books on the market and on consumer practices is still unclear and uncertain, in countries that saw the highest initial uptake, such as USA and UK, included. On closer inspection, in these countries, after some years of sales progresses and industry's euphoria, ebook sales started to visibly decrease: in the USA, in 2012 ebooks accounted for around 21% (215 million) of total book sales, a percentage that had risen to 27% in 2014 (234 million), but then had dropped to 24% in 2015 (204 million), to further decrease to 21% in 2016 (179 million) (source: US Nielsen/NPD BookScan); in the UK too, in 2015 digital book sales for the first time dropped off 4% over previous year figures, prompting pessimism about the sector's growth expectations (source: UK Nielsen Bookscan).

But what is really surprising is the fact that, during this same time frame, *paper* book sales have raised in various countries: in the USA, for example, traditional book sales rose from 591 million copies in 2012 to 674 million in 2016 (source: US Nielsen/NPD BookScan). Even if this is a short time frame and the trend may invert once again, the scenario shows that the digitization process is neither linear nor to be taken for granted and that there is a constant tension between changes generated by digital innovation and continuities in devices, market assets and readers' practices.

The realm of book printing, perhaps to an even greater extent than music or cinema, is characterized by co-existence and stratification between analog and digital, old and new technologies, luminous screens and yellowed pages. This co-existence brings with it at least two interesting consequences. First, paper book technology in the digital age is still seen as one of the best and most efficient: it does not need electricity, is distinctly hard wearing (shock, cold and partially water resistant) and is made of simple materials available in many parts of the world. Second, the current historical juncture is the apex of the paper book's dissemination because digital technologies in production and printing terms and internet sites such as Amazon encourage the purchase and exchange of paper books via an old medium—the postal service. The death of paper books is a recurring theme in media history but, in this case, digital media seem to have had a positive impact on the dissemination of analog media, as we saw in the case of records.

The newspaper and magazine publishing sector gives us a very different scenario but one that once again highlights a powerful dialectic between change and continuity, just as with books. If printed books coexist with digital books, rather than being replaced by them, the impact of the popularization of the internet on newspaper publication has been more rapid and far-reaching especially on its economic assets and news consumption practices. Newspapers were, in fact, among the first traditional media to try their luck on the internet as early as the latter half of the 1990s. The *New York Times*, for example, launched its online edition in 1996, although it only began to update its site 24 hours a day in the year 2000 (Boczkowski, 2004). It has only been from the year 2000 onwards that digital media dissemination began to generate profound transformations in the journalistic world. These transformations can be traced to the shaking up of certain well-established distinctions and hierarchies, which had been fundamental to news production in earlier decades (Schudson, 2011). The digitization of news making casts doubt on other distinctions, such as that among the various formats and journalistic reports and between new and old media. In an era of online journalism, it is increasingly common for important news items to circulate via tweets or Facebook posts before being commented on in a YouTube video, being turned into a printed paper newspaper and quickly being made into an instant ebook.

A frequently cited phenomenon is change in the previously clearly dis-tinct roles of producers and consumers of news, with the latter increasingly generators of images and news in their own right and also playing a fundamental role in the circulation of articles, which can potentially be shared by individuals via their own social network contacts. The phenomenon of *citizen journalism* is thus increasingly significant as a consequence of the ever more direct involvement of ordinary people and non-professionals in news production (Fenton, 2010). Although this did not originate with the digital media, but dates back at least to the paper pamphlets produced during the late-eighteenth-century American War of Independence (Gillmor, 2006), there is no doubt that the dissemination of the internet, personal digital devices and social networks have transformed the scope and pace of citizen involvement in news generation and distribution.

However, the multiplication of available sources and of uncontrolled and potentially false or inaccurate news (the so-called *fake news*) via social networks, has led to a *post-truth scenario*: "circumstances in which objective facts are less influential in shaping public opinion than appeals to emotion and personal belief", as the Oxford English Dictionary described it for the first time in 2016. It is a scenario which, to some extent, conjures up George Orwell's political sci-fi novel *1984*, directly associated with a set of phenomena characteristic of news circulation in the digital world including the *24-hour news cycle* (Cushion & Lewis, 2010), the omnipresence of the social media and the ever more pronounced tendency by readers to rely on social networks as privileged sources of information. Research in 2016 by the Reuters Institute for the Study of Journalism into 26 countries found that a growing number of people use social networks as their main source of news with admittedly significant variations from country to country: 26% in France, 35% in the USA and as much as 55% in Brazil. Further research in the same year by the Pew Research Center found that in the USA as many as 62% of adults use social network platforms—Facebook, Twitter and Reddit in particular—for news and that the majority of these get their news from only one of these sites (Gottfried & Shearer, 2016).

These transformations in news flow and the multiplication of news sources has obviously been accompanied by a reconfiguration of the economic frameworks of traditional media and has had consequences, in particular, on paper format sales. The crisis in printed newspaper sales came to the fore only from the latter half of the noughties onwards taking the concrete form, on the one hand, of a drop in sales in some parts of the world and, on the other, in reductions in advertising investment in the newspaper industry, which has only partially been redirected to the internet. From 2012 to 2016 printed newspaper circulation dropped in five of the six areas of the world where the market has been segmented, excluding Asia: in particular in Australia and Oceania 30.7% fewer paper newspapers circulated in 2016 than in 2012, while in Europe and North America the figures were 20.5% and 11.6% respectively (Source: WAN-IFRA, 2017). These data, however, show a contrary trend in Asia, where in the same period printed newspaper sales grew by 40%, largely due to increased literacy and economic growth in China and India, which together account for more than half of global paper newspaper sales. Thus, global daily print newspaper circulation increased by more than 140 million copies from 2012 to 2016 thanks precisely to these populous Asian countries (Source: WAN-IFRA, 2017). These figures show once again that worldwide digitization is a contradictory phenomenon and that analog and traditional media are not simply replaced by digital technologies, but are sometimes even reinforced by them.

Newspapers advertising is another sector affected by digitization. In recent years a contraction in investment in printed newspapers has taken place together with an exponential growth in digital advertising revenues that, from 2012 to 2016, increased by 32% globally (Source: WAN-IFRA, 2017). This means that a significant proportion of advertising investors, at least in the journalism sector, has shifted from paper to digital prompting a reconfiguration of the sector's business models. This reconfiguration has first and foremost consisted in the fact that the reduction in advertising revenues has been partially offset by the growth of circulation revenues (for the first time in history sales revenues overtook advertising revenues in 2013) especially thanks to the growth in sales in the Asian countries mentioned earlier. Second, and an even more significant aspect capable of summing up the contradictions of the contemporary publishing world, the World Association of Newspapers and News Publishers estimated that globally, in 2015, 92% of all daily newspaper revenues was generated by paper-based and not by digital editions. In global terms, then, digital today is still largely a minority contribution to the newspaper market, which is still overwhelmingly paper based.

Overall the publishing sector revolves around intermedia logic in a clear tension between change and continuity. On the one hand, digital devices and infrastructure have ushered in significant transformations in written contents and writing and reading practices, generating new cultural formats such as hypertext and blogs, as well as a widening of access to written contents on an ever more global basis. On the other hand, the most long-lived media support—paper—has maintained much of its presence both in written book form—which shows no sign of disappearing—and in print newspapers, which have remained central to the economic framework of this sector despite powerful competition from digital newspapers.

5.4 Cinema and Video

Digitization has had significant consequences in the world of cinema and the moving image, too, in terms of working methods, film contents, democratization of production and ways of watching moving pictures. As Henry Jenkins (1999) noted some years ago, the cinema-digital technologies relationship functions on various levels, dimensions and issues that cinematic theory has only recently succeeded in putting into focus. These transformations have impacted not only on the type of support used for film circulation and their aesthetic, but also—as cinema scholar Lev Manovich (2001) has highlighted—placed the digital cinema paradigm center-stage in the whole new digital media ecology, thus underlining yet again the digitization process's intermedia trajectory.

Cinema digitization has impacted on the production sphere, in the first place introducing new creative possibilities thanks especially to digital special effects developments. 1977 was the year when digital techniques were used to a significant extent for the first time in George Lucas's sci-fi epic *Star Wars*. In 1979, the director's production company, Lucas Film, set up an independent division exclusively dedicated to digital effects. In the late 1980s and early 1990s, the role of special effects became increasingly important to the production of many highly successful films (the classic example here is Steven Spielberg's 1993 blockbuster movie *Jurassic Park*) and their technical evolution probably achieved maturity in 1995, when the first cartoon made entirely with digitally generated images, *Toy Story*, was made by Pixar Animation Studios (Rodowick, 2007).

Pixar's story is interesting not simply because it was the first company to make a whole film using digital techniques but also for its industrial trajectory. Indeed, Pixar arose from the ashes of the digital special effects division of Lucas Film which, in 1986, sold the company to Steve Jobs, who had that year lost control of Apple and was in search of new computer projects. What Jobs was interested in was not the creative digital animation implications of Pixar (he had no intention of entering the film-making world) but the technological infrastructure required to create such effects. To improve its animation Pixar had, in fact, developed the best workstation then available for animation graphics, the Pixar Image Computer, which made its appearance on the computer market under Jobs's management: in other terms Jobs adopted the same philosophy borrowed from his ten-year experience in personal computers in the film sector concentrating on making and selling *hardware* components.

However, making profits from selling an expensive computer for visual effects proved more difficult than selling PCs and, in 1990, the idea of making computers exclusively for animated film was set aside. The selling workstation approach having failed, Pixar returned to its focus on making digital cartoon films such as *Toy Story* and other later films meeting with extraordinary box office success and transforming this small firm into the second most important animated film producer in the world. However, Pixar's manufacturing and economic trajectory generated no true "revolution" in the sector and its fate was, by contrast, common to that of other twentieth-century media firms: in

2006, this digital animation firm was bought up by the sector's main player, Walt Disney Company, a firm that had been founded in 1923 when cartoons were still being drawn by hand, photogram by photogram. Digitization of film techniques was the basis not solely of the sector's manufacturing and industrial frame-work but also its aesthetic and narrative outcomes. The very first attempt to make a realistic computer-generated character in a commercial was Michael Crichton's movie *Looker* (1981) starring a computer-based model named Cindy (see Figure 5.3). In 1989, the first seamless character, perfectly matched to its action environment, a so-called "digital character", was presented in the form of the alien creature starring in James Cameron's film *The Abyss* (O'Neil, 2016, pp. 24–25). Cameron is part of movie digital history because he was also the director responsible for *Avatar* in 2009, a 3D film made with digital tech-niques and the greatest box office success in the world, but one that remained an isolated case proving incapable of opening the way to a new wave of films made and distributed using a three-dimensional recording and viewing system. By the way, digital 3D cinema was another case of "double birth" (see Box 4.1 in Chapter 4), because all analog versions of this technique first appeared in the 1950s to counteract the seductive power of the then recently established TV.

The creative consequences triggered by digital techniques were not felt only in the great Hollywood studios and sci-fi and action films but also influenced the

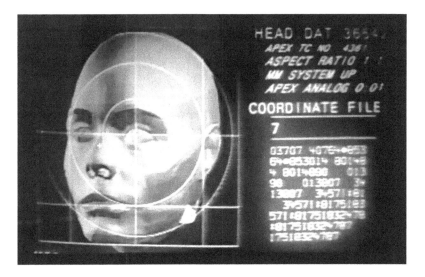

Figure 5.3 A still frame of Cindy, one of the first digital characters, appearing in Michael Crichton's movie *Looker* (1981)

creativity of niche movie sectors such as certain European avant-garde films (for example Thomas Vinterberg's 1998 Danish film *Festen*) and independent US films (such as Steven Soderbergh's 2002 film *Full Frontal*). But even in the matter of aesthetics and creativity, some exceptions notwithstanding, digital techniques were incorporated into film making without prompting radical change. As Lev Manovich (1999), once again, has observed, the growing import-ance of special effects in digital cinema constitutes a return to the traditions of the first decades of cinema history, in the age of George Méliès movies, when photograms were frequently made one-by-one and sometimes colored in by hand. In the case of film making, too, then, digital techniques have not generated a "disruptive revolution" overturning the analog past, but rather returned to and updated logics and methods characteristic even of the earliest phases in cinema history.

A digitization dimension that is less visible to audiences but equally important to sector organization relates to film screening and in particular the digital transformation of movie theatres themselves, a process that got under way in the early noughties. Cinema screen digitization has not been a uniform process in the various parts of the world, partly because it implied a series of expensive investments, which led initially in the USA and elsewhere to the closure of many cinema chains (Belton, 2002). Despite these initial difficulties, globally speaking in 2014 around 90% of cinemas were no longer using 35mm analog film and had changed to screening systems based on digital copies (Data: IHS Markit). Thus, without the majority of viewers even noticing, the film support that had characterized the movie industry since the very first Lumiére brothers screening in 1895, disappeared from mainstream cinemas, replaced by digital copies. On the distribution chain level, too, digital had a significant impact on earlier traditions. Remaining with the movie theaters themselves, from traditional distribution models involving films printed in limited editions and sent by courier (costly in both time and practical terms), over the last decade with the pro-gressive disappearance of film, a digital distribution system based on portable supports or via a central server sending out copies to the various cinemas has come to the fore.

In addition to professional film making, digital has had a profound impact on amateur film making in terms of the democratization of the potential for record-ing and sharing personal videos. In the first place, digitization has facilitated the creation of private, amateur and home-made contents and their dissemination via the digital media platforms. In this case too, amateur film making pre-dates the digital era. Although only in 1983 Sony released a simple camcorder expressly designed for domestic consumers (Willett, 2009), video recording of family events was popular in the wealthier classes from the mid twentieth century onwards and became even more common in the 1970s, thanks to the commercialization of practical and affordable Super8 film cameras and, later, video cameras recording analog video signals in Betamax and VHS formats. If on the one hand these devices simplified recording and made it more immediate for non-expert users, these systems still required complex and time-consuming equipment for editing the films and making copies for friends and families.

From the second half of the 1990s onwards, the dissemination of digital video cameras for non-professional use—a category that no longer encompassed only the conventional "amateurs"—was an important step because it meant images could then easily be modified with video cutting and editing programs managed on home PCs. One of the first video digital cutting and editing programs for PCs (which allowed for *non-linear* cutting and editing, i.e. the potential to recover and insert video sequences without forwarding or re-winding a support) was Adobe Premiere, available for Apple systems in 1991 and Windows systems from 1993. The outcomes of the democratization process generated by reductions in digital recording and editing costs are embodied by low-cost films meeting with considerable box office success such as the 1999 *The Blair Witch Project*, which was not only a low-budget movie (bringing in over $150 million from an initial investment of $30,000) but one in which the use of amateur video cameras also played a central part in the plot (Willett, 2009, p. 9).

Despite this success, a technical problem was the huge memory required to store video sequences, until, at the end of the 1990s, video cameras began to be sold using compressed digital video formats such as MiniDV and home PCs began to be connected up directly to video cameras. At the beginning of the new millennium the dissemination of these innovations—cutting and editing programs, affordable video cameras, larger and less costly memories—enabled home users to manage their video recordings relatively simply and transfer them to CD-ROMs and DVDs for friends. This took place as a result of improvements in PCs' technical performance capabilities and following on from the fact that in these years some of the main computer industries focused on digital video to increase hardware sales. In 1999, for example, Apple integrated both hardware and software for video cutting and editing into its new PC models and Microsoft took the same approach the following year, distributing the cutting and editing program Movie Maker. In the early noughties, then, creating and editing video sequences was increasingly accessible to anyone with a computer and a video camera.

Smartphones, too, took their place in the history of audio-visual video leading to a further leap forward in the potential for recording and sharing amateur videos. In fact, the most characteristic trait of the further democratization prompted by smartphones has been a mushrooming of videos created and, above all, shared by users on the web. There is nothing random about the fact that this transformation in video's social dissemination has coincided with the success of contents sharing web platforms and the best known of these in particular: YouTube. If we interpret the digitization of video making as a complex and progressive process—from almost exclusively professionally created to generalized user access—YouTube has undoubtedly represented a crucial passage in it, allowing users to distribute their videos free-of-charge and in real time to a virtually global public. It is for this reason, too, that in the space of just a few years YouTube has become one of the most popular platforms in the world (as seen in Chapter 3) and, specifically, has contributed to transforming videos into one of the most characteristic forms of communication in the digital media environment. The intermedia logic referred to previously in relation to other sectors thus re-emerges here. The presence and relevance of the audio-visual in the contemporary digital universe can be explained only by the intertwining of conventional film making, "smart" telecommunications and the distribution permitted by the Web and, naturally, by TV, as YouTube's "Broadcast yourself!" claim help to underline.

In addition to new possibilities in creating and sharing video contents, another consequence of digitization on consumption practices has been the *domestication* of film viewing, i.e. the increasingly central importance of the home as the film consumption sphere *par excellence*. This can be considered, once again, a digital strengthening of a trend already under way since the 1970s, with analog VHS and Betamax video recording technology. Over recent years this process has been further reinforced by a series of services developed on the internet, which have made traditional forms of distribution and access to film contents obsolete. This process is exemplified by the alternation of two consumer film rental models represented by two central US companies: Block-buster and Netflix. In 2010, the well-known film rental multinational Blockbuster, set up in 1985 in the wake of the success of VHS and peaking in the 1990s with DVDs, was obliged to file for bankruptcy as a result of the contraction of the film rental market. Netflix was set up in 1997, initially to rent out DVDs by post and, thus, still relying on physical DVD circulation, but then flourished following an alternative business strategy implemented from 2007: "renting" films digitally by online streaming thus eliminating physical copies and rental return costs. The next step in Netflix's evolution, starting in 2013, was the launching of its own independent production, movies and TV series, a step that other digital companies such as Amazon have also undertaken with the latter launching its streaming video service in 2006 and its own film production in 2010. The fact that a DVD rental company has become the largest producer of TV series distributed globally and the greatest investor in the TV series pro-duction sector (approximately 6 billion in 2016) in just about a decade speaks

Box 5.4 Documents

Ryan Singel, *Wired, "Video Killed the Video Store"* (2009)

In this excerpt from a 2007 article in the magazine *Wired*, journalist Ryan Singel announced the bankruptcy of Blockbuster, the video rental chain that had ridden the wave of film vision privatization in the 1990s. The article is emblematic in its focus on the discourses that accompanied the passage from DVD to the then embryonic Netflix streaming system.

The Blockbuster is dead, long live the blockbuster. At least that's what the technology omens are saying. *The Wall Street Journal* reported Tuesday that Blockbuster Video, whose shares are trading below $1, is seeking advice on how to file for bankruptcy. Blockbuster counters it's only trying to get help to restructure its debt. No matter. The days of tromping to the video store to find the night's entertainment are past. Now the question is only how long will it be until walking to the mailbox to get a DVD is considered antiquarian. Driving or walking to the video store to bring home less than a gig of data–data that may or may not even be in stock–just doesn't make much sense anymore. At least not when compared to Netflix's easy ordering system, its recommendation engine, lack of late fees, deeper inventory and clever use of the Postal Service to have movies delivered quickly. Blockbuster tried to keep up, with an innovative mail rental plan that let people trade in movies at the store as well, but the plan turned out to be too complicated and too late.

But even the notion of even leaving the room to get a movie, doesn't make sense if you have a fat internet connection and the willingness to explore some legal and less-legal ways to download movies to a computer. [. . .] Think YouTube, Hulu, Netflix's streaming movies, iTunes and Amazon overpriced rentals on demand, as well as dozens of others striving–yet again–to find a way to stream Hollywood video across the internet. No one has created a popular computer-in-the-living room solution yet–which makes DVDs still very practical, but that's just details. Some company–or several–will and then the notion of leaving the house to get a movie to watch will seem as quaint as writing a check at the grocery store.

Source: Singel, R. (2009). "Video killed the video store".
Wired, May 3

volumes of the transformational scope of the contents distribution sector and the central importance of Web platforms in this process.

As has frequently occurred in media history, the emergence of new apparently disruptive technologies has encouraged premature death knells to be sounded for earlier media. In this case the digitization and domestication of film watching led to forecasts that spectators were on the point of abandoning the movie theaters and that the latter would soon close down–incidentally, exactly the same narrative spread when TV sets invaded the living rooms in the 1950s and 1960s and then proved to be wrong. Looking at the effects of digital home movies on movie theaters at the global level once again shows a number of contradictions. While it is true that contraction in cinema box office sales has occurred in the United States and Europe over the last decade, in other parts of the world the opposite happened with box office sales in ongoing, breath-taking rise. For example, from 2005 to 2011 cinema revenues rose 135% in China, 82% in Russia and 71% in Brazil, while even in a European country with a strong movie culture such as France, ticket sales increased too in the same timeframe by 23% (UNESCO, 2013). Once again, then, the consequences of digitization have been neither uniform geographically nor definable as an overall trend.

Let us now return to file sharing and streaming services, which have done for film what we saw earlier happening in the music sector, i.e. acted as an inno-vative circulation method for audio-visual contents on the Web. In the first place these new services have been accused of having worsened and increased on a mass-scale a pre-existing problem: copyright infringements also known as *piracy*. This is another dimension which, after amateur production and home consumption practices, has had the greatest impact on video circulation. From the first half of the noughties onwards file sharing networks multiplied, allowing users to download both music and films free-of-charge. In the case of films, the availability of a *codec* (a video format encoding software) able to compress big movie files into lighter ones was of determinant importance. The most common of these codecs was DivX, which was created in 1998 by a French hacker who modified an official Microsoft video file format and later created a company to exploit it commercially. As frequently occurs in the hacking scene, a *fork project* was launched in 2001 to release an open source version, Xvid, enabling the heavy contents of a DVD to be extracted, compressed and masterized onto a CD and/or shared free-of-charge on the Web with relative ease.

If peer-to-peer software played a center stage role in the early years of the history of digital film piracy, online services allowing pirated video films to be viewed without them having previously been downloaded has dominated a second phase, the so-called *cyberlockers* platforms. This kind of Web site allows copies of films to be uploaded by users from servers frequently located in countries where copyright law is difficult to enforce. In the first years of their dissemination, the best-known video cyberlocker was Megavideo, a service set up in 2005 and shut down in 2012 for violations of copyright law following on from an international police operation orchestrated by the US FBI. At its apex, Megavideo had 5 million visitors daily and alone accounted for around 4% of the whole of North America's internet traffic. The authorities originally hoped that closing down the platform would have slowed down digital film piracy but in actual fact other similar systems have replaced it and achieved even higher user figures than their predecessor (Peukert, Claussen, & Kretschmer, 2017).

The economic effects of piracy on the film industry have been at the heart of a heated debate where ambivalent phenomena and interpretations have emerged. Certain researchers have underlined that piracy's effect on legal film product sales and turnover has not been purely negative but has also indirectly promoted films and contents: the more films circulate, even in pirated form, the better they are known and the more spectators, who might otherwise never have come into contact with them, get involved (Smith & Telang, 2012). In general, film copyright debates have contributed to laying bare the fact that current copyright laws designed for a technological universe pre-dating the Web are unlikely to be able to effectively reconcile the demands and needs of the various cultural content production and consumption players. On the one hand, in fact, a film market that demands adequate protection and remuneration for their investments and creative efforts are legitimate. On the other, users want to be able to exchange, re-work and enjoy contents circulating freely thus multiplying the resulting creative and artistic possibilities (Lessig, 2004). These contrasting demands are difficult to reconcile and underline the fact that systemic and intermedia interaction between cinema and the internet has cast such doubt on the technology–creativity protection relationship. This will probably require a radical rethinking of the very concept of copyright in the near future.

The video and film sectors have taken a full part in an intermedia tendency, which has also emerged for other sectors—just think of the complex interplay between cinema, internet and digital devices in mobile TV viewing underlined here. Furthermore, we have observed that the digitization of traditional film, above all, has brought out clear change-continuity tensions. While it has had a significant impact on cinema infrastructure (think of the digitization of movie theatres themselves), in this case too digitization has not generated a "disruptive revolution" while it seems to have had more decisive consequences for the everyday practices of users and consumers: from infrequently used goods, videos have become one of the most popular "currencies" on the Web and, more generally, in digital society as a whole.

5.5 Photography

Taking and sharing pictures online has become one of the most ubiquitous digital practices thanks to smartphones cameras and thus the chance to take photos at any time and upload them immediately on social networks and other platforms. The digitization of photography is, however, older and more complex and its roots go back to at least the 1970s with some of the first experiments taking place in an important US research center, which we have already identified as one of PC history's reference places, Xerox Park in Palo Alto California (see Chapter 2).

It was here that SuperPaint was designed in the early 1970s, the first digital system dedicated to graphic elaboration for film and TV products and used in particular to make film and TV program credits (Shoup, 2001). For the whole of the 1980s, digital image manipulation was almost exclusively the preserve of the professional TV and film realms (such as in the case already discussed of Lucas Film) and it was only in the early 1990s that programs designed to modify digital images on home PCs began to be available. The best known of these was Photoshop–still today a benchmark for amateur and professional photography–whose first version was distributed in 1990. Over the years manipulating images has become such common practice as to prompt a new colloquial use verb–"to photoshop"–for the increasingly frequent creative use of images and photographs.

Culturally speaking, the image digitization process is part of a longer story rooted in the evolution of the social perception in photography. Since the invention of photography in the first half of the nineteenth century such techniques have existed in a constant tension between reality and fiction, factual representation of concrete situations and the potential for creating unreal images by falsifying them with sophisticated analog, often hand-made techniques. Digitization has made the artificial manipulation of pictures and images even more commonplace for non-professionals too thus throwing into crisis the very reputation of photography as a realistic and credible medium. In the early 1990s, scholars such as William Mitchell (1992) and Martin Lister (1995) started to perceive that the shift from analog to digital photographic techniques would soon lead to a *post-photographic* era, a situation where the very meaning and social role of photographers would undergo radical change. However, the most thoroughgoing implications for radical change in photography's social status was yet to emerge: the transformations later ushered in by social media and smartphones led to photographic practices no longer based on the specific technology of the photo camera, but rather dependent on–in science and technology studies terms–a *socio-technical network*, resulting from the alignment process between new digital technologies, novel aesthetic codes and emerging user-generated practices (Lister, 2013, p. 4).

But what might seem another "disruptive revolution" produced by digital technologies was actually part of a longer-term process, which saw a gradual, multi-decade transformation in image perception. Indeed, already in the early 1990s, magazines and newspapers were beginning to make widespread use of digital retouches thus launching a redefinition process of the reality–image relationship in the direction of a new concept of photography: American scholar Fred Ritchin (2009) defined it as a paradigm shift adopting the term *hyper-photography*, i.e. a model of photographic creativity increasingly interdependent on other digital media logics and characterized by a disconnection from any realistic methods of representation. In the noughties, photo manipulation became one of the most characteristic traits of modern visual culture and it was increasingly taken for granted that the images circulating in the media and on the internet had been computer modified. All this soon led to controversy and consequent attempts at regulation. For example, in the wake of certain scandals linked to the manipulation of war reportage photos, the main photo agencies and photo-journalism awards, such as the prestigious World Press Photo Award, introduced regulations and codes that banned or at least limited the use of Photoshop in detail (dos Santos Silva, 2013).

We are thus living in an apparently contradictory and ambivalent visual era, in which in the front of increasing possibilities of image manipulation we have learned to be more sensitive to pictures' counterfeiting, but at the same time these manipulated images play a central and veridical communicative role in today's global and interconnected society. Even if everybody knows that digital pictures can be easily manipulated, photographic and filmic images are often cited as evidence of events in mainstream media and social media posts–repurposing in digital photography pre-existing tensions between technologies, images and realism typical of analog photography since its invention in the nineteenth century. These tensions can be recognized manifestly when, for example, the editing and processing of images deal with wars and conflicts (Alper, 2014): heavily edited pictures about military interventions question the role that circulation of digital images across newspapers, TV and social networks has for the shaping of public opinion and the development of democratic processes.

As mentioned in the previous paragraph, while digitization modified social perceptions of photographic realism it is important to remember that the habit of "correcting" photographs was born together with photographic techniques in the mid-nineteenth century and its roots, once again, lay deep in analog film technologies, dark rooms and photographic developers (Fineman, 2012). As early as the 1970s, the amateur photography sub-culture, historically an important photography sector, popularized the use of amateur darkrooms and contributed to disseminating a particular sensitivity to manipulation techniques, which with Photoshop became even more popular and commonplace.

Evidence of the intersection between analog and digital in photography is also there in the ability to see images immediately after taking a photo. Polaroid instant cameras made this possible in 1948 and these became very popular in the 1960s and 1970s (Buse, 2015). In this case too, then, it is clear that certain contemporary digital photography practices are grounded in a series of techniques, groups of users and availability already established in the analog era.

The development of full digital cameras was a decades-long process. The first digital camera prototype dates to 1975, when a Kodak engineer made a—never sold but functioning—model capable of recording black and white images with a 100x100 pixel resolution. A further ten years passed before the first digital camera appeared in the mid 1980s when another of the leading analog photography firms of the day, Japanese Canon, released the RC-701, a camera that saved images onto floppy disks. These were used above all in photo-journalism, a context in which the ability to send photographic files in short time frames, for example to cover political and sports events, was and still is crucially important. The first digital cameras designed for a non-professional public were released in the early 1990s and soon adopted the Jpeg standard for image recording developed in 1992 by the International Organization for Standardization (ISO). Initially these were single mega pixel resolution cameras, a quality that was a world away from that provided by analog photographic film, but in any case, sufficient to produce images destined to be embedded into the first World Wide Web sites.

The first digital reflex camera, which aspired to attract the interest of amateur photographers and replace traditional analog cameras was sold only in 1999 by a further historic analog photography firm, Nikon, who succeeded in taking image resolution to around 3 megapixels. Quality was still a long way from that of analog photography as further confirmation of the fact that new media are not always a purely technical improvement on old ones (Gitelman & Pingree, 2003). For several years analog photography thus remained qualitatively superior to its digital counterpart but the latter had other advantages over the former: to mention just three, digital photos could be immediately transferred to computers and could thus be modified with graphic software and, finally, shared on the Web or through smartphones.

Over the years, the cost of digital cameras progressively went down and resolutions were such as to permit printing on good quality paper and digital photography thus made its way, in the first half of the noughties, onto the PCs of non-expert computer and photo retouching software users. US data show that digital camera sales overtook that of their analog counterparts in 2003, when approximately 13 million digital cameras as against 11.2 million analog cameras were bought (PMA, 2005). This transition to digital photography generated considerable changes in the photographic industry's equilibria. However, in contrast to the music world, where previously dominant firms lost control over certain important business sectors, in photography the main firms of the sector were front rank exponents of the transition to digital. Some of these even managed to consolidate their dominant positions further contrasting newcomers from the computer and IT sectors. This is certainly the case of two of the most important Japanese camera manufacturers, Canon and Nikon, who reinforced their dominance above all in upper market segments such as reflex cameras (otherwise called DSLR), a sector in which they controlled around 95% of the global market in 2015 (Source: NPD Group).

However, not all of the companies who had dominated analog photography managed successfully to make the move to digital. A case in point is the oldest and most important of the US photography sector companies, Kodak, founded in 1888 by the inventor of roll film, George Eastman. In the twentieth century, Kodak established itself as the main manufacturer of photographic rolls in the US (where it controlled about 90% of the market in the 1970s) and its name was for many years synonymous with photography itself, at least in the West (while in Asia, Japanese Fuji had similar economic dominance and symbolic prestige). While, as we have seen, Kodak had been the first to create a digital camera in the 1970s, in the two decades that followed many of the firm's strategic decisions in the transition to digital turned out to have been misguided (Lucas & Goh, 2009). One reason for the difficulties experienced by Kodak lay in the radical change that took place in the sector's business models: digital photography made photo printing unnecessary (or at least secondary), totally transforming a sector chain previously bound to paper printing processes, which Kodak dominated right from the start. In the mid noughties, following on from the mass abandonment of traditional film rolls in favor of digital cameras, the Kodak name virtually disappeared from consumer photography. In 2012, after a grand total of 124 years of business, Kodak was obliged to file for bankruptcy, left the consumer photography sector and sold its patents to IT firms such as Apple, Google and Microsoft. These latter companies evidently saw photography as a growing sector and one that overlapped with mobile telecommunications, the internet and the software market, underlining once again that photography, too, experienced an intermedia trajectory.

In fact, in around the mid noughties, some of the equilibria that had emerged in this first transition phase changed in response to the popularization of smartphones with top quality photographic lenses capable of dialoguing directly with the new forms of communication offered by the Net. These smartphones were initially given a specific and "photographic" name–cameraphones–but just a few years later good quality photography was a feature of even the cheaper mobile phones. To understand the scope of this change from traditional photographic devices to smartphones with lenses consider that in 2005 Nokia, then telephone sector leader but with no photographic sector history, sold more photo lenses (in its telephones) than Canon sold digital cameras, thus becoming the top world producer of photographic lenses. In the space of just a few years, with the sale of new smartphone models including, primarily, iPhones, mobile media became the main photographic devices for ordinary users sharing photos on social networks, blogs and photosharing platforms. Thanks in part to the first iPhone models, for the first time a single device enabled users to control the entire photographic process from photographs to image creation, elaboration, distribution and final circulation of the results (Gómez Cruz & Meyer, 2012). A fully intermedia transformation in digital photography has thus taken shape by "assembling" the characteristic traits of a range of technologies, devices and creative processes into a new, increasingly socially widespread practice (Hand, 2012).

Social network sites have also played a decisive role in fashioning this new photography practice infrastructure for ordinary people. The transformations in photography generated by the shift to the digital world, which we have witnessed in recent years, are based on three major pre-conditions: an explosion in portable devices equipped with lenses (smartphones and digital cameras); the dissemination of broadband internet connections, above all in their mobile versions by means of smartphones; and, the increasingly central role played by the habit of sharing everyday events on social media. The availability of smartphones able to take pictures and upload them on the internet-made platforms, where a growing quantity of user-generated images have started to be stored, was necessary. These sharing platforms have favored a sort of rebirth in the social role of the photographic medium, moving it in the direction of a widespread tool used to maintain everyday relationships and thus creating new forms of collective visual memory organized on Web photo sharing services and social networks (van Dijk, 2008). From the mid noughties onwards, Web photographic applications have developed rapidly, parallel to the success of blogs and platforms sharing user generated contents. One of the main platforms to offer users the opportunity to conserve and share their digital photos was Flickr: created in 2004 and bought by *Yahoo!* in 2005, in 2015 Flickr announced that it had a grand total of 10 billion photos on its database organized through about 53 million tags (Hai-Jew, 2017).

Another platform of particular significance for the change in photography's social role is Facebook, launched in 2004. Born from a specifically photographic

Box 5.5 In-depth Theory

The Socio-technical Network of the iPhone

The use of iPhones in photography lends itself to a socio-technical network concept explanation, as photography scholars Gómez Cruz and Meyer (2012) have pointed out. In science and technology studies, the notion of *socio-technical network* was developed to describe the way in which certain human activities are organized not around a single technology, but rather on the basis of a network of relationships made up of both artefacts and people (Latour, 1987). It can thus be observed that the success of Apple iPhone 4 was not just the result of a single technology but rather the outcome of a specific socio-technical network made up of contemporary digital photography practices.

The importance of the 2010 iPhone 4 model to photography's evolution was due not so much to the fact that its photographic quality was higher than that of other devices (there were higher quality ones available at the time). On the contrary, iPhone 4 represented a key element in an emerging digital photography socio-technical network, specifically supporting new photography circulation methods and making uploading images on Web platforms easy and immediate directly from devices. Creating an inter-media waterfall effect, these new practices impacted on the rise and use of 3G networks and, more generally, in a reconfiguration of mobile telephone operator products. It was thanks to this emerging socio-technical network that photographic practices previously associated above all with amateur photographers became attractive to people who were less involved in photography's technical aspects, thus contributing to "enrolling" new types of users. iPhone's lower photographic quality, compared to "real" digital cameras, also prompted the development of new creative practices exploiting the smartphone's technological limitations such as the vintage effects available with the Instagram app, created in late 2010 precisely in the wake of iPhone 4's photographic success, exclusively to be used on the iOS operating system. Hence, iPhones and the iOS operational system represented a new platform that attracted a great many developers who created new specific software for photography thus enabling users to modify photos directly on their phones. As Gómez Cruz and Meyer (2012, p. 14) have summarized,

> for the first time in photographic history, a single device has made it possible to control the whole process, not only of image production and distribution of those images (like any mobile phone) but also the

possibility of processing those images, in the same device, to obtain different results.

It is thus clear that transformations generated by iPhones were not so much a matter of photo-taking or photo quality differences, something related to a single device, but rather the ability of these gadgets to constitute a node in the construction of a new socio-technical network. iPhone has built an entirely new configuration of relationships in photography practices that holds together a new technological device, novel amateur photographer categories, new software and their developers, online sharing platforms and the infrastructure for the transmission of images through these increasingly common smartphones.

Further Reading

Gómez Cruz, E., & Lehmuskallio, A. (Eds.). (2016). *Digital Photography and Everyday Life: Empirical Studies on Material Visual Practices.* London: Routledge.
Gómez Cruz, E., & Meyer, E.T. (2012). Creation and control in the photographic process: iPhones and the emerging fifth moment of photography. *Photographies, 5*(2), 203-221.

metaphor—it was a digital version of the paper school year book, commonly known as a *face book*, which collects the photographs of American university students (Kirkpatrick, 2011)—over the years Facebook has become the largest photo archive on the planet. While official numbers on the volume of photos held by Facebook do not exist, it is believed that it contained around 250 billion in 2013, while daily photo uploads on this California company's platform were estimated at 350 million (Source: internet.org).

In recent years, the importance of photos to Facebook and other social networks has increased further and, in recognition of the central importance of photographs for its business model, Facebook further reinforced the role of images in 2012 by buying up Instagram, created just two years before. Instagram is a good example of the change-continuity tension in digital photography's evolution, as its initial success was due to digital emulation of the effects of analog photo lenses and the square format typical of Polaroid. The success of a service like Instagram once again highlights the cultural bond between analog and digital: on the one hand the nostalgia for the old analog technologies phenomenon seems to permeate the digital world as a whole and photography in particular (see Niemeyer, 2014; Menke & Schwarzenegger, 2016); on the other, cultural appropriation of the old analog systems has taken on new meanings in the digital era. An example is the so-called *selfies*, a neologism entered in the Oxford English Dictionary in 2013 defining "a photograph that one has taken of oneself, typically one taken with a smartphone or webcam and uploaded to a social media website". If, apparently, the selfie looks like a new photographic category closely bound up with the new digital technologies, on closer examination it is part of a longer process of self-portraits' redefinition in modern society. This process began at least in seventeenth-century painting, for example with the famous Diego Velázquez's *Las Meninas* in 1656 (Mirzoeff, 2016, p. 31), and intersects with many other old photographic uses and practices such as the nineteenth-century visiting cards (Saltz, 2014).

The tendency of digital technologies to emulate or return to analog aesthetics further highlights not only the profound interweaving of digital and analog technologies in photography but also the logic of change and the logic of continuity in the photographic medium, which can be fully understood only from a historical and intermedia perspective sensitive to the interaction between photography, its historical practices and other forms of digital communication.

5.6 Television

In the latter half of the twentieth century, television was the medium that transformed the daily experiences of audiences and citizens more than any other contributing to modifying—as sociologist Joshua Meyrowitz (1985) has shown—not simply social relationships but also perceptions of the world as a whole. However, in the wake of the digitization process, debates on the presumed *end of* TV have become increasingly frequent in recent years: for example, TV is less and less seen as a medium capable of structuring collective social life time frames or a *death of channels* scenario—in which the organization of contents by TV programmers loses significance as "consumers will be their own editors, going from passive to active and choosing freely between programs, films and other services" (Ytreberg, 2002, p. 284)—has often emerged.

If, on the one hand, the fragmentation of TV's time frames, rhythms and audiences, encouraged by the mushrooming of systems, channels and devices, has undermined the historic "social clock" role played by TV, on the other, contemporary TV consumption appears not to have declined in the digitization era. From 2004 to 2014, the hours spent watching TV by a hypothetical world citizen increased by an average of 10 minutes passing from 3 hours and 3 minutes to 3 hours and 13 minutes (Source: Eurodata TV Worldwide 2015). And in the US, a country with one of the world's highest viewing figures average, family viewing figures increased even more passing from 7 hours and 20 minutes to 8 hours and 50 minutes per day (OECD, 2013, p. 184) from 1997 to 2011. In sum, in a reconfigured digital scenario, TV is still a centrally important medium in social terms.

Nevertheless, digitization has had a multi-faceted impact on TV, generating significant consequences in at least five ways: a) the evolution, from the 1990s onwards, of TV ownership frameworks towards so-called *media convergence* characterized by integration between TV and other companies in different communication sectors; b) the digitization of traditional analog broadcasting signals set in motion in many parts of the world from the early 2000s onwards; c) the transformation of TV sets as viewing devices, accompanied by a multiplication of digital accessories and tools; d) changes in social viewing habits by audiences both in spatial terms—with mobile viewing—and in time frame terms with access to on demand viewing; e) the translation of cultural forms typical of TV into internet-based formats, in particular by means of the dissemination of TV production and consumption linked to video sharing platforms such as YouTube.

These various dimensions are not distinct but have together built an inter-media digital TV environment whose complexity can be understood by analyzing specific experiences, as Joshua Braun (2016) has done by focusing on the evolution of the North American satellite TV network MSNBC. By looking at this specific trajectory, Braun highlighted the way in which changes in the distribution of digital TV contents have been driven by a complex network of technologies, economic forces, social norms and institutional actors. But, for the sake of simplicity, let us attempt to impose some order on this, analyzing the five dimensions referred to above one-by-one.

A first impact of digitization on TV was grafted onto a more generalized process of media convergence, which began in the 1980s in what was still an analog dominated scenario. This media convergence macro-phenomenon has a long history (Balbi, 2017a) and has transformed three substantially distinct media sectors for most of the twentieth century: telecommunications, informatics and the producers of creative contents. The assumption underlying the notion of media convergence is that these three sectors would overlap and integrate primarily as a result of their progressive digitization. This was the notion that guided governmental policies and media corporations' business strategies in the 1990s and noughties generating direct consequences for the world of TV. In particular, telecommunications and broadcasting were identified in neo-liberal policies as two sectors to be liberalized, freeing them of public control or at least opening them up to free market competition. In Europe, the end of the public radio-TV monopolies took place in the 1970s and 1980s, while telecommunications were privatized more gradually first in the UK and then, from the late 1990s onwards, in most other European countries (Hesmondhalgh, 2007).

One of the main effects of the free market policies of the 1980s and 1990s was the end of the historic separation between broadcasting and telecommunications, a distinction that had been a political imposition designed to prevent firms potentially capable of working in both sectors from acquiring dominant positions. The decisive shift in the US occurred in 1982, when the American Justice Department authorized telecommunication company AT&T to enter the broadcasting sector, which had previously been closed off to it, obliging AT&T at the same time to give up its dominant position in the telephone market (Baldwin, Stevens McVoy, & Steinfield, 1996, p. 6).

This was the beginning, first in the US and then in Europe and other parts of the world, of an overall reconfiguration of media ownership and business, generating various types of integration between originally TV-based firms and those that had traditionally worked in other media sectors (Doyle, 2013). In sum, if we examine the trajectory of these companies and the structure of their markets, it is evident that TV digitization has partly coincided with a tendency towards convergence between the various media sectors whose most significant consequence has been the fall of barriers which had existed for decades.

A second dimension in the TV digitization process has related to the transformation of the technologies underlying TV broadcasting, which originated in the 1940s and 1950s in analog form mainly via airwaves or cable. The digitization process in TV signals developed from the 1990s onwards in different ways and time frames in various parts of the world, but it has in any case been the most incisive change in broadcasting technology since the arrival of color at least. The standards currently used globally for digital TV were set out in the 1990s once again by ISO's Mpeg working group. The digital audio-visual signal standard used by TV, called Mpeg 2, was approved in 1994 and adopted as the benchmark for the digital TV system called DVB, which became the standard adopted by all European states in the years that followed. The countries of North America, together with others such as South Korea, on the other hand, adopted a different version of this standard, called ATSC. Variants of a third system called ISDB-T were used in Japan and the countries of South America while yet another version called DTMB was adopted by the Peoples' Republic of China. The geography of the digitization process in TV broadcasting technologies was, then, anything but homogeneous with even greater variations than had occurred for TV's analog era in which there were three main standards worldwide: PAL, NTSC and SECAM. From this point of view, then, the digitization of TV signals would seem to have followed a recurrent framework in globalization processes: a global scope change that has taken different forms in the various regions of the world according to their diverse political, cultural and geographic characteristics.

Alongside the proliferation of digital standards, a similar multiplication took place in the ways in which these TV signals were broadcast to audiences: in North America, Asia and the Pacific digital TV was broadcast mainly via cable; in Western Europe airways systems via terrestrial antennas were the most commonly used; in Eastern Europe satellite transmission was the most frequent and the same was true of Latin America and the Middle East where cable transmission was also important. This proliferation of both standards and TV signal distribution methods highlights the fact that—in contrast to what is generally believed—the transition to digital did not favor progressive technological standardization but actually heightened existing worldwide fragmentation and dis-homogeneity. These differences underline once again the relevance of the political economy of communication dimension and, specifically, the determinant role played by local policies and cultural peculiarities in the transition to digital. In the case of TV, given the importance played by this medium in national public opinion formation processes, the transition was often a considerably sensitive issue for political equilibria themselves.

In Europe, for example, TV digitization was encompassed within more complex European common political and cultural space building processes. From the early 1990s onwards, in fact, European Union institutions pushed its member

---

Box 5.6 Documents

European Commission, *The Advantages of Digital TV for the European Consumer* (2005)

> In this communication, the Commission examines the transition from analog to digital broadcasting. The phase in which the two broadcasting systems co-exist, based to a large extent on terrestrial platforms, must give way to a phase in which the conversion to digital is accelerated. One of the advantages of digital TV is that it offers a growing range of fully interactive applications allowing for interaction between viewer and broadcaster.
>
> The Commission proposes that the beginning of 2012 be agreed for switch-off in all Member States. The national switchover plans should therefore all be completed by 2012. It expects that by the end of 2010 the switchover process should be well advanced in the EU as a whole.
> [. . .]

The Advantages of the Switchover Process

Aside from providing better picture and sound quality, the switchover to digital broadcasting offers clear advantages for both consumers and operators.

These advantages stem from the fact that it is possible to process and compress digital data in a more efficient manner than was the case for analog signals.

Consumer benefits from digital TV compared with analog TV are as follows:

- a wider choice of programmes from a greater number of channels and radio stations;
- improved flexibility of use thanks to better portable and mobile reception;
- services that are more interactive thanks to the improvement in IT services;
- the potential to contribute to serving the specific needs of the elderly or disabled by providing them with services such as better subtitling, audio commentaries or signing;
- lower sale prices for digital receivers and integrated TV receivers; Price is increasingly becoming less of a barrier to acquiring such equipment.

> Source: Communication from the Commission to the Council, the European Parliament, the European Economic and Social committee and the Committee of the Regions on accelerating the transition from analog to digital broadcasting (2005)

states in the direction of a progressive adoption of common standards for terrestrial digital, DVB-T, but it was only in the year 2000, during the Lisbon Conference on digital terrestrial TV, that this strategy was made explicit. The EU's principal political and economic objective was to push the whole continent in the direction of the so-called *IT society* guaranteeing universal access to digital services to all citizens with the goal of minimizing the risk of a digital divide developing. The fundamental idea was that digital services were to be made accessible on a more familiar medium than computers and one that was already used in millions of European homes—TV. In this political vision, terrestrial digital TV would, on the one hand, have allowed new digital services to be brought into the home and, on the other, enabled a rationalization of airspace spectrum use, reducing TV frequencies in favor of internet and mobile telecommunication service frequencies. In sum, the political economy directives played a decisive role in shaping the transition from analog to digital TV systems in Europe.

Also in virtue of political drives in the direction of common TV digitization, many European countries began experimenting or transmitting in digital form as early as the beginning of the noughties but take up time frames varied from country to country. Some smaller states, many of which were first in line to take up Europe-wide integration, such as Finland, Holland and Sweden, fully implemented the new standards in 2006–2007, while other countries that had signed up to European policies more recently, such as Poland, Bulgaria or Hungary, delayed until after 2012, the date named by the European Union (Commission Recommendation 2009/848/EC) for the completion of the so-called switch-over and the definitive switching off of old analog signals (see Box 5.6).

On a global level, too, adaptation to digital signals highlighted a series of differences and peculiarities due to diverse degrees of economic development in the various countries and the specific features of their media systems. In India, for example, the old analog system (common in rural or non-urban areas) continues to co-exist with the new digital broadcasting system prevalent in the richer and larger cities. In the USA, digital completely replaced analog in 2008, but the opportunity to use a variant of the old analog signals remained open for about 2,500 exclusively local TV channels. Large countries such as China and Brazil have been slow to digitize completely and implemented the switch-over from analog broadcasting dividing up the transition into phases for the various parts of their vast territories. Thus, not only is digitization of TV broadcasting still a long way from completion but it also required a long transition and followed different trajectories and rhythms in accordance with the specific features of each individual country, once again proving wrong those who saw digitization as an irresistible force automatically favoring forms of global homologation and standardization.

With digitization, TV widened audience opportunities. One of the clearest signs of this transformation is the multiplication of TV channels: according to the European Audiovisual Observatory, in the European Union total channel numbers have increased considerably over the years passing from 3,615 channels in 2009 to 5,370 in 2015 (a total that does not include local broadcasters). Certainly, from an analog-continuum perspective it should also be underlined that a considerable share of the programs broadcasted on these "new" channels is simply "old" TV shows kept in archives and reused to fill the schedule. Analog TV contents have thus found new forms of distribution thanks to digital.

The third important TV digitization dimension relates to the technical evolution of traditional TV sets as main reception devices. Right from its invention

TV has undergone multiple technological turning points: invention in the 1920s, the mid 1930s triumph of the electronic over the mechanical paradigm, rapid popularization in the West in the 1950s and 1960s, the arrival of color, satellite and cables between the 1960s and 1970s up to the introduction of remote controls in the 1970s and 1980s (Winston, 1998). Over recent years attempts to widen the classical functions of TV (in order to get it dialoguing with the Web) have contributed to defining a new generation of devices often with marketing labels such as Smart or Hybrid TVs. These new devices integrate internet connections and Web digital film rental, enable audiences to watch more than one channel at the same time, watch TV on the move or access various forms of on-demand contents. While these opportunities may appear "revolutionary", they are actually on a continuum with the latest developments in analog TV. Let's have a look at the last two examples from the list above.

First, watching TV on the move was actually not an invention of digitization but goes back at least to the portable analog TV era of the 1960s, such as the Italian Brionvega Algol now exhibited at MoMA in New York as an example of artistic design, or the 4.7 inch portable TV Universum, produced since 1968

Figure 5.4 A promotional picture from 1968 of the Universum FK 100R, one of the early portable TVs, with a weight of 3.8 kgs, produced by the German firm Quelle

Source: Courtesy of Stiftung Deutsches Technikmuseum Berlin, Photo: Historisches Archiv

by the German firm Quelle (see Figure 5.4). These 1960s portable TVs evolved into the liquid crystal analog TVs launched in the early 1980s (such as Sony's Watchman introduced in 1982; on portable TV see also Box 4.6 in Chapter 4 on mobile privatization): TV portablility is indeed a half-century old idea.

Second, in the analog era as well, traditional TVs had already made attempts to expand their base functions to offer additional content types and user models. One case in point is undoubtedly Teletext (Moe & Van den Bulck, 2016), a written TV service originating in the UK in the 1970s, which then spread to the whole of Europe and other parts of the world in the decade preceding the popularization of the Web but is still active in many countries today. With pages that can be commanded via remote control, Teletext's wide range of text services became ubiquitous: real time news, useful info for citizens and TV program subtitling. The huge range of services it offered made Teletext, according to some scholars, a sort of *ante litteram* low-tech internet: on the one hand, it fulfilled (and still fulfils) some of the information and entertainment functions that were later popularized on the Web; on the other it represented (and still represents) a user-friendly system with which to access editorial contents by means of the twentieth century's most widespread and popular medium, TV.

If we have identified many elements of continuity between analog and digital TV thus far, it is also important to underline the most important change and intermedia elements. Thanks to the dissemination of personal digital devices such as smartphones and tablets "watching TV" is partially and progressively breaking away from "watching a TV set".

The first moves in this direction date to the first half of the noughties, as we saw in Chapter 4, with the implementation of new digital telephone standards, which turned out to be dead ends. Thanks to the UMTS (Universal Mobile Telecommunications System) infrastructure, which represented a development of GSM, mobile phones became capable of receiving DVB-H mobile TV signals. One of the first countries to implement it was Finland, where Nokia began to offer this type of additional service from 2005 onwards. Many of the firms that decided to experiment with the 3G networks saw mobile TV (and secondarily, also video-calls) as one of the killer applications of the new standard (see Chapter 4). Very soon, however, initial interest in watching TV on telephone screens weakened, only to re-emerge with the recent dissemination of smartphones and tablets and the more direct integration of TV with the internet world.

This leads us to the fourth dimension to be examined in relation to TV digitization: changes in TV content consumption models. The partial obsolescence of the TV set and the dissemination of new digital devices capable of offering TV contents in *mobility* and with more marked *individualism* is in fact at the heart of new forms of consumption, both spatial and temporal. As we have seen, from a spatial point of view, TV consumption is now easier outside the home and far away from fixed TVs themselves. Temporally speaking, on the other hand, the new technical possibilities allowing for on-demand TV contents and time-shifted TV viewing have begun to modify the central importance of TV scheduling (Strangelove, 2015). However, at a closer look, these new possibilities have reconfigured, rather than revolutionized, the central importance of channel programming and TV schedules. In fact, while opportunities for audiences to personalize and adapt contents to their own time frames are now manifold, TV scheduling has remained a powerful tool in the hands of TV broadcasters with which to shape TV contents, advertising and visibility and continues to function as a strategy used to "tame" the most innovative forms of TV and target them towards a more generalist, mass audience. In addition, looking at recent strategies of TV series release in streaming services like Netflix, some sort of *scheduling logic* survives, for example by releasing weekly one-by-one episodes, which creates expectations by resembling "traditional" TV scheduling.

Looking at audience practices, TV viewing emerges as a powerfully generationally-based activity. Recent research has shown that in the US a sharp generational gap is opening up as far as traditional TV viewing styles are concerned. According to Nielsen's data, the hours per week young people spent watching TV at home dropped from around 27 in 2011 to 16 in 2016 (source: Nielsen). More generally, what this data tells us is that changes in TV contents' consumption with digital media over the coming years will certainly be influenced by the different relationship which younger generations will establish not solely with TV itself but also with the whole system of digital media contents, thus highlighting the intermedia character of the digitization process once again.

Indeed, a fifth and final dimension of TV digitization relates to forms of integration between TV and internet contents. The best known and most characteristic example of this integration is undoubtedly once again YouTube, a platform already examined in the music industry and video production and has effectively shown itself to be one of the nerve centers of the digitization process in many cultural sectors. As William Uricchio (2009) has argued, YouTube has threatened traditional TV as it is not based, as traditional TV was, on the expressive power of the live transmission, continual content flow or the ability to act as social aggregator around a shared content with a dispersed and highly differentiated public. This watershed notwithstanding, however, YouTube represents the most characteristic form of TV–internet conversion, culturally speaking: think of the thousands of segments drawn from traditional broadcasting uploaded every day onto this platform, which are then saved and re-framed in new digital media contexts. There is nothing random, moreover, about the fact that YouTube has chosen to use TV terminology to define itself: think of the term "channels" used for specific themed spaces in the portal or its battle-cry "Broadcast yourself!", which echoes broadcasting language in personalized form.

In addition to YouTube, other typically TV-based content consumption models have been re-adapted to the internet context often starting with the potential for using on-demand contents on the move too with tablets or smart-phones. In our section on cinema and video we referred to the Netflix platform, which began producing and disseminating new TV contents on the Web in 2013 and now accounts for more than a third of US evening internet traffic, according to their own data, which also says that in 2017 the platform had about 115 million subscribers globally, half of whom are in 130 countries other than the US.

It is precisely TV series that offer an insight into some of the developments generated by interaction between traditional TV and Web communication and collaboration practices otherwise defined as *participatory cultures* (Jenkins, 1992). The success of TV series frequently depends not only on the moment they are viewed on TV but also, and primarily, on the way in which TV contents are appropriated, collected and reworked by fans with Web tools. One of the first and best-known examples of this was the TV series *Lost* whose cryptic events fans shared their own interpretations of from 2005 onwards on a highly successful Web site called Lostpedia, which was built using the participation structure and form characteristic of the Wiki site (Mittell, 2009). As these participatory cultures come to the fore on the Web, the relationship between TV programming and audiences has changed, beginning with the active participation of especially highly motivated viewers. This tendency has been described by Jenkins and Ford (2013), highlighting the mixed-type dissemination model, in which top-down provision is integrated with bottom-up sharing practices and in which TV content success thus depends on how and to what extent these are disseminated by fans on the Web. A further dimension introduced by participatory cultures regards the fact that broadcasters have access to increasingly varied and accurate (big) data on the public's tastes, choices and consumption trends (Napoli, 2010). In the digital realm, broadcasters know their audience much better than any other time in history and this is a significant change from the analog past.

Thus, returning to one of the questions posed at the outset of this chapter on the meaning to be attributed to the watching of a TV series on Netflix, there is no doubt that we are faced with a media experience markedly different from the TV use models of just a few decades ago. This new experience highlights all the pressure towards intermediality in which the various media sectors are implicated: internet infrastructure, TV, computers, social networks, mobile device apps and so on. At the same time, however, the TV sector has also remained in many aspects anchored to a series of infrastructures, cultural forms and national boundaries established in the analog era, underlining the profound continuity with the past. Three examples of this are the increase in hours spent watching TV, the continuing importance of scheduling and the dependence on wide-reaching national and regional policies in TV market management. Above all, it is surprising that, when we speak of "watching TV", we still know approximately what we mean (and we often refer to practices that are surprisingly similar to those of some decades ago) but, at the same time, this whole of taken-for-granted assumptions has been subject to many different changes. How new audiences will metabolize these changes is not yet clear.

5.7 Radio

Radio's history is a long one. The first experiments with sound transmission on the airwaves date as far back as the first decade of the twentieth century. In its *golden age* from the 1920s to the 1940s, it became a central tool in the building of political masses in both democratic and totalitarian countries. In the 1950s and 1960s, radio had to measure up to TV's success and thus modified some of its distinctive features relieving also a new moment of glory from the 1970s and 1980s onwards. Radio as a medium has thus changed radically more than once in the course of its history, creating new formats for a more segmented audience, and digitization can be seen as only one further stage. It is perhaps precisely as a result of this metamorphic nature that radio has frequently anticipated uses and characteristics that have then become common in other media and the same has been true of digital. An example is the adoption of transistors in the late 1950s, when radio became the first truly mobile means of communication encouraging the birth of *mobile* and *street cultures*, decades before the mass mobility facilitated by mobile phones and more generally by digital media.

The radio digitization process can be illustrated by focusing on two different aspects: the digitization of the traditional radio system and, more from an intermedia perspective, radio's integration into internet communication models.

The historical roots and "spirit" of digital radio can be retraced to the creation of the European Broadcasting Union (EBU) in 1950, supporting the political vision according to which Europe should be considered a common broadcasting sphere, prevalently based on the principle of public service (O'Neill, Ala-Fossi, Jauert, Lax, Nyre, & Shaw, 2010; Jauert, 2017). Radio's technical digitization process began in the mid 1980s, parallel to TV's but it then distinguished itself from this latter in its diverse growth rhythms and the effective dissemination of the new system. Digital radio transmission was born in the 1980s as an explicitly European project driven by a consortium of German language broadcasters who studied and experimented with it. Then, in 1987, the European Community funded the Eureka-147 research project with the goal of creating a digital audio broadcasting system. The results obtained by this project were then taken up once again by ISO's Mpeg working group who developed, together with the MP3 music format, a new digital encoding standard for radio broadcasting called DAB from 1989 to 1994 (O'Neil, 2009).

Initially the European Union interpreted radio (like TV) digitization not only as a further step to regional integration but also as an opportunity for European technological industries to play a front-rank role in the global communications sector as had occurred a few years earlier with the GSM mobile phone standard (see Chapter 4). It was, in fact, believed that defining a common European standard for radio would translate into a more general development opportunity for other home electronics consumption sectors (Lembke, 2003, p. 213). Despite this significant institutional support, radio digitization resulted in a much-delayed adoption, above all if compared with digital TV. Not only did DAB not succeed, despite initial hopes, in establishing itself as a global digital radio standard but even within the European Union the transition to digital radio was fragmented and partial, moving forward slowly and uncertainly. This partly happened because the advantages of the digital radio system over the FM/AM analog system turned out not to be particularly attractive to radio listeners, in contrast to digital TV (Lax, Ala-Fossi, Jauert, & Shaw, 2008).

DAB's political economy trajectory did not help to support radio digitization in the way it did for TV either. One of DAB's first disappointments was the US's decision not to adopt it with the latter opting to develop an alternative format. The trajectory of digital radio in US reveals how digitization represented a divisive element, rather than a uniforming force for the radio sector. In the early 1990s, the US National Association of Broadcasters (NAB) gave an initial endorsement for the European DAB, but soon the US radio industry refused the system. Indeed, DAB was designed reflecting interests and power structures typical of the European broadcasting context and it was therefore judged to be excessively challenging for the stability of the American radio industry (Ala-Fossi, 2016, p. 276). As a consequence, the US industry developed its own digital radio standard based on a different technical paradigm. In contrast to European DAB, the American standard was indeed partially compatible with the analog FM signal and did not require the complete replacement of all the country's broadcasting towers. Initially labelled IBOC (In-Band, On Channel), this system took later the marketing name of HD radio and was officially approved by the

U.S. Federal Communications Commission (FCC) in 2002 as the main digital radio standard. However, in the US digital transmission was adopted only by a minority of radio stations and consequently was only marginally taken up at by consumers (Anderson, 2014).

With the US alternative choice, hopes of global adoption thus waned and consequently the EU's interest in DAB also weakened considerably. While a switch off agenda had been drawn up for TV in the year 2000 (during the Lisbon Conference), nothing similar happened in the radio sector. A number of European countries did not even launch regular broadcasts in DAB and sales of radios fitted out to receive these signals remained marginal. For example, by 2015 only three European countries (the UK, Denmark and Switzerland) had achieved 50% DAB home penetration while, in the majority of other countries, radio dissemination remained low (13% in Germany) or verging on non-existent (3% in Italy).

Outside Europe the adoption of digital radio has been even slower. In China, DAB was introduced in 2008, but up to 2016 it has been available only in the urban area of Beijing. In Hong Kong, for example, after a short period of experimentation, the service was interrupted. A massively populated country, India experimented with DAB in the late 1990s, but then refused to embrace this standard for several reasons, including the fact that the great majority of its population could not afford new digital devices. A notable exception to the slow adoption of DAB outside of Europe is South Korea, where it was estimated that, up to 2015, more than 60 million DAB devices had been sold. This success is due to two main reasons: the support of huge consumer electronics producers such as LG and Samsung and the massive adoption of DAB smartphones and portable digital TVs, compatible with digital radio reception (source: WorldDAB). The "smartland Korean" (Jin, 2017) shows itself once more to be a country of celebratory achievement of technological advancement, quick adoption of new digital devices and ideas, and extensive use of mobile communications as digital radio embedded in the smartphones is.

These delays and uncertainties have prompted observers to consider digital radio at the very least as a disappointing innovation compared to initial hopes if not as an outright technological failure (Goddard, 2010). These difficulties may seem surprising if we bear in mind that a twin medium such as TV—which over the course of its history has frequently emulated radio's trajectory in terms of regulation, business models and innovations in language—followed a relatively successful innovation trajectory. However, on closer examination some of the reasons behind digital radio's lack of success emerge precisely from a comparison with TV. From a political economy point of view, the TV system has always been considered more important than radio and this has had implications for the lack of institutional support for the transition to digital radio. From a technical point of view, digital TV involved innovative potential for consumers beginning with forms of on-demand and Web contents access while digital radio could only partially, if at all, guarantee improved sound quality and, in its satellite version, the chance to reach areas with limited cover. From a cultural point of view, as we have seen, digitization has enabled TV to conserve its primary role within the family and in the living rooms, an aspect which encouraged families to invest in replacing analog with digital. Radio, on the other hand, has played a subsidiary role in home spaces and preserved its consumer appeal above all in cars in the majorities of countries. These and other reasons are at the heart of digital radio's limited success to date and make it a good example of the fact that overall digitization is not a linear, "natural" process but depends on the fluctuating interests of political and economic actors as well as peculiarities of use and practice in the context of the everyday lives of users.

In contrast to the "conservative" transition of traditional analog radio to a digital infrastructure, the new possibilities offered by the WWW opened innovative ways to this medium, in terms of formats, contents and listening practices. And for this very reason, the radio was undoubtedly one of the driving forces behind the social dissemination of the internet in the mid 1990s. In a period when neither the Web nor computers were technically ready to manage video and image distribution, Web enthusiasts' attention focused heavily on the opportunities for free audio broadcasting. One of the first radios to broadcast on the Web was Internet Talk Radio, set up in 1993 by American technology expert Carl Malamud who recognized the new opportunities represented by the cross fertilization between internet transmission and radio formats. An early radio show was *Geek of the Week*, a space devoted to interviews with computer experts (Sawhney & Lee, 2005; see also Box 5.7). In the mid 1990s, both specifically Web-based broadcasters and traditional radio stations offering contents on their Web sites, too, began riding the Internet Talk Radio wave. The explosion of Web radio from the late 1990s was also the result of the dissemination of RealAudio Player, a software that allowed easy access to good quality audio streaming, which could also be produced live. In the years that followed, Web radio became an increasing Web trend: in the year 2000 in the US alone there were an estimated 20,000 Web radio stations broadcasting exclusively via internet.

Web radio's success was the outcome of a number of different factors in which the pre-existing cultural background also played a part, as well as technical innovations and the opportunities offered by the internet communication model. On the one hand, the idea of developing independent, low-cost radio had a long history frequently on the cusp between political activism and cultural creativity—a well-known example of this form of continuity were the *pirate*

Box 5.7 Documents

Carl Malamud, *The Metaphor of the First Internet Radio* **(1997)**

In this short excerpt from his book *A World's Fair for the Global Village* (1997), Carl Malamud reflects on the first internet radio he contributed to creating, pointing out two powerful aspects of it: the arbitrary decision to call what he was doing "radio" and the power of metaphors in shaping the appropriation of new digital internet-based forms of communication.

> This book is the result of a four-year odyssey during which I thought I was building a radio station and found instead that it had turned into a world's fair. With the Internet, many metaphors are possible. With an invisible infrastructure, we can easily call ourselves as a global schoolhouse, a telephone company or a radio station. Sometimes, though, chance intervenes and we are able to go beyond metaphor and create something tangible. In January 1993, I started work on a new project. The idea was simple enough: I would record interviews with people who were building the Internet, package these interviews as a series of audio files and let people download and then listen to them on their comparers. I called my program *Geek of the Week* and threw in the label *Internet Talk Radio* for good measure. The *New York Times* wasn't impressed with the *Geek of the Week* label, but they sure went for the Internet Talk Radio metaphor, writing a front-page story that went into national syndication [...] The thing about it was, we weren't a radio station. What we were really doing was communicating with our audience using a new technology. Our programs were audio intensive, but this wasn't radio. This wasn't radio any more than television was, as David Sarnoff said in his initiation of service for RCA, "radio sight" added to "radio sound". The Internet is a new medium and we were feeling our way trying to understand what that meant.
>
> Source: Malamud, C. (1997). *A World's Fair for the Global Village*. Cambridge, MA: The MIT Press, p. xv

radio or *free radio* stations set up in many countries from the 1960s onwards (Johns, 2010).

Not only did the interweaving between radio and the Web replicate classic radio broadcasting's linear model of live consumption but it also put forward new asynchronic content use models: program time-shifting and, in particular, so-called *podcasting* (Dubber, 2013). The origin of the term podcasting was not in radio but rather MP3 format files, supported by iPods, the portable Apple devices referred to previously. Today's podcasts are audio contents distributed by means of a hybrid on-demand broadcasting system that can be used on a range of platforms, including the iTunes Store, which integrated this distribution model from 2005 onwards. As models of communication, Web radio and podcasting have become fully integrated into the contents circulating on the Web over the last decade; these new ways to listen to radio content increasingly produced a *networked radio audience*, now able to access these contents in different times and with multiple devices, as they remain always online, can be easily searchable and are effortlessly delivered to a wide set of portable digital devices, including in first place smartphones (Bonini, 2014).

In terms of broadcasting models, podcasting is a turning point in the traditional radio (and TV) linear models, which have become ingrained into broadcasting history since its birth in the 1920s: the programming schedule. With program schedules (a technique that, as we have seen in the case of TV, has not disappeared and to some extent has been even reinforced) broadcasters set out a daily and weekly program thus structuring the everyday lives of their audiences. For example, as radio or TV main night news was broadcast at 8 pm (or at other times depending on country) and there was no way this could be viewed at an alternative time, listeners had to tune in to that channel at that time if they wanted to hear it (Berry, 2006). Sociologist John Thompson (1995) has argued that the fact that physically unconnected individuals watched or listened to the same program at the same time was twentieth-century broadcasting's most characteristic feature and called it *despatialized simultaneity*. With the ability to listen to or watch programs whenever we like on whatever support and pause them when we like, podcasts have thus contributed to diluting this broadcaster–audience negotiation in favor of the greater listening freedom offered by the latter.

However, these relevant changes introduced by digital technologies in radio broadcasting have only partially influenced the strategies of radio networks and the assets of national radio industries, making evident, once more, that the logic of continuity coexist with the logic of change triggered by digitization. Indeed, even if radio networks have been fast in expanding their activities over the internet, conversely the radio industry's strategies and assets have changed only marginally with digitization. In the great majority of countries, radio stations and networks have preserved their pre-digital assets, with a clear distinction of roles between public and commercial services lasting since the introduction of broadcasting in the 1920s. Also, the business models have hardly changed with the digitization of radio: public radios are still mainly financed by the states and commercial networks by advertising, while selling radio receivers (with or without digital capabilities) still represents an eco-nomically viable sector. In the UK, for instance, a major consequence of radio digitization has been mainly the increasing pressure to develop a new market for manufacturing in the domestic electronic sector, with a lack of attention toward listeners' desires and interests (Rudin, 2006). A report by the European Broadcasting Union (EBU, 2017) shows that in 2017, over the 1,206 official radio stations active in Europe, only 369 were transmitting DAB only, while the majority of them used DAB as complement to the traditional FM frequency. Also the radio schedule can be considered one of the most telling continuities from analog to digital radio (and another sign of the business models' conservative attitude): despite the increasing podcasts' consumption, radio is today mostly listened to live, surfing linearly the schedules provided by radio networks via different devices such as mobile phones, personal computers, tablets, and especially traditional radio sets and car radios.

The digital radio trajectory helps to understand quite clearly some of the major ambiguities and contradictions of the digitization phenomenon: on the one hand, radio can be considered the traditional medium that has been able to inte-grate earlier and more deeply with digital formats and systems (i.e. with streaming and podcasts); on the other hand, not only conventional radio listen-ing practices have largely remained the same in the digital landscape (for example the centrality of live listening in cars), but the process of digitization of the analog FM/AM signal has revealed itself as a partial failure, given that, after about 30 years since its initial design, the DAB system and its variants still remain poorly adopted in most of the world regions, including in Europe, where DAB had been originally conceived.

5.8 Digitization and the Interweaving of Different Media

As seen in this chapter, the digitization of analog media has shown distinctive features in each of the various sectors considered, but a common trend towards an intermedia and systemic reconfiguration has developed over recent decades by means of a constant tension between the two logics—continuity and change—which we have highlighted right from Chapter 1 of this book.

In the first place, digitization has favored the interweaving of different media and, more generally, a growing interdependence between politics, technologies, aesthetics, markets and practices, which were previously distinct and separate. This does not mean—despite the *überbox* rhetoric of the 1980s (Fagerjord, 2002)—that we are using a single device for *all* our media needs and activities in the digital world. Quite the contrary, in fact: digitization has generated a multiplication of devices, platforms and infrastructures *each of which*, however, contains and encompasses a mixture of diverse media and is tied to increasingly specific practices. The intermedia trend is a phenomenon driving the various media to interweave generating a consequent change in our media activities and needs. If it is true that listening to a song, watching a film, taking and looking at a photograph, reading a newspaper or a book or watching TV have remained to some extent identifiable activities in our daily lives, these are, however, rarely linked to a single and recognizable medium but are rather part of a wider communication ecology that we defined *digital media pattern* at the beginning of this chapter. This digital pattern is a complex and stratified interweaving of different and previously distinct and separate media that converge and thus cross-fertilize. It is thus clear that today's songs are less and less a matter of a single audio content and more frequently a YouTube video flow, sent to us via Facebook. A photograph can circulate on a range of platforms or be exchanged by means of WhatsApp or WeChat message services becoming something other than classic images. A Saturday evening TV show can still be watched on our home TV sets but now makes sense only with smartphones in our hands following Twitter comments. The dominant logic is thus osmosis between different media, the interweaving of media practices less frequently linked to a single, recognizable medium or device.

The digital media pattern has emerged over the time from a constant tension between a force for change (the *logic of change*) and the urge for stability in existing media models (the *logic of continuity*): all the media sectors considered in this chapter evolved by means of trajectories where both sides of this coin have alternated. The presence of this constant tension between change and continuity enables us to make at least a couple of further and final considerations.

In the first place, digitization had profound consequences for analog media in all the three basic phases of media production, distribution and consumption. New forms of frequently bottom-up production (from citizen journalism to YouTube videos), novel and often free-of-charge opportunities to get contents circulating on the Web (the effects of streaming and file sharing on music and cinema) and new opportunities for personalized consumption (radio-TV on-demand and podcasts) suggest that we are living in a media universe, quite different from the analog world. The most striking example of this is social network contents, generated in part by what were once "consumers", and increasingly used (also) by what would once have been defined "producers" to segment their markets with ever greater precision.

But, on the flip side, it is also interesting to note that digitization does not appear to have swept away the analog media universe. Quite the contrary, digitization seems to have encouraged *analog rebirth* as in the case of vinyl records, whose second life (a further case of *double birth* in addition to that of mobile phones referred to in Chapter 4) represents an emblematic case of the way in which the old analog media can take on new meanings and cultural values in the digital context. The survival of analog media into the digital age is a growing phenomenon linked to various practices of media consumption, which is crystal clear in relation to the so-called *retro-technologies* (Sarpong, Dong, & Appiah, 2016) and the effective return, generally in niche contexts, of technologies considered obsolete and frequently (mistakenly) declared dead: from Polaroid and 35mm film in photography (Minniti, 2016) to the cassettes, records and analog synthesizers used by musicians (Pinch & Trocco, 2002) and retro-gaming among videogame fans (Heineman, 2014). The digital pattern that emerges from these processes is thus made up not only of the intermingling of previously distinct and separate media, not only of recombination of exclusively digital media, but also of old analog tools and new digital technologies. In other words, the digital media pattern is also made up of analog media and practices and the two, analog and digital, not only co-exist side by side but actually gain new meaning and use from this coexistence.

An overview of the old analog media's digitization progression, then, shows a process that has been anything but coherent or linear or a "disruptive revolution" but rather a sometimes untidy but nonetheless recognizable co-evolution between forces, tendencies and orientations within a common digital pattern. It is certainly an ambivalent and controversial process, which has operated on different, sometimes conflicting rhythms and logics depending on the sector that the new media technologies have developed and the different geographical and cultural articulations in which they have taken root.

LEARNING MATERIALS

Key Points to Focus on

- Intermediality as a framework for understanding the digital media pattern.
- The digitization of music:
  - The differences between compact discs and MP3s.
  - The MP3 creation process.
  - Four internet-based digital music circulation models.
  - The survival of records and other analog formats.

- The digitization of books:
  - Four main phases in the digitization of written words.
  - The history of personal readers: from Dynabook to Kindle.
  - The crisis of digital ebooks and the survival of printed contents.
  - The consequences of digital on journalism and newspapers at the global level.
- The rise of digital cinema and video:
  - From special effects to digital cinema.
  - Non-professional user video creation.
  - Home movies from VHS and DVD to streaming.
  - The controversy over digital piracy.
- Digital photography:
  - The digital challenge to the realistic perception of images.
  - Kodak's bankruptcy.
  - From digital cameras to cameraphones and smartphones.
  - Image sharing on social network sites.
- The rise of digital TV: five dimensions:
  - The convergence of TV, telecommunications and informatics.
  - TV signals: from analog to dis-homogenous digital.
  - From home-based TV to hybrid and mobile TV viewing.
  - Changes in consumption patterns.
  - Integration between TV and internet contents (YouTube).
- The development of digital radio:
  - The slow development of digital radio infrastructure (DAB).
  - The rise of early digital radio stations on the internet.
  - Podcasting and new radio consumption patterns.
  - The "conservative" radio market and audience.

Questions to Answer

- Explain the differences between the notion of media convergence and the idea of intermediality.
- Why did music compact discs, although they were already digital, not generate a radical change in the music sector while MP3s later did so?
- In what sense are digital ebooks part of a wider *reading infrastructure*?
- What kind of consequences have digital technologies had on video amateurs and non-professional users?
- What does cameraphones, such as the iPhone 4, triggering the rise of a new socio-technical network in photographic practices mean?
- How is digital TV transforming and how maintaining TV consumption patterns?
- Why was there a delay in digital radio take-up as compared to TV?

A Few Books for Further Study

Bartmanski, D., & Woodward, I. (2015). *Vinyl: The Analogue Record in the Digital Age*. London & New York: Bloomsbury Academic.

Boczkowski, P. (2004). *Digitizing the News: Innovation in Online Newspapers*. Cambridge, MA: The MIT Press.

Braun, J.A. (2016). *This Program is Brought to You By . . .: Distributing Television News Online*. New Haven, CT: Yale University Press.

Burgess, J. & Green, J. (2009). *YouTube: Online Video and Participatory Culture*. Cambridge: Polity Press.

Dubber, A. (2013). *Radio in the Digital Age*. Cambridge: Polity Press.

Gillespie, T. (2007). *Wired Shut: Copyright and the Shape of Digital Culture*. Cambridge, MA: The MIT Press.

Hand, M. (2012). *Ubiquitous Photography*. Cambridge: Polity Press.

Napoli, P.M. (2010). *Audience Evolution: New Technologies and the Transformation of Media Audiences*. New York: Columbia University Press.

Sterne, J. (2012). *MP3. The Meaning of a Format*. Durham, NC: Duke University Press.

Strangelove, M. (2015). *Post-TV: Piracy, Cord-Cutting, and the Future of Television*. Toronto: University of Toronto Press.

Wikström, P. (2013). *The Music Industry: Music in the Cloud* (2nd edition). Cambridge: Polity.

Conclusion
Myths and Counter-hegemonic Narratives in Digital Media History

In this book, we have adopted diverse theoretical perspectives to retrace digitization's multiform process, highlighting certain characteristics and underlining some of the main *mythologies* that have fed into the analog to digital media transformation. The word *myth* is a highly complex one and a fundamental mechanism in human culture, as Bronislaw Malinowski, one of the fathers of anthropology, argued almost a century ago: myth "is not of the nature of fiction, such as we read today in a novel, but it is a living reality, believed to have once happened in primeval times, and continuing ever since to influence the world and human destinies" (1925/1948, p. 78). In these final considerations, we address the issue of mythology, exploring at least two dimensions that encompass digital media's myths. In the first place, myths emerge as *symbolic narratives* whose goal is to legitimize existing social and cultural practices that, in general, feature divinities or heroes performing exemplary, exceptional or fascinating acts or those that are in themselves reference points or inspirations. In the second place, myths can also be concepts or ideas that do not correspond to the real world, but whose groundlessness does not stop them from influencing collective thought. Digitization and digital media history encompasses all these two dimensions and constitutes a full-blown mythology with its own heroes, example legacy and narratives, which frequently do not correspond to what *actually* occurred but are fundamental all the same to an understanding of the real present. As we have noted on several occasions, digitization has acquired a symbolic role in contemporary society thus itself becoming a sort of present day *founding myth*, an interpretative key to a definition of our own world as compared to that of the past.

Over recent decades, the digitization phenomenon has exerted huge appeal and generated a long sequence of heroes in various sectors and historic eras. These can be thought of as digitization's pantheon of founding fathers (and very rarely founding mothers): inventors, politicians, hackers, university students, entrepreneurs who have had explosive ideas, have frequently been seen as geniuses or at least ahead of their times and capable of disseminating the digitization poetic. Beside humans, devices and infrastructures such as the ENIAC computer, ARPANET, Napster or the Google algorithm are no less mythological, becoming symbols of a new model of technology, circulation of information and, broadly, society and culture. Finally, market processes and companies characteristic of the digital world are no less heroic: on the one hand small, innovative firms and start-ups (another of digital's legends) who managed by dint of shrewdness and a new technological vision to defeat big and established companies; on the other, large corporations sometimes with deep roots in the analog media panorama and the ability to manage millions of users worldwide. Think about how IBM, AT&T, Nokia, Ericsson or, more recently, Tencent, Google, Apple, Facebook, Amazon, Uber and many others have all played a starring role in the digital tale.

Deepening the last point, one of the most appealing aspects of this mythology lies precisely in the fact that at the time when digital culture began building its heroes, these were to be sought above all in the worlds of business and technological innovation. Steve Jobs and, to an extent, Bill Gates are two of the most evident examples of legendary figures spawned at the source of digital techno-capitalism. But more than any other it has been a single company, Apple, that has personified the digital media mythology at various historical junctures: think of the idea of transforming computers into mass personal, home media (Chapter 2), integrating computers, telephones and internet into a single device with the iPhone (Chapter 4), and changing the music industry sector as the iPod music reader and the iTunes virtual shop did (Chapter 5). The entrepreneurial dimension shoring up the digital myth has been fed not solely by inventions and commercial strategies but also by Apple's ability to build images and narratives capable of supplying digital society with legends to admire and—as occurred in 2011 with the global outpouring of grief at the death of Steve Jobs—idolized on a par with rock or film stars. This legendary dimension of digitization accompanied the classic technological narrative step by step too with inventor "geniuses" frequently put on a pedestal as exceptional figures with special "powers". If, however, the ancient Prometheus rebelled against the gods and stole fire from them and Mary Shelley's modern Prometheus (a.k.a. Dr. Victor Frankenstein) used science to overcome life's limitations, the *digital Prometheus* frequently takes the form of a businessman vanquishing his free market rivals thus conjuring up a further powerful contemporary social myth, that of the *self-made man*, the hero of the American dream. From this perspective, then, digitization has reworked a classic archetype solidly rooted in Western culture at its current historical-cultural juncture characterized by technological innovation guided by late or neo-capitalist free market and consumer economy processes.

As we saw, a further dimension of the myth concept is a matter of the driving force behind certain ideas that can emerge as groundless or only partially true but are no less significant for this. In fact, myths are neither true nor false but simply living or dead and some alive and kicking myths have emerged as driven by digital media in the book. The role of these myths can be addressed by adopting a notion of cultural *hegemony*, elaborated by Italian Marxist thinker Antonio Gramsci (1948/1977): these myths are powerful narratives that support the construction of the cultural hegemony of digitization as a dominant discourse in today's capitalist society. Consequently, these hegemonic narratives about digital media can be contrasted by other corresponding *counter-hegemonic narratives* or *counter-myths*, which become tools for a better understanding of the cultural role of digital media and the building of an alternative critical perspective.

In different chapters, we have identified various myths. Think about the *infrastructural mythology*, according to which internet and wireless networks and infrastructures are brand new and digital born, eco-friendly and with a completely different structure compared to analog past; a historically rooted and counter-hegemonic tale has helped to reconsider this myth, underlining the continuity with past networks (especially the telephone network, but think also about electrical ones) and the pollution caused by them. Think also about the *participation mythology*, which we considered in Chapter 3, a narrative construction claiming that, in Web 2.0 especially, users are more engaged than in the past and co-produce digital contents; again, more recently, counter-hegemonic tales are emerging and underline the fact that a tiny minority of users are really engaged—like in the era of "classic" mass media.

Beside these (and other) digital myths, we want to focus the book's conclusive reflections on other three distinctive mythologies, emerged in different times and in different media sectors, that deserve a deep and final reconsideration: the digital as an *irresistible force*, its *global character* and its *revolutionary nature*.

Myth 1: Digitization as an Irresistible Force

First, the myth of digitization as an irresistible force has formed above all the political-economic sphere. Digitization has frequently been seen as an inexorable one-way macro-phenomenon and governments and international bodies of various political orientations have promoted this idea for decades. Digitization has frequently been seen as a force for change and progress capable of taking humanity on a great leap forward: see the US *information highways* rhetoric and, more generally, digitization cited as an effective democracy and wellbeing export. This mythological dimension also appeared, on the contrary, when looking at the internet as an effective tool with which to control freedom and democracy impulses: think of internet control in China and the so-called Datagate scandal, which brought out the US government's anti-democratic and controlling use of the Web. Both apparently conflicting political visions have shared a common hope rooted in *technological determinism*: that digital technologies are inherently capable of fundamentally modifying current political forms, structures and logics.

The belief that digitization is irresistible also underlies the idea that it will supplant analog media and, more generally, that it will shortly free contemporary society of old and awkward supports such as paper. From a quantitative point of view, the progressive digitization of analog media is incontrovertible and it seems likely that this process will speed up in future. That digitization is advancing everywhere at the same pace and with the same implications and that it will overthrow and kill off all earlier media sectors is highly debatable, however. In the course of this book we have, in fact, cited many cases of indecision, digital failures and forms of nostalgia or even return to analog practices–these all can be considered examples of counter-hegemonic visions of digitization.

The failures have included full blown blunders in interpreting new business models but also expectations that typically Western innovation logics are exportable to other parts of the world as if social metabolization of new technologies was a "natural" process: think about the "One laptop per child" *colonialist* idea of technological transfer described in Chapter 2. We have also seen technological "setbacks" such as WAP (Chapter 4) and digital radio (Chapter 5) take-up in the West, but also media models that initially seemed to have lost out but then re-emerged like underground currents in other periods (the mobile phone story recounted in Chapter 4 is an example of this technological *double birth*). Of the many forms of nostalgia for and even return to analog, we examined the return of records within the digitized music panorama and the continuing importance of paper (in books but also newspapers) in a universe that forecasts foresaw as the exclusive preserve of bits for some decades. This is probably linked with another hegemonic narrative, which has emerged in this book: the idea that digitization can favor a progressive and irresistible de-materialization of infrastructures, objects, and finally also personal relationships. As we have seen in Chapter 1 especially, from a theoretical perspective, Chapters 2 and 5 with devices and Chapters 3 and 4 with infrastructures and private relationships, digitization is now no longer considered in opposition to "real" and "material" structures but rather critically tangible and embedded in the everyday lives of billions of people.

The frequency of flawed prophesies is a further symptom of digitization's non-irresistibility. Take, for example, the 1980s media convergence forecasts according to which we would soon have been using a single device to access all our media contents: this *überbox* rhetoric saw digital as a one way, one directional and linear force tending to kill off the earlier media universe's differences. As we have seen, digitization actually emerges as in constant dialectic with the past and its tools, ready to reabsorb and be reabsorbed into various cultural practices.

Myth 2: Digitization as a Levelling-out Force

The second myth to be further discussed is the global character of digitization, the belief that its impact has been uniform and standardizing the world over. This connotation derives both from the interweaving of digital and global over time (from the starting point of Marshall McLuhan's *global village* concept) and from the economic, political and cultural consequences of digital media, which immediately demonstrated an ability to cross national boundaries and confines. Digital media has indeed effectively widened out access to communication contents: digitization has simplified and reduced production, distribution and consumption costs as compared to the past, granted greater audience finding opportunities and, above all, amplified the global stage exponentially enabling people in areas of the world where this was previously impossible to access information. It is equally clear that digitization is neither moving forward uniformly *in all countries of the world* nor, to an even greater extent, *across all regions of each individual country*. We have, in this book, observed on multiple occasions that the peculiar features of political economies and national cultural re-appropriation practices are capable of taking the media, and digital in particular, in country and region-specific directions. Internet's history is a profoundly nation-specific one in the sense that both its structure and access opportunities and the uses made of it are profoundly nation-specific or even local (Chapter 3). Mobile telephone history, and the relevant case of US backwardness until the noughties, was influenced by decision-making processes whose roots lay in federal or state logics but also in cultural specificities of the USA (Chapter 4). Even the process by which analog's media moved over to digital has developed in different ways in the diverse sectors and areas of the globe frequently generating even greater standard and format deformities than existed under analog as in the case of TV digital standards (Chapter 5). The global dimension of the change processes under way—to which we have referred repeatedly in this book—must thus measure up to national or local dimensions, which draw digitization back into the specific fold of the culture, economics and politics of the various regions of the world. The three-factor equation that sees digitization as equaling standardization (and elimination of the differences) and homogenization of digital tastes, styles and practices is thus not confirmed by the facts. And for this reason, in recent decades a counter-hegemonic narrative has emerged. This looks at digitization as a cultural product, focusing on the differences in political economy management (the internet in China, as we saw in Chapter 3, is politically different from the US internet, for example) or the differences in cultural re-appropriation of similar digital technologies (the mobile telephone in some African countries has cultural meanings which are very different from those of Western cultures, as discussed in Chapter 4).

Myth 3: Digitization as a Permanent Revolutionary Force

The last digitization-related mythological dimension is that which has featured most in this book: the "digital revolution" rhetoric. Indeed, the label of digital revolution has emerged as one of the main interpretative keys giving meaning to contemporary society's most important technological and cultural transformations (Chapter 1). On the one hand, this book has stressed digital media's "revolutionary" dimension and the extent to which its dissemination has constituted a break with the communication universe preceding it. To cite a few key passages, in contrast to just a few decades ago we now have access to vast databases containing every conceivable sort of information, are contactable while on the move and, in the lion's share of the world, can perform operations such as booking a train ticket or buying a book in just a few clicks, listen to a radio station broadcasting from the far side of the world or watch a film at whatever time and in whatever way suits us and much more. Even more important is the fact that the *intensity* and *frequency* of communication has sped up over recent decades and now effectively encompasses the whole human day: we are permanently available for communication via digital media at any time of day or night, fostering a progressive mediatization of everyday life (Couldry & Hepp, 2016). Finally a further significant change prompted by digitization concerns the scale of access to communications cited earlier. As we have seen, in particular, with mobile communications (and to some extent, without forgetting the digital divide, internet) for the first time in history even regions historically lacking in communication tools and opportunities are now covered by networks enabling humans to exchange information and communicate in real time. Digitization *is* effectively a profound transformation for billions of people in many parts of the world and in many everyday communication practices, which are now more intense and constant.

On the other hand, over the course of this book we have repeatedly asked ourselves whether it is really true that digitization has revolutionized old analog communication practices and, more generally speaking, our daily lives. Do we really live in a *completely* different world compared to some decades ago, before the macro-phenomenon of digitization emerged? Posed in this way the very existence of a clear break with the analog past shows all its cracks. In this book, we have repeatedly emphasized that the roots and assumptions of this supposed revolution are in actual fact the fruit of a long process (what we have called *longue durée*) with strong historical roots. In other words, if we want to understand digital media in-depth, we should at least start to understand phenomena that emerged at the end of the nineteenth century, if not earlier. To name just a few, we have mentioned the need to count contemporary societies through automatic machines (Chapter 2), the first wireless telegraphy and telephony communications (Chapter 4), the construction of mass production, distribution and consumption markets in music and the audiovisual industry (Chapter 5), and, more generally, the growth of privatization emerged at least from the Victorian age. The cultural realms in which digital media emerged were heavily shaped by two twentieth-century wars like the Second World War and the Cold War, which are crucial to an understanding of the origins and need for computers and what we call the internet today (Chapters 2 and 3). In sum, digitization was first inspired and shaped by cultural phenomena that emerged long before the "digitization" word and concept itself was conceived.

Furthermore, the continuities with the analog media world are manifold and multiform and it is difficult to sustain the idea of a clear watershed between the *analog past* and the *digital future*. A first, prosaic continuity consists in the fact that the principal digital media were analog in the first phase of their existence and thus, in a sense, digital's roots lie directly in a non-numeric past: computer's calculation machine ancestors; the use the internet made of the telephone network; the substantial identification of mobile telephones and radio telephones or the use of 1G analog networks until the 1990s—all this shows how difficult it is to identify a precise *terminus ad quem* marking the end of analog (and thus the beginning of digital). The business mentalities of the various companies mentioned in this book clearly show how the digitization *breakthrough* was integrated into a more comprehensive and analog/digital strategy. Companies producing calculators, typewriters, copy machines, pagers, electronic organizers, TV sets and many other analog devices were among the first building digital tools (Chapters 2, 4 and 5) thus showing that the transition from analog to digital was far from being a complete revolution. Finally, as we have seen, it is clear in a number of fields that analog has in actual fact never been swept away by digital and continues to co-exist with it. The old formats and supports have not disappeared but co-habit with new ones and are sometimes even born again thanks to digital: as we saw mainly in Chapter 5 paper books coexist with ebooks (and are in better shape than their younger relatives), we still print photographs (perhaps the most precious to us) and more generally analog photography practices are still important and vinyl records convey new, not simply nostalgia related, consumption meanings and emotions.

Despite the rhetoric, then, an extinct, or soon to be so, analog past and irresistible digital present does not reflect the true state of affairs.

In line with recent counter-hegemonic scientific research, we would argue that in many cases the old analog media have been modified but not entirely revolutionized in their reference models by the digitization process. Think, to give a single example, of TV's cultural value (Chapter 5). That thanks to digitization TV is not simply a home, one-to-many and relatively non-interactive medium whose rigid schedules and *liveness* rule audiences' lives just as they did in the past, is certainly true. It is, however, equally undeniable that certain "classic" cultural traits of this medium still prevail in modern consumption methods and, by contrast, that TV has directly influenced the Web world, as YouTube demonstrates. Essentially, while the digitization of the old analog media has certainly thrown certain consolidated structures into crisis, it is more difficult to argue, above all in the short term, that the cultural role of these media with their decades long social roots have been radically changed by digital.

More generally speaking, then, the so-called digital revolution would seem, on the one hand, to be firmly anchored to developments, needs and logics already established along the nineteenth and twentieth century and maintaining numerous elements of continuity with the analog past. But, on the other hand, there are certainly truly transformative aspects to this process, which have prompted a new relationship with our media environment at a global scale, even transforming the existing ideas about what media are and which role they can have in our increasingly globalized world.

Thus, looking at the myths of the media digitization process gives us a better understanding of one of the principal reasons behind the adoption of a historical approach to the digital universe: the need to *normalize* digitization, scale down its exceptional nature and study it as just one phenomenon among others in the media and communication history panorama. As we noted in Chapter 1, historian Fernand Braudel argued that deep undercurrents merit scholarly attention and not simply the sea's surface waves, however more visible these latter are. To begin to understand the profound nature of digital media in its various cultural and social contexts, then, we must not fall into the innovation and digital myth rhetoric traps where everything is "naturally" constantly new (this is the so-called presentism), "innovative" and better than in the past but rather focus on a more profound level encompassing thought and mentalities, which take account of cultural differences. This dimension can be understood only from a long-term perspective and only by a discipline whose slow analysis process is capable of bringing out changes and continuities—in short only by history.

This book is just a first step in this direction (the "normalization" of digital media) and further steps will need to be taken in the future. Nevertheless, our hope is that this volume may inspire students and future media historians to "stretch out" the digital media history field considering other interrelated media, other geographical case studies, other historical continuities and breaks (perhaps with a *longer longue durée* than we have been able to provide in this book). For this reason, at the end of our *History of Digital Media*, we provide a list of topics and questions that we hope may serve as starting points for the work of future digital media scholars:

1. An intermedia perspective is crucial, as we have said, to a better under-standing of (analog or digital) media histories and the outcomes of their complex interconnections we addressed by means of the "digital media pattern" notion. But many questions remain: how will this intermediality evolve? Is what we are experiencing simply the beginning of an "augmented intermediality" or, even more radically, are we now facing the end of digital *media* history specificity simply because the word "medium" is on the verge of disappearing and disintegrating into an overwhelming digital matrix? And, if this latter scenario does take place, then how are we to transform the conceptual tools we have used to date to define *media* as distinctive entities in our society? In any case, a more in-depth consideration on intermediality itself would be interesting, one that questions, for instance, if it is a satisfactory notion or whether we should perhaps extend it to include non-communication technologies. In other words, how should the notion of intermediality be readdressed in today's fast changing digital innovation scenario? How can we historicize media's reciprocal interconnections by studying the presence of old media in digital media con-sidering, for example, how telegraphy influenced the development of the internet or how letters, telegrams, text messages and tweets are part of a single remediation history? Finally, if we have to include non-communication techno-logies in the history of digitization, we should also explore the ways in which transportation, food, energy and waste technologies as well as emerging issues in robotics, nanotechnology or synthetic biology should further be brought into an expanded digital media history.

2. This book also aims to supply sensitivity to the global changes which digital media are subject to in an attempt to enable our history to swing between what are considered "innovation centers" and their technological peripheries. This is probably the most difficult task taken on by this book and our efforts in this respect are to be considered partial and provisional. Therefore, we would like to see future digital media scholars pursuing this further, asking themselves: how can global history(ies) of digital media be written? By whom and in which languages? To what extent can the countries in which the industrial and IT revolutions began (primarily the US) still be considered the centers of digital society—as we tend to believe today? Which are the consequences of the

"Asianization" of digital media, shown in relation to several media sectors across the book? Clearly, we should be motivated by increasing pressure to establish a *postcolonial digital media history* capable of discovering and making sense of the various origins, trajectories and stories connected to digital technologies and digitization.

3. A historical and long-term perspective is another major distinctive feature of the book although our main focus has been *simply* the last two centuries and the post World War Two period in particular. Nevertheless, we strongly believe that a *longer longue durée* approach is not only possible but also a necessary "add-on" to digital media history. This raises several questions requiring answers: how can digital media history be "stretched out", temporally speaking, and why? Are there past (communication) history periods that resemble recent digital hyper-innovation decades and are thus comparable with them? Is "digitization" a key term that can be applied to human history as a whole– as Ben Peters (2016a) recently suggested–and how would this be beneficial to digital media studies? Answering these questions requires scrutinizing what we mean by expressions such as "communication", "mediation/mediatization" and "new/digital media" and also wondering whether these are distinctive definitions of our "digital present" and if so how (as we have outlined that most of these are mythological such as ideas relating to the end of spaces and distances, networking, participation, etc.)? Historians will probably answer "no" but this simply raises other questions: has nothing really changed then? Unexpected long-term continuities and unnoticed/hidden changes will probably need to be rediscovered and updated by future media historians.

4. In addition to intermedia, global and *longue durée* perspectives, future digital media historians (and, more generally, digital scholars) will also have to reflect in a more nuanced way on how digital media history should be done and told. This raises methodological and historiographical questions such as: which are the most useful and telling theoretical traditions potentially informing this narrative (we provide *our* partial answer in Chapter 1, but there are many other options)? Which are the historical sources to look at, where are they kept and how can they be accessed especially if they are owned by private companies? Finally, how can the history of digital media interact with other fields inside and outside media and communication studies?

A History of Digital Media has tried to provide initial, tentative and partial answers to some of these questions. But, as we have said, much remains to be done and this book is simply a starting point, the first line in a long, as yet unwritten, dialogue, one of the first bricks in what is soon to be a recognized as a new house (or better field) of media studies: digital media history.

Chronology

1951   The first computer enters the market: UNIVAC

1952   In the US, the first hydrogen bomb is released thanks to calculations made by ENIAC

1957   Japan supports local computer industry by levying a tax on computer imports

The USSR launches the Sputnik, its first artificial military satellite, into orbit

1959   First USSR project to build a computer network

1960   Ted Nelson elaborates the concept of hypertext in the unfinished project Xanadu

1962   Time-sharing for mainframes is experimented with

The first known video game, *Spacewar*, is launched

1963   ARPA launches the ARPANET project

1964   An early desktop computer is created by Olivetti: P101

1965   Gordon Moore formulates Moore's First Law

1968   *2001: A Space Odyssey* by Stanley Kubrick costarring the computer Hal 9000 is released

1969   ARPANET network has four nodes

1971   Intel markets the first microprocessor, the 4004

Email begins to be used as a communication tool between ARPANET researchers

Michael Hart launches the Gutenberg Project Online Library

1972   INRIA launches the Cyclades project in France

Japan Computer Usage Development Institute plans to computerize Japanese society

1973   Xerox creates the Alto terminal, the first computer with a graphics interface, and Superpaint, the first digital image software

Daniel Bell publishes *The Post-Industrial Society*, assigning to computers a key role in this emerging social configuration

Lee Felsenstein sets up Computer Memory at Berkeley, CA, to share "alternative" content

1974   Altair 8800, one of the first PCs for hobbyists and enthusiasts, is created

1975   On April 4, Bill Gates and Paul Allen found Microsoft

Kodak sets up the first digital camera

1976   Steve Jobs and Steve Wozniak create Apple I

In an open letter, Bill Gates advises hobbyists to pay for, and not simply copy, his software

1977   George Lucas uses digital techniques and digital special effects in the movie *Star Wars*

Apple II, Commodore's PET and TRS-80 are marketed

1978   Vinton Cerf and Bob Kahn set up the TCP/IP protocol

The movie *Convoy* makes CB, the forerunner of the mobile phone, a popular and symbolic device

Nora and Minc's report (in French) foresees the advent of a "telematic society"

1979   Japanese NTT launches the first mobile phone network for consumers

1982   Minitel launches in France (closes in 2012)

Compact Discs start to be sold

Ridley Scott's *Blade Runner* released

At the end of the year, *Time* appoints the PC as the "machine of the year"

1983   The movie *War Games* popularizes computers as devices for teenagers

Microsoft makes the first version of Word (a word processing program)

US video games industry collapses and Japan's starts to acquire dominance in the sector

1984   Apple markets the first Macintosh with a graphic user interface

William Gibson publishes the novel *Neuromancer* and invents the word "cyberspace"

1985   Microsoft introduces the first version of Windows

Stewart Brand creates the WELL virtual community

The CD-Rom comes onto the market

Mobile phone networks start to be launched in major EU countries

1987   The European Community funds the Eureka-147 research project

Oliver Stone's *Wall Street* contributes to the hype of mobile phones

The Chinese academic community connects to the Net through Germany

1989   Tim Berners-Lee presents to CERN his idea of the WWW, which is then released in 1993

James Cameron's *The Abyss* presents the first fully digital character

1990   The first version of the software Photoshop is released

EU's Bangemann Report starts to build a digital narrative for a connected Europe

ARPANET is closed down

1991   Linus Torvalds begins work to create Linux

The video software Premiere is released by Adobe

1992   GSM standard, created in Stockholm, is adopted by eight European countries

The mobile phone standard 3G, later launched in 2001, begins implementation

Jpeg standard for image recording is developed by ISO

1993   Clinton administration presents *The National Information Infrastructure: Agenda for Action*

CERN releases the WWW software as a gift to the international community

PDF format is created

Internet Talk Radio, one of the first radios on the Web, starts to broadcast

1994   Netscape is the first browser used to surf the Net

The Chinese government starts the Golden Shield Project, concluding in 2002-2003

ISO's Mpeg group releases the digital encoding system for radio broadcasting, DAB

De Digitale Stad (DDS, Amsterdam's Digital City) pilot project is launched

1995   Nicholas Negroponte's and Mark Poster's books *Being Digital* and *The Second Media Age* respectively, contribute to raise enthusiasm about digital society

Internet sales are legalized, leading to the commercialization of the Net

NSF sells its academic structure to private firms

Netscape Corporation is listed on the Stock Exchange with great success eBay is set up

Amazon opens its online bookshop

The MP3 format is officially released by ISO

Toy Story is the first cartoon made entirely with digitally generated images

Marketing of the DVD begins

1996 The *New York Times* inaugurates its online edition

The Real Player software makes the internet radio phenomenon possible

John Perry Barlow makes *A Declaration of the Independence of Cyberspace*

1997 Ericsson, Motorola, Nokia and Unwired Planet set up the WAP standard to access online content with mobile phones

The domain name for Google is registered on September 15

1998 Tencent, a Chinese company owning WeChat, is founded

The software Open Diary, allowing blogging functions, is released

The WAP standard is implemented, creating the base for mobile internet connection

ICANN, a US-based non-profit organization, is set up in order to assign internet addresses and domains globally

1999 Napster is created (then shut down in 2001 for copyright violation)

Apple, followed the next year by Microsoft, integrates video editing into their PCs

The movie *Matrix* makes digital media and media concepts popular

Alibaba, the most important Chinese website for e-commerce, is founded

EU project *eEurope 2005* is launched to promote the creation of a "European internet"

2000 The legal case *Yahoo!* vs. French Government makes evident the "national" governance over internet contents

The Lisbon Conference establishes the EU strategy for digital terrestrial TV

2001 Apple iPod 1st Generation is released on the market on June 23

Dotcom financial bubble crashes

For the first time since the 1970s world computer sales slow down

Wikipedia is launched

2002   In the US, FCC officially approves a radio format called HD Radio (an alternative to DAB)

RIM releases the mobile phone BlackBerry 5810 with a QWERTY keyword

2003   Apple iTunes Store opens its online space to sell digital music

In the US, digital cameras sold exceed analog ones

The platform Second Life allows users to interact online through avatars

2004   Dale Dougherty invents the term "Web 2.0"

Facebook and Flickr are launched

2005   Chinese firm Lenovo buys up IBM's computer division

YouTube has its first video uploaded on April 23

Nokia becomes the largest producer of photographic lenses with the cameraphone

Radio podcasts integrated with iTunes

Megavideo, the most famous cyberlocker platform (later shut down in 2012 for copyright infringement) starts to operate

Nicholas Negroponte launches a non-profit project called One Laptop per Child

2007   Apple launches the iPhone and the iOS mobile operating system

Kindle is introduced to the market by Amazon

M-Pesa, a system to exchange money via SMS, starts to be used in a few African countries

Netflix starts to move from DVD renting to online streaming

Taiwanese PC companies start to market the short-lived netbooks

2008   Apple's iTunes Store becomes the world's largest music retailer

Spotify, the most popular platform for music streaming services, starts to operate

2009   Music companies create the platform Vevo on YouTube to regain control over digital music distribution

2010   Apple's iPad tablet is launched

Blockbuster, set up in 1985 to rent VHS tapes, goes bankrupt

Instagram is launched

2011 Smartphones surpass PCs in terms of the number of units sold globally

In the US, digital music sales surpass physical ones

First season of the TV series *Black Mirror* is released in the UK

Steve Jobs dies on October 5

2012 Kodak, obliged to file for bankruptcy, sells its patents to US IT firms

Date is set by the EU for full passage to digital TV

China overtakes the United States as the world's largest global smartphone market

2013 Netflix starts to produce original TV content

The number of PCs sold globally begins decreasing structurally

Chinese Lenovo is the primary worldwide personal computer manufacturer

Data analyst and ex-CIA employee Edward Snowden triggers a scandal about digital mass surveillance in the US

2014 The IPO of Alibaba in the US is the largest IPO ever worldwide

The Director of the Chinese State Internet Information Office Lu Wei sends a letter to the *Huffington Post* to clarify the Chinese view on global internet governance

2015 Google restructures, changing its name to Alphabet

For the first time in history, there is an average of one mobile phone for every person on the earth

Appendix
Statistical and Quantitative Data

Table A.1 The internet: evolution of internet users in seven world regions and proportion over the total of world users (2000, 2005, 2010, 2015)

	2000		2005		2010		2015	
	Total users (mil.)	World (%)	Total users (mil.)	World (%)	Total users (mil.)	World (%)	Total users (mil.)	World (%)
North America	108	29.9	223.3	23.8	271.3	13.2	313.8	9.4
Oceania	7.6	2.1	16.4	1.7	21.2	1.1	27.2	0.8
Europe	103	28.5	269.0	28.7	475.1	23.1	604.1	18.1
Latin America & Caribbean	18	5	68.1	7.3	211.6	10.3	339.2	10.1
Asia	114.3	31.7	323.7	34.4	891.5	43.4	1,611.0	48.1
Middle East	5.2	1.5	21.7	2.3	67.7	3.3	123.1	3.7
Africa	4.5	1.3	16.1	1.7	115.6	5.6	327.1	9.8
Total	360.9	100.0	938.7	100.0	2,054	100.0	3,345	100.0
Over world population	5.9%		14.4%		29.6%		45.4%	

Source: Authors' elaboration on Internet World Stats data (internet users) and World Bank (world population)

Table A.2 Mobile phone: evolution of mobile phones subscriptions in six world regions and proportion over the entire population (2005, 2010, 2015)

	2005		2010		2015	
	Total (million)	Per 100 inhabitants	Total (million)	Per 100 inhabitants	Total (million)	Per 100 inhabitants
Africa	87	12.4	366	45.4	710	76,2
Arab States	84	26.8	310	87.9	421	110,5
Asia & Pacific	833	22.6	2,614	67.3	3,795	93
Russian States	166	59.7	377	134.2	400	142.8
Europe	550	91.7	709	115	752	119.8
The Americas	459	52.1	881	94	1,102	111.8
Total	2,179		5,257		7,180	

Source: authors' elaboration on ITU data

Table A.3 Personal computer: proportion of households with a PC in six world regions (2005, 2010, 2015)

	2005	2010	2015	Difference 2005-2015
	(%)	(%)	(%)	(%)
Africa	2.9	5.4	9.7	+334
Arab States	14.7	28.3	41.9	+285
Asia & Pacific	19.8	26.7	36	+182
Russian States	16.6	42.4	64.4	+388
Europe	52.4	71.9	79.8	+152
The Americas	40.9	51.6	65.4	+160

Source: authors' elaboration on ITU data

Table A.4 The internet: fixed broadband subscriptions per 100 inhabitants in 30 major countries (2000, 2005, 2010, 2015)

Country	2000	2005	2010	2015
Argentina	–	2.4	10.0	16.3
Australia	–	9.8	24.6	28.5
Bangladesh	–	–	0.3	3.1
Brazil	0.1	1.7	7.2	12.2
Canada	4.6	21.7	31.7	36.3
China	<0.1	2.8	9.3	19.8
Congo (Rep.)	–	–	<0.1	<0.1
Egypt	–	0.2	1.9	4.5
Ethiopia	–	<0.1	<0.1	0.5
Finland	0.7	22.4	29.1	31.7
France	0.3	15.4	33.7	41.3
Germany	0.3	12.9	31.5	37.2
India	–	0.1	0.9	1.3
Indonesia	<0.1	<0.1	0.9	1.1
Iran	<0.1	<0.1	1.3	10.9
Italy	0.2	11.6	21.6	24.4
Japan	0.7	18.4	26.8	30.7
Korea (Rep.)	8.4	25.9	35.5	40.2
Mexico	<0.1	1.7	9.0	11.6
Nigeria	–	<0.1	0.1	<0.1
Pakistan	–	<0.1	0.5	1.0
Philippines	–	0.1	1.9[1]	4.8
Russian Fed.	–	1.1	10.9	18.9
South Africa	–	0.3	1.4	2.6
Spain	0.2	11.6	23.1	28.7
Sweden	2.8	27.9	32.0	36.1
Switzerland	0.8	22.5	37.2	45.1
Turkey	–	2.3	9.8	12.4
UK	0.1	16.4	30.9	38.6
US	2.5	17.2	27.1	31.0

[1] 2011

Source: our elaboration on ITU data

Table A.5 Mobile phone: subscriptions per 100 inhabitants in 30 major countries
(1990, 1995, 2000, 2005, 2010, 2015)

Country	1990	1995	2000	2005	2010	2015
Argentina	<0.1	1.2	17.6	57.3	141.4	146.7
Australia	1.1	12.4	44.5	89.8	100.4	132.8
Bangladesh	<0.1	<0.1	0.2	6.3	44.9	81.9
Brazil	0.0	0.8	13.3	46.3	100.9	126.6
Canada	2.1	8.8	28.4	52.8	75.7	83.0
China	0.0	0.3	6.7	29.8	63.2	92.2
Congo (Rep.)	<0.1	<0.1	2.2	15.8	90.4	111.7
Egypt	<0.1	<0.1	2.1	19.0	90.5	111.0
Ethiopia	0.0	0.0	0.0	0.5	7.9	42.8
Finland	5.2	20.3	72.0	100.5	156.3	135.4
France	0.5	2.2	49.1	78.3	91.4	102.6
Germany	0.3	4.5	57.7	94.6	106.5	116.7
India	<0.1	<0.1	0.3	8.0	62.4	78.1
Indonesia	<0,.1	0.1	1.8	20.9	87.8	132.3
Iran	<0.1	<0.1	1.5	12.1	72.6	93.4
Italy	0.5	6.9	74.1	121.9	154.8	142.1
Japan	0.7	9.4	53.1	76.0	96.8	126.5
Korea (Rep.)	0.2	3.7	58.3	81.5	104.8	118.5
Mexico	0.1	0.7	13.6	42.6	77.5	86.0
Nigeria	<0.1	<0.1	<0.1	13.3	54.7	82.2
Pakistan	<0.1	<0.1	0.2	8.1	57.3	66.9
Philippines	<0.1	0.7	8.3	40.5	89.0	115.8
Russian Fed.	<0.1	0.1	2.2	83.4	165.5	160.0
South Africa	<0.1	1.3	18.6	70.4	97.9	164.5
Spain	0.1	2.4	60.2	98.4	111.3	108.2
Sweden	5.4	22.7	71.8	100.8	117.2	130.4
Switzerland	1.9	6.4	64.7	92.2	123.2	136.5
Turkey	0.1	0.7	25.5	64.4	85.6	96.0
UK	1.9	9.9	73.7	108.6	123.6	124.1
US	2.1	12.6	38.5	68.3	91.3	117.6

Source: our elaboration on ITU data

Table A.6 Computer: estimated proportion of households with a computer in 30 major countries (1990, 1995, 2000, 2005, 2010, 2015)

Country	1990	1995	2000	2005	2010	2015
Argentina	–	–	20.5[3]	32.0	47.0	65.1
Australia	–	34.0[2]	53.0	67.0	81.1	83.0
Bangladesh	–	–	–	1.4	3.0	8.2
Brazil	–	–	12.6[3]	18.5	34.9	53.5
Canada	–	28.8	54.9	72.0	82.7	85.1
China	–	–	–	25.0	35.4	49.6
Congo (Rep.)	–	–	–	1.4	3.5	5.2
Egypt	–	–	–	–	31.3	50.9
Ethiopia	–	–	–	–	1.4	3.5
Finland	–	–	47.0	63.9	82.0	89.3
France	–	14.0	27.0	54.3	76.4	81.5
Germany	–	19.0	47.3	7.0	85.7	91.0
India	–	–	–	2.0	6.7	14.1
Indonesia	–	–	–	3.7	10.8	18.7
Iran	–	2.0	–	19.0	35.2	57.4
Italy	–	–	29.4	46.0	64.8	72.5
Japan	–	15.6	50.5	80.5	83.4	79.7
Korea (Rep.)	–	14.5[2]	71.0	79.7	81.8	77.1
Mexico	–	–	9.3	18.6	29.8	44.9
Nigeria	–	–	–	4.0	7.6	9.8
Pakistan	–	–	–	–	9.7	19.0
Philippines	–	–	–	6.6	13.6	27.0
Russian Fed.	–	–	8.6[3]	25.0	55.0	72.5
South Africa	–	–	8.6[3]	13.0	18.3	20.1
Spain	11.0	18.0	30.4	55.0	68.7	75.9
Sweden	–	32.0[2]	59.9	80.0	89.5	88.3
Switzerland	14.5	–	57.7	76.5	83.7	88.4
Turkey	–	–	–	12.0	44.2	55.6
UK	–	25.0	38.0	70.0	82.6	89.9
US	–	24.1[1]	51.0	67.1	75.5	86.8

[1] 1994; [2] 1996; [3] 2001

Source: our elaboration on ITU data

Table A.7 Internet: estimated proportion of users over the whole population in 30 major countries (1990, 1995, 2000, 2005, 2010, 2015)

Country	1990	1995	2000	2005	2010	2015
Argentina	0.0	0.1	7.0	17.7	45.0	69.4
Australia	0.6	2.8	46.8	63.0	76.0	84.6
Bangladesh	–	–	0.1	0.2	3.7	14.4
Brazil	–	0.1	2.9	21.0	40.7	59.1
Canada	0.4	4.2	51.3	71.7	80.3	88.5
China	–	–	1.8	8.5	34.3	50.3
Congo (Rep.)	–	–	<0.1	1.5	5.0	7.6
Egypt	–	<0.1	0.6	12.8	21.6	37.8
Ethiopia	–	<0.1	<0.1	0.2	0.8	11.6
Finland	0.4	13.9	37.2	74.5	86.9	92.7
France	0.1	1.6	14.3	42.9	77.3	84.7
Germany	0.1	1.8	30.2	68.7	82.0	87.6
India	–	<0.1	0.5	2.4	7.5	26.0
Indonesia	–	<0.1	0.9	3.6	10.9	22.0
Iran	–	<0.1	0.9	8.1	15.9	45.3
Italy	–	0.5	23.1	35.0	53.7	65.6
Japan	–	1.6	30.0	66.9	78.2	91.1
Korea (Rep.)	–	0.8	44.7	73.5	83.7	89.6
Mexico	–	0.1	5.1	17.2	31.1	57.4
Nigeria	–	–	0.1	3.5	24.0	47.4
Pakistan	–	–	1.3[1]	6.3	8.0	18.0
Philippines	–	–	2.0	5.4	25.0	40.7
Russian Fed.	–	0.1	2.0	15.2	43.0	70.1
South Africa	–	0.7	5.3	7.5	24.0	51.9
Spain	–	0.4	13.6	47.9	65.8	78.7
Sweden	0.6	5.1	45.7	84.8	90.0	90.6
Switzerland	0.6	3.6	47.1	70.1	83.9	87.5
Turkey	–	0.1	3.8	15.5	39.8	53.7
UK	0.1	1.9	26.8	70.0	85.0	92.0
US	0.8	9.2	43.1	68.0	71.7	74.5

[1] 2001

Source: our elaboration on ITU data

Table A.8 Internet: estimated proportion of households with internet access in 30 major countries (2000, 2005, 2010, 2015)

Country	2000	2005	2010	2015
Argentina	9.1[1]	13.3	34.0	55.5
Australia	33.0	56.0	74.1	85.9
Bangladesh	–	0.2	1.4	11.0
Brazil	8.6[1]	13.6	27.1	54.5
Canada	42.6	64.3	78.4	86.6
China	–	11.0	23.7	54.2
Congo (Rep.)	–	0.1	0.7	2.3
Egypt	–	15.3	25.3	42.3
Ethiopia	–	–	1.1	9.8
Finland	30.0	54.1	80.5	89.9
France	15.7	34.4	73.6	82.6
Germany	24.6	61.6	82.5	90.3
India	–	1.6	4.5	20.0
Indonesia	–	1.0	4.6	38.4
Iran	–	6.6	21.4	55.5
Italy	15.4	38.6	59.0	75.4
Japan	34.0	57.0	81.3	97.2
Korea (Rep.)	49.8	92.7	96.8	98.8
Mexico	6.1[1]	8.9	22.2	39.2
Nigeria	–	2.0	6.1	11.4
Pakistan	–	–	5.7	24.0
Philippines	–	4.3	9.5	28.3
Russian Fed.	–	17.0	41.3	72.1
South Africa	–	3.0	10.1	50.0
Spain	–	35.5	59.1	78.7
Sweden	48.0	72.5	88.3	91.0
Switzerland	36.5	67.0	80.7	84.7
Turkey	–	7.7	41.6	69.5
UK	30.0	60.2	79.6	91.3
US	41.5	58.1	71.1	81.5

[1] 2001

Source: our elaboration from ITU data

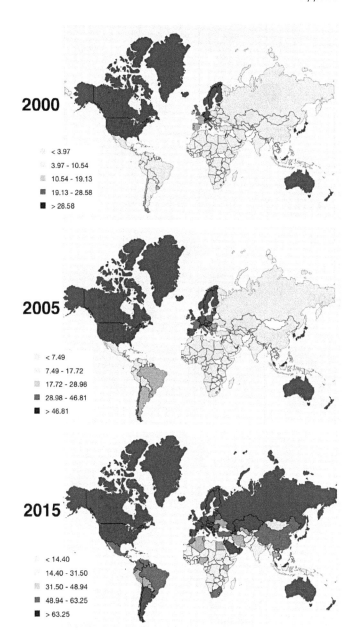

Figure A.1 Internet: historical world maps of the proportion of internet users over population in different countries (2000, 2005, 2015)

Source: authors' graphical elaboration on World Bank/ITU data

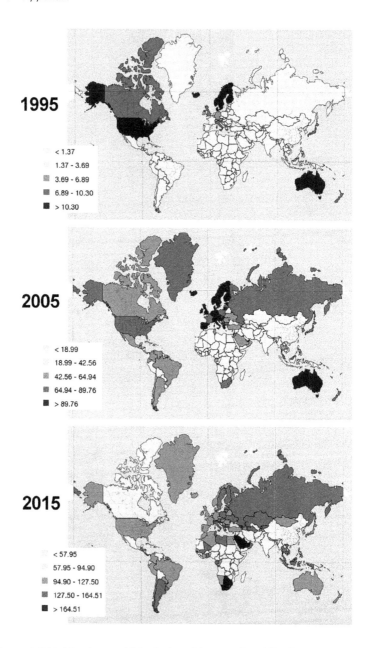

Figure A.2 Mobile phones: historical world maps of mobile phone subscriptions per 100 people in different countries (1995, 2005, 2015)

Source: authors' graphical elaboration on World Bank/ITU data

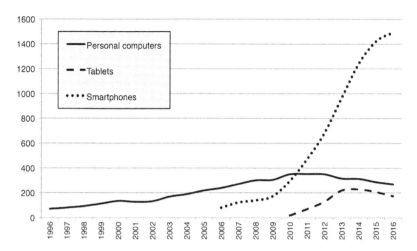

Figure A.3 Digital devices: evolution of global sales of personal computers, smartphone and tables (1996-2016). Million of units

Source: authors' elaboration on Gartner data for computers and smartphones and on IDC data for tablets

Acronyms

1G/2G/3G/ 4G/5G	First, second, third, etc. generation (of wireless telephone technology)
ARPA	Advanced Research Projects Agency (US)
ATSC	Advanced Television System Committee
AT&T	American Telephone and Telegraph
BBS	Bulletin Board System
Bit	Binary Digit
BRICS	Association of five emerging national economies of Brazil, Russia, India, China and South Africa
CB	Citizen Band
CD-ROM	Compact Disc Read-Only Memory
CERN	Conseil Européen pour la Recherche Nucléaire [European Organization for Nuclear Research] (Switzerland)
CISAC	International Confederation of Societies of Authors and Composers
Cnet	Centre national d'études des télécommunications (France)
CTI	Chung T'ien TV [中天電視] (Taiwan, China)
DAB	Digital Audio Broadcasting
DARPA	Defense Advanced Research Projects Agency (US)
DCA	Defense Communications Agency (US)
DDS	The Digital City [De Digitale Stad] (the Netherlands)
DSLR	Digital single-lens reflex
DTMB	Digital Terrestrial Multimedia Broadcasting
DVB	Digital Video Broadcasting

DVD	Digital Versatile Disc
EBU	European Broadcasting Union
EEC	European Economic Community
EIN	European Informatics Network
ENIAC	Electronic Numerical Integrator and Computer
EU	European Union
FBI	Federal Bureau of Investigation (US)
FCC	Federal Communication Commission
FM/AM	Frequency Modulation / Amplitude Modulation
GNU	GNU is Not Unix
GOSPLAN	[Госплан СССР], State Planning Committee [Государственный комитет по планированию] (USSR)
GPS	Global Positioning System
GSM	Global System for Mobile Communication [Groupe Spécial Mobile]
GUI	Graphic User Interface
(X)HTML	(Extensible) HyperText Markup Language
IBM	International Business Machines
ICANN	Internet Corporation for Assigned Names and Numbers
ICT	Information & Communication Technology
INRIA	Institut National de Recherche en Informatique et en Automatique (France)
IPO	Initial Public Offering
ISDB	Integrated Services Digital Broadcasting
ISDN	Integrated Services Digital Network
ISO	International Organization for Standardization
IT	Information Technology
ITU	International Telecommunication Union
MIR	[МИР], Machine for Engineering Calculations [Машина для Инженерных Расчётов], (USSR)
MIT	Massachusetts Institute of Technology (US)
MoMA	Museum of Modern Art (US)
MP3	MPEG-2 Audio Layer III
MPEG	Moving Picture Experts Group

M-Pesa	Mobile Pesa ("money" in Swahili)
MS-DOS	Microsoft Disk Operating System
MUD	Multi-User Dungeon
NAB	National Association of Broadcasters (US)
NASA	National Aeronautics and Space Administration (US)
NASDAQ	National Association of Securities Dealers Automated Quotation
NII	National Information Infrastructure
NMT	Nordic Mobile Telephony [Nordisk MobilTelefoni] (Scandinavia)
NSA	National Security Agency (US)
NSF	National Science Foundation (US)
NTSC	National Television System Committee
NTT	Nippon Telegraph and Telephone [日本電信電話株式会社](Japan)
NWCO	New World Communication Order
OECD	Organization for Economic Cooperation and Development
OGAS	[ОГАС], All-State Automated System [Общегосударственная автоматизированная система учёта и обработки информации] (USSR)
OLPC	One Laptop per Child
OS	Operating System
PAL	Phase Alternating Line
PC	Personal Computer
PCS	Personal Communication Services
PDF	Portable Document Format
PSB	Public Service Broadcasting
RTMS	Second generation mobile radiotelephone [radio telefono mobile di seconda generazione] (Italy)
SECAM	Sequential Colour with Memory [Séquentiel Couleur à Mémoire] (France)
SMS	Short Message Service
TCP/IP	Transmission Control Protocol/Internet Protocol
Tim	Telecom Italia Mobile (Italy)
UGC	User Generated Contents
UMTS	Universal Mobile Telecommunications System
UNESCO	United Nations Educational, Scientific and Cultural Organization

UNIVAC	UNIVersal Automatic Computer I
URL	Uniform Resource Locator
VHS	Video Home System
VPN	Virtual Private Network
WAN-IFRA	World Association of Newspapers and News Publishers
WAP	Wireless Application Protocol
WELL	Whole Earth 'Lectronic Link
Wi-Fi	Wireless networking technology based on the IEEE 802.11 standards
WWW	World Wide Web

References

Abbate, J. (1999). *Inventing the Internet*. Cambridge, MA: The MIT Press.

Agar, J. (2003). *The Government Machine: a Revolutionary History of the Computer*. Cambridge, MA: The MIT Press.

Agar, J. (2013). *Constant Touch: A Global History of the Mobile Phone*. London: Icon.

Aguiar, L., & Waldfogel, J. (2015). *Streaming Reaches Flood Stage: Does Spotify Stimulate or Depress Music Sales?* Institute for Prospective Technological Studies Digital Economy Working Paper 2015/05, Seville, European Commission, Joint Research Centre. Retrieved from *https://ec.europa.eu/jrc/sites/jrcsh/files/JRC96951.pdf*.

Akrich, M. (1992). The De-scription of Technical Objects. In W. Bijker & J. Law (Eds.), *Shaping Technology/Building Society: Studies in Sociotechnical Change* (pp. 205-224). Cambridge, MA: The MIT Press.

Akrich, M., & Latour, B. (1992). A Summary of a Convenient Vocabulary for the Semiotics of Human and Nonhuman Assemblies. In W. Bijker & J. Law (Eds.), *Shaping Technology/Building Society: Studies in Sociotechnical Change* (pp. 259-265). Cambridge, MA: The MIT Press.

Ala-Fossi, M. (2016). Why Did TV Bits and Radio Bits Not Fit Together? Digitalization and Divergence of Broadcast Media. In A. Lugmayr & C. Dal Zotto (Eds.), *Media Convergence Handbook Vol. 1* (pp. 265-285). Berlin: Springer.

Alderman, J. (2001). *Sonic Boom: Napster, MP3, and the New Pioneers of Music*. Cambridge, MA: Perseus Publishing.

Allan, R.A. (2001). *A History of the Personal Computer. The People and the Technology:* London, Allan Publishing.

Allan, S. (2008). Media History. In W. Donsbach (Ed.), *The International Encyclopedia of Communication Vol. VII* (pp. 2915-2926). Malden, MA and Oxford: Wiley-Blackwell.

Allen, M. (2013). What was Web 2.0? Versions as the dominant mode of internet history. *New Media & Society, 15*(2), 260-275.

Allen-Robertson, J. (2013). *Digital Culture Industry: A History of Digital Distribution*. London: Palgrave Macmillan.

Alper, M. (2014). War on Instagram: Framing conflict photojournalism with mobile photography apps. *New Media & Society, 16*(8), 1233-1248.

Alzouma, G. (2008). Téléphone mobile, Internet et développement: L'Afrique dans la société de l'information? *tic&société, 2*(2).

Anderson, J.N. (2014). *Radio's Digital Dilemma: Broadcasting in the Twenty-First Century*. London: Routledge.

Anderson, M. (1988). *The American Census: A Social History.* New Haven, CT: Yale University Press.

Arthur, W.B. (1989). Competing technologies, increasing returns, and lock-in by historical small events. *Economic Journal, 99*(394), 116-131.

Balbi, G. (2008). Dappertutto telefonini. Per una storia sociale della telefonia mobile in Italia. *Intersezioni, 3,* 465-488.

Balbi, G. (2015). Old and New Media. Theorizing Their Relationships in Media Historiography. In S. Kinnebrock, C. Schwarzenegger, & T. Birkner (Eds.), *Theorien des Medienwandels* (pp. 231-249). Köln: Halem.

Balbi, G. (2016). *Nothing really changes vs. everything is constantly changing. Reflections on two determinisms.* Paper presented at the 66th ICA Annual Conference, Fukuoka, Japan, June 9-13.

Balbi, G. (2017a). Deconstructing "Media Convergence": A Cultural History of the Buzzword, 1980s-2010s. In S. Sparviero, C. Peil, & G. Balbi (Eds.), *Media Convergence and Deconvergence.* London: Palgrave.

Balbi, G. (2017b). Wireless's "critical flaw": The Marconi Company, corporation mentalities, and the broadcasting option. *Journalism & Mass Communication Quarterly, 94*(4), 1239-1260.

Balbi, G., Delfanti, A., & Magaudda, P. (2016). Digital circulation: Media, materiality←1, infrastructures. An introduction. *Tecnoscienza: Italian Journal of Science & Technology Studies, 7*(1), 7-16.

Baldwin, T.F., Stevens McVoy, D., & Steinfield, C. (1996). *Convergence: Integrating Media, Information & Communication.* Thousand Oaks, CA: Sage.

Banerjee, U.K. (1996). *Computer Education in India: Past, Present and Future.* New Delhi: Concept Publishing Company.

Barabási, A.-L. (2002). *Linked: The New Science of Networks.* Cambridge, MA: Perseus Pub.

Baran, P. (1964). *Memorandum RM-3420-PR On Distributed Communications. I. Introduction to Distributed Communications Networks.* Retrieved from www.rand.org/content/dam/rand/pubs/research_memoranda/2006/RM3420.pdf.

Barbrook, R. (2007). *Imaginary Futures: From Thinking Machines to the Global Village.* London: Pluto.

Barbrook, R., & Cameron, A. (1996). The Californian ideology. *Science as Culture, 6*(1), 44-72.

Barlow, J.P. (1995). Is there a there in cyberspace? *Utne Reader* (March-April), 50-56.

Barlow, J.P. (1996). *A Declaration of the Independence of Cyberspace.* Retrieved from www.eff.org/it/cyberspace-independence.

Bartmanski, D., & Woodward, I. (2015). *Vinyl: The Analogue Record in the Digital Age.* London and New York: Bloomsbury Academic.

Behringer, W. (2006). Communications revolutions: A historiographical concept. *German History, 24*(3), 333-374.

Bell, D. (1973). *The Coming of Post-Industrial Society. A Venture in Social. Forecasting.* New York: Basic Books.

Belton, J. (2002). Digital cinema: A false revolution. *October, 100,* 98-114.

Beniger, J. (1986). *The Control Revolution: Technological and Economic Origins of The Information Society.* Cambridge, MA: Harvard University Press.

Bergin, T.J. (2006). The origins of word processing software for personal computers: 1976-1985. *Annals of the History of Computing, 28*(4), 32-47.

Berker, T., Hartmann, M., Punie, Y., & Ward, K. (2005). *Domestication of Media and Technology*. Maidenhead, UK: Open University Press.

Berners-Lee, T. (1999). *Weaving the Web: The Original Design and Ultimate Destiny of the World Wide Web by Its Inventor*. San Francisco, CA: HarperSanFrancisco.

Berry, R. (2006). Will the iPod kill the radio star? Profiling podcasting as radio. *Convergence: The International Journal of Research into New Media Technologies, 12*(2), 143-162.

Bertel, T.F., & Ling, R. (2016). "It's just not that exciting anymore": The changing centrality of SMS in the everyday lives of young Danes. *New Media & Society, 18*(7), 1293-1309.

Bijker, W.E. (1987). The Social Construction of Bakelite: Toward a Theory of Invention. In W.E. Bijker, T. Hughes, & T. Pinch (Eds.), *The Social Construction of Technological Systems* (pp. 159-187). Cambridge, MA: The MIT Press.

Bijker, W.E. (1997). *Of Bicycles, Bakelites, and Bulbs: Toward a Theory of Sociotechnical Change*. Cambridge, MA: The MIT Press.

Bijker, W.E., Hughes, T.P., & Pinch, T. (Eds.). (1987). *The Social Construction of Technological Systems*. Cambridge, MA: The MIT Press.

Birke, D., & Swann, G.M.P. (2006). Network effects in mobile telecommunications. An empirical analysis. *Journal of Evolutionary Economics, 16*(1), 65-68.

Boczkowski, P. (2004). *Digitizing the News: Innovation in Online Newspapers*. Cambridge, MA: The MIT Press.

Boczkowski, P., & Lievrouw, L. (2007). Bridging STS and Communication Studies: Scholarship on Media and Information Technologies. In O. Amsterdamska, E. Hackett, M. Lynch, & J. Wajcman (Eds.), *The Handbook of Science and Technology Studies* (pp. 949-977). Cambridge, MA: The MIT Press.

Boltanski, L., & Chiapello, E. (2005). *The New Spirit of Capitalism*. London and New York: Verso (original French version 1999).

Bolter, J.D. (1991). *Writing Space: The Computer, Hypertext, and the History of Writing*. London: Routledge.

Bolter, J.D., & Grusin, R. (1999). *Remediation: Understanding New Media*. Cambridge, MA: The MIT Press.

Bonini, T. (2014). The new role of radio and its public in the age of social network sites. *First Monday, 19*(6).

Bonner, A. (2007). *The Art and Logic of Ramon Llull: A User's Guide*. Leiden: Brill.

Bory, P., Benecchi, E., & Balbi, G. (2016). How the Web was told: Continuity and change in the founding fathers' narratives on the origins of the WWW. *New Media and Society, 18*(7), 1066-1087.

Bouwman, H., Akademi, A., Carlsson, C., Carlsson, J., Nikou, S., Sell, A., & Walden, P. (2014). *How Nokia failed to nail the Smartphone market*. 25th European Regional Conference of the International Telecommunications Society (ITS), Brussels, Belgium, 22-25 June. Retrieved from www.econstor.eu/bitstream/10419/101414/1/794346243.pdf.

Bowker, G.C., Baker, K., Millerand, F., & Ribes, D. (2010). Toward Information Infrastructure Studies: Ways of Knowing in a Networked Environment. In J. Hunsinger, L. Klastrup, & M. Allen (Eds.), *International Handbook of Internet Research* (pp. 97-117). Dordrecht: Springer.

Braudel, F. (1960). History and the social sciences: The long duration. *American Behavioral Scientist, 3*(6), 3-13 (original French version 1958).

Braun, J.A. (2016). *This Program Is Brought to You by . . . : Distributing Television News Online*. New Haven, CT: Yale University Press.

Bresnahan, T.F., & Yin, P.-L. (2007). Standard Setting in the Market: The Browser War. In S. Greenstein & V. Stango (Eds.), *Standards and Public Policy* (pp. 18–59). Cambridge, MA: Cambridge University Press.

Brügger, N. (Ed.). (2017). *Web 25: Histories from the First 25 Years of the World Wide Web*. New York: Peter Lang.

Brügger, N., & Kolstrup, S. (Eds.). (2002) *Media History. Theories, Methods, Analysis*. Aarhus: Aarhus University Press.

Brunton, F. (2013). *Spam: A Shadow History of the Internet*. Cambridge, MA: The MIT Press.

Burgess, J., & Green, J. (2009). *YouTube: Online Video and Participatory Culture*. Cambridge: Polity Press.

Buse, P. (2015). *The Camera Does the Rest: How Polaroid Changed Photograph*. Chicago, IL: University of Chicago Press.

Bush, V. (1945). As we may think. *The Atlantic Monthly*, July, 101–108.

Butsch, R. (2007). *The Citizen Audience: Crowds, Publics and Individuals*. London and New York: Routledge.

Callon, M., & Law, J. (1982). On interests and their transformation: Enrollment and counter-enrollment. *Social Studies of Science, 12*(4), 615–625.

Calvino, I. (1988). *Six Memos for the Next Millennium*. Cambridge, MA: Harvard University Press.

Campbell-Kelly, M. (2003). *From Airline Reservations to Sonic the Hedgehog. A History of the Software Industry*. Cambridge, MA: The MIT Press.

Campbell-Kelly, M., & Garcia-Swartz, D.D. (2008). Economic perspectives on the history of the computer time-sharing industry, 1965–1985. *IEEE Annals of the History of Computing, 30*(1), 16–36.

Carey, J. (1989). *Communication as Culture: Essays on Media and Society*. Boston, MA: Unwin Hyman.

Carey, J., & Elton, M.C.J. (2010). *When Media Are New: Understanding the Dynamics of New Media Adoption and Use*. Ann Arbor: University of Michigan Press.

Castells, M. (1996). *The Rise of the Network Society*. Cambridge, MA: Blackwell Publishers.

Castells, M., & Himanen, P. (2002). *The Information Society and the Welfare State: The Finnish Model*. Cambridge: Oxford University Press.

Castells, M., Fernandz-Ardevol, M., Qiu, J.L., & Sey, A. (2007). *Mobile Communication and Society: A Global Perspective*. Cambridge, MA: The MIT Press.

Cavanagh, A. (2007). Contesting media history. *Westminister Papers in Communication and Culture, 4*(4), 5–23.

Ceruzzi, P. (2003). *A History of Modern Computing*. Cambridge, MA: The MIT Press.

Chakravartty, P., & Zhao, Y. (Eds.). (2008). *Global Communication: Toward a Transcultural Political Economy*. Lanham, MD: Rowman and Littlefield.

Chandler, A.D. (2005). *Inventing the Electronic Century*. Cambridge, MA: Harvard University Press.

Chen, S.-H., & Wen P.-C. (2016). The Evolution of China's Mobile Phone Industry and Good-enough Innovation. In Y. Zhou, W. Lazonick, & Y. Sun (Eds.), *China as an Innovation Nation* (pp. 261–282). Oxford: Oxford University Press.

Chéneau-Loquay, A. (2010). *Innovative Ways of Appropriating Mobile Telephony in Africa*. Report published by the French Ministry of Foreign and European Affairs and the

International Telecommunication Union (ITU). Retrieved from www.itu.int/ITU-D/cyb/app/docs/itu-maee-mobile-innovation-africa-e.pdf.

Chiariglione, L., & Magaudda, P. (2012). Formatting culture. The Mpeg group and the technoscientific innovation by digital formats. *Tecnoscienza: Italian Journal of Science & Technology Studies, 3*(2), 125–146.

Christensen, C.M. (1997). *The Innovator's Dilemma: When New Technologies Cause Great Firms to Fail.* Chicago, IL: Harvard Business School Press.

Coit Murphy, P. (2003). Books are Dead, Long Live Books. In D. Thorburn & H. Jenkins (Eds.), *Rethinking Media Change: The Aesthetics of Transition* (pp. 81–93). Cambridge, MA: The MIT Press.

Copeland, B.J. (2010). *Colossus: The Secrets of Bletchley Park's Code-Breaking Computers.* Oxford: Oxford University Press.

Couldry, N. (2012). *Media, Society, World. Social Theory and Digital Media Practice.* Cambridge: Polity Press.

Couldry, N., & Hepp, A. (2017). *The Mediated Construction of Reality.* Cambridge: Polity Press.

Crawford, K. (2011). Listening, not Lurking: The Neglected Form of Participation. In H. Grief, L. Hjorth, & A. Lasén (Eds.), *Cultures of Participation* (pp. 63–77). Berlin: Peter Lang.

Cubitt, S. (2017). *Finite Media Environmental Implications of Digital Technologies.* Durham, NC and London: Duke University Press.

Curien, N. (2005). *Economie des Réseaux.* Paris: La Découverte.

Curran, J. (2012). Rethinking Internet History. In J. Curran, N. Fenton, & D. Freedman (Eds.), *Misunderstanding the Internet* (pp. 34–65). London: Routledge.

Cushion, S., & Lewis, J. (Eds.). (2010). *The Rise of 24-hour News Television: Global Perspectives.* New York: Peter Lang.

Dahl, H.F. (1994). The pursuit of media history. *Media, Culture & Society, 16*, 551–563.

Dasgupta, S. (2014). *It Began with Babbage: The Genesis of Computer Science.* Cambridge: Oxford University Press.

David, P.A. (1985). Clio and the economics of QWERTY. *American Economic Review, 75*, 332–337.

Davies, H., & Bressan, B. (Eds.). (2010). *A History of International Research Networking: The People Who Made It Happen.* Weinheim: Wiley-VCH.

Davis, J. (2007). Going analog: Vinylphiles and the consumption of the 'obsolete' vinyl record. In C.R. Acland (Ed.), *Residual Media* (pp. 222–238). Minneapolis, MN: University of Minnesota Press.

de Bruijn, M., Nyamnjoh, F., & Brinkman, I. (Eds.). (2009). *Mobile Phones: The New Talking Drums of Everyday Africa.* Bamenda, Cameroon: Langaa and Leiden, the Netherlands: African Studies Centre.

de Gourney C., Tarrius A., & Missaoui L. (1997). The Structure of Communication Usage of Travelling Managers. In L. Haddon (Ed.), *Communications on the Move: The Experience of Mobile Telephony in the 1990s* (pp. 51–72). Telia: Farsta.

de Sola Pool, I. (Ed.). (1977). *The Social Impact of the Telephone.* Cambridge, MA: The MIT Press.

Dedrick, J., & Kraemer, K.L. (2005). The impacts of IT on firm and industry structure: The personal computer industry. *California Management Review, 47*(3), 122–142.

Delfanti, A. (2013). *Biohackers. The Politics of Open Science.* London: Pluto Press.

DeNardis, L. (2014). *The Global War for Internet Governance.* New Haven, CT: Yale University Press.

Doms, M. (2004, January). The boom and bust in information technology investment. *FRBSF Economic Review*, 19–34.

Dordick, H.S., & Wang, G. (1993). *The Information Society: A Retrospective View*. Thousand Oaks, CA: Sage.

Doron, A., & Jeffrey, R. (2013). *The Great Indian Phone-Book: How the Cheap Cell Phone Changes Business, Politics, and Daily Life*. Cambridge, MA: Harvard University Press.

dos Santos Silva, M.F. (2013). Gaza burial, World Press photo 2013: Between ethics and forensics. *Journal of Applied Journalism & Media Studies*, *2*(2), 347–354.

Dourish, P., & Bell, G. (2011). *Divining a Digital Future: Mess and Mythology in Ubiquitous Computing*. Cambridge, MA: The MIT Press.

Doyle, G. (2013). *Understanding Media Economics*. Thousand Oaks, CA: Sage.

Driscoll, K. (2014). *Hobbyist Inter-Networking and the Popular Internet Imaginary: Forgotten Histories of Networked Personal Computing, 1978-1998*. PhD Dissertation, University of Southern California. Retrieved from http://digitallibrary.usc.edu/cdm/compoundobject/collection/p15799coll3/id/444362/rec/2

Driscoll, K. (2016). Social Media's Dial-Up Ancestor: The Bulletin Board System. *IEEE Spectrum, 53*(11), 54-60.

Dubber, A. (2013). *Radio in the Digital Age*. Cambridge: Polity Press.

Dutta-Roy, A., & Segoshi, N. (1996). Going online with the Internet in Brazil. *Spectrum, 33*(7), 54-58.

Dutton, W.H., Gillett, S.E., McKnight, L.W., & Peltu, M. (2004). Bridging broadband internet divides: Reconfiguring access to enhance communicative power. *Journal of Information Technology*, 19, 28–38.

EBU (2017). *Market insights digital radio 2017*. Geneve: European Broadcasting Union.

Edgerton, D. (2007). *The Shock of the Old: Technology and Global History since 1900*. London: Profile-books.

Edwards, P.N. (1996). *The Closed World: Computers and the Politics of Discourse in Cold War America*. Cambridge, MA: The MIT Press.

Eisenstein, E.L. (1979). *The Printing Press as an Agent of Change: Communications and Cultural Transformations in Early Modern Europe*. Cambridge and New York: Cambridge University Press.

Eko, L.S. (2012). *New Media, Old Regimes: Case Studies in Comparative Communication Law and Policy*. Lanham, MD: Lexington Books.

Ekström, A., Jülich, S., Lundgren, F., & Wisselgren, P. (Eds.). (2011). *History of Participatory Media: Politics and Publics, 1750-2000*. New York: Routledge.

English, J. (2005). *The Economy of Prestige: Prizes, Awards and the Circulation of Cultural Value*. Cambridge, MA: Harvard University Press.

Ensafi, R., Winter, P., Mueen, A., & Crandall, J.R. (2015). Analyzing the Great Firewall of China over space and time. *Proceedings on Privacy Enhancing Technologies*, 1, 61-76.

Eurodata TV Worldwide. (2015). *One Television Year in the World*. Levallois, France: Eurodata TV-Cedex.

Fagerjord, A. (2002). Reading-View(s)ing the Über-Box: A Critical View on a Popular Prediction. In M. Eskelinen & R. Koskimaa (Eds.), *Cybertext Yearbook 2001* (pp. 99–110). Jyväskylä: Publication of the Research Centre for Contemporary Culture.

Fanon, F. (1963). *The Wretched of the Earth*. New York: Grove Press (original French version 1961).

Farley, T. (2005). Mobile telephone history. *Telektronikk, 3*(4), 22–34.

Fenton, N. (Ed.). (2010) *New Media, Old News: Journalism and Democracy in the Digital Age*. Los Angeles, CA and London: Sage.

Fickers, A. (2012). The emergence of television as a conservative media revolution: Historicizing a process of remediation in the post-war western European mass media ensemble. *Journal of Modern European History, 10*(1), 49–75.

Fineman, M. (2012). *Faking It: Manipulated Photography before Photoshop*. New York: Metropolitan Museum of Art.

Flichy, P. (1995). *Dynamics of Modern Communication: The Shaping and Impact of New Communication Technologies*. London and Thousand Oaks, CA: Sage (original version in French 1991).

Flichy, P. (2007). *The Internet Imaginaire*. Cambridge, MA: The MIT Press (original version in French 2001).

Forester, T. (1993). *Silicon Samurai: How Japan Conquered the World's IT Industry*. Oxford: Wiley-Blackwell.

Fouché, R. (2012). From Black Inventors to One Laptop Per Child. In L. Nakamura and P.A. Chow-White (Eds.), *Race after the Internet* (pp. 61–84), New York, Routledge.

Franke, H.-C. (2014). "Alter Draht"-"Neue Kommunikation": Die Umnutzung des doppel-drahtigen Kupferkabels in der Entwicklung der digitalen Telekommunikation ["Old Wire"-"New Communication". The Conversion of the Double-Stranded Copper Cable in the Development of Digital Telecommunications]. *Diagonal, 35*, 97–112.

Fransman, M. (1995). *Japan's Computer and Communications Industry: The Evolution of Industrial Giants and Global Competitiveness*. Oxford: Oxford University Press.

Freiberger, P., & Swaine, M. (2000). *Fire in the Valley: The Making of the Personal Computer*. New York: McGraw-Hill.

Friedman, T. (2005). *Electric Dreams: Computers in American Culture*. New York: New York University Press.

Friedrich, O. (1983). Machine of the year. The Computer moves in. *Time, 121*(1), January 3.

Fuchs, C. (2014). *Digital Labour and Karl Marx*. New York: Routledge.

Gabrys, J. (2011). *Digital Rubbish: A Natural History of Electronics*. Ann Arbor: University of Michigan Press.

Gadrey, J. (2003). *New Economy, New Myth*. London and New York: Routledge (original version in French 2001).

Gaudreault, A., & Marion, P. (2002). The cinema as a model for the genealogy of media. *Convergence: The International Journal of Research into New Media Technologies, 8*(4), 12–18.

Gaudreault, A., & Marion, P. (2005). A Medium is always born twice. *Early Popular Visual Culture, 3*(1), 3–15.

Gaudreault, A., & Marion, P. (2013). Measuring the 'double birth' model against the digital age. *Early Popular Visual Culture, 11*(2), 158–177.

Gelenter, D. (1998). *The Aestetichs of Computing*. London: Weidenfeld & Nicolson.

Gerovitch, S. (2008). InterNyet: Why the Soviet Union did not build a nationwide computer network. *History and Technology, 24* (4): 335–350.

Geser, H. (2004). Towards a Sociological Theory of the Mobile Phone. In *Sociology in Switzerland: Sociology of the mobile phone*. Retrieved from http://socio.ch/mobile/t_geser1.pdf.

Gillespie, T. (2007). *Wired Shut: Copyright and the Shape of Digital Culture*. Cambridge, MA: The MIT Press.

Gillespie, T., Boczkowski, P.J., & Foot, K.A. (Eds.). (2014). *Media Technologies: Essays on Communication, Materiality and Society*. Cambridge, MA: The MIT Press.

Gillies, J., & Cailliau, R. (2000). *How the Web Was Born: The Story of the World Wide Web*. Oxford: Oxford University Press.

Gillmor, D. (2006). *We the Media: Grassroots Journalism by the People, for the People*. Sebastopol, CA: O'Reilly Media.

Gilroy, P. (1993). *The Black Atlantic: Modernity and Double Consciousness*. Cambridge, MA: Harvard University Press.

Gitelman, L. (2006). *Always Already New: Media, History and the Data of Culture*. Cambridge, MA: The MIT Press.

Gitelman, L., & Pingree, G.B. (Eds.). (2003). *New Media, 1740-1915*. Cambridge, MA: The MIT Press.

Gleick, J. (2011). *The Information: A History, a Theory, a Flood*. New York: Pantheon Books.

Glenn, J. (2006). A brief history of mobile telephony: The story of phones and cars. *Southern Review: Communication, Politics & Culture, 38*(3), 43-60.

Goddard, G. (2010). *DAB Digital Radio: Licensed to Fail*. London: Radio Books.

Goggin, G. (2006). *Cell Phone Culture. Mobile Technology in Everyday Life*. London: Routledge.

Goggin, G. (2011). *Global Mobile Media*. London: Routledge.

Goggin, G. (2012). Google phone rising: The Android and the politics of open source. *Continuum, 26*(5), 741-752.

Goggin, G., & McLelland, M. (Eds.). (2017). *Routledge Companion to Global Internet Histories*. New York: Routledge.

Goldsmith, J., & Wu, T. (2006). *Who Controls the Internet? Illusions of a Borderless World*. Oxford: Oxford University Press.

Goldstine, H.H. (1972). *The Computer from Pascal to Von Neumann*. Princeton, NJ: Princeton University Press.

Gómez Cruz, E., & Lehmuskallio, A. (Eds.). (2016). *Digital Photography and Everyday Life: Empirical Studies on Material Visual Practices*. London: Routledge.

Gómez Cruz, E., & Meyer, E.T. (2012). Creation and control in the photographic process: iPhones and the emerging fifth moment of photography. *Photographies, 5*(2), 203-221.

Gonzalez, G.R., & Cox, A. (2012). Redefining Participation in Online Communities: Some Neglected Topics. In H. Li (Ed.), *Virtual Community Participation and Motivation: Cross Disciplinary Theories* (pp. 72-89). Hershey, PA: IGI Global.

Goody, J. (1986). *The Logic of Writing and the Organization of Society*. Cambridge, MA: Cambridge University Press.

Google (2016). *Employer information Report 2016*. Internal Report, 29 September.

Gotkin, K. (2014). When computers were amateur. *IEEE Annals of the History of Computing, 36*(2), 4-14.

Gottfried, J., & Shearer, E. (2016). *News use across social media platforms 2016*. Pew Research Center, May 26 Retrieved from www.journalism.org/2016/05/26/news-use-across-social-media-platforms-2016/.

Gow, G., & Smith, R. (2006). *Mobile and Wireless Communications: An Introduction*. Maidenhead, UK: Open University Press.

Graetz, J.M. (1981). The origin of Spacewar. *Creative Computing, 7*(8), 56-67.

Gramsci, A. (1977). *Selections from Political Writings, 1910-1920*. London: Lawrence & Wishart (original Italian version 1948).

Green, N., & Haddon, L. (2009). *Mobile Communications: An Introduction to New Media*. Oxford: Berg.

Greenstein, S. (2015). *How the Internet Became Commercial: Innovation, Privatization, and the Birth of a New Network*. Princeton, NJ: Princeton University Press.

Griset, P., & Schafer, V. (2011). Hosting the World Wide Web Consortium for Europe: From CERN to INRIA. *History and Technology, 27*(3), 353–370.

Groening, S. (2010). From "a box in the theater of the world" to "the world as your living room": Cellular phones, television and mobile privatization. *New Media & Society, 12*(8), 1331–1347.

Habermas, J. (1989). *The Structural Transformation of the Public Sphere: An Inquiry into a Category of Bourgeois Society*. Cambridge, MA: The MIT Press (original German version 1962).

Haddon, L. (1988). The home computer. The making of a consumer electronic. *Science as Culture, 1*(2), 7–51.

Hafner, K., & Matthew, L. (1996). *Where Wizards Stay Up Late: The Origins of the Internet*. New York: Simon & Schuster.

Hahn, H.P., & Kibora, L. (2008). The domestication of the mobile phone: Oral society and new ICT in Burkina Faso. *The Journal of Modern African Studies, 46*, 87–109.

Hai-Jew, S. (2017). Flickering Emotions: Feeling-Based Associations from Related Tag Networks on Flickr. In S. Hai-Jew (Ed.), *Social Media Data Extraction and Content Analysis* (pp. 296–341). Hershey, PA: IGI Global.

Halfaker, A., Gieger, R.S., Morgan, J., & Riedl, J. (2013). The rise and decline of an open collaboration system: How Wikipedia's reaction to sudden popularity is causing its decline. *American Behavioral Scientist, 57*(5), 664–688.

Hall, S. (1980). Encoding and Decoding in the Television Discourse. In S. Hall, D. Hobson, A. Lowe, & P. Willis (Eds.). *Culture, Media, Language* (pp. 128–138). London: Hutchinson (Original work published 1973).

Hall, S. (1990). *Cultural Identity and Diaspora*. In J. Rutherford (Ed.), *Identity: Community, Culture, Difference* (pp. 222–237). London: Lawrence & Wishart.

Hallin, D.C., & Mancini, P. (2004). *Comparing Media Systems: Three Models of Media and Politics*. Cambridge and New York: Cambridge University Press.

Han, S. (2011). *Web 2.0*. London: Routledge.

Hand, M. (2012). *Ubiquitous Photography*. Cambridge: Polity Press.

Haring, K. (2008). *Ham Radio's Technical Culture*. Cambridge, MA: The MIT Press.

Harrison, A.K. (2006). 'Cheaper than a CD, plus we really mean it': Bay Area underground hip hop tapes as subcultural artefacts'. *Popular Music, 25*(2), 283–301.

Harwit, E., & Clark, D. (2001). Shaping the Internet in China. Evolution of political control over network infrastructure and content. *Asian Survey, 41*(3), 377–408.

Hasebrink, U., & Hepp, A. (2017). How to research cross-media practices? Investigating media repertoires and media ensembles. *Convergence. The International Journal of Research into New Media Technologies, 23*(4), 362–377.

Hauben, J. (2005). "Across the Great Wall": The China-Germany e-mail connection 1987–1994. *The Amateur Computerist, 13*(1): 25–28.

Hauben, R. (2000). ARPANET Mailing lists and usenet newsgroups creating an open and scientific process for technology development and diffusion. *The Amateur Computerist, 10*(1): 28–35.

Heineman, D.S. (2014). Public memory and gamer identity: Retrogaming as nostalgia. *Journal of Games Criticism, 1*(1), 1–24.

Herkman, J. (2012). Introduction: Intermediality as a Theory and Methodology. In J. Herkman, T. Hujanen, & P. Oinonen (Eds.), *Intermediality and Media Change* (pp. 10–27). Tampere, Finland: Tampere University Press.

Herkman, J., Hujanen, T., & Oinonen, P. (Eds.). (2012). *Intermediality and Media Change.* Tampere, Finland: Tampere University Press.

Herman, E.S., & McChesney R. W. (1997). *The Global Media: The New Missionaries of Corporate Capitalism.* London and Washington, DC: Cassell.

Hesmondhalgh, D. (1997). Post-Punk's attempt to democratise the music industry: The success and failure of Rough Trade. *Popular Music, 16*(3), 255–274.

Hesmondhalgh, D. (2007). *The Cultural Industries.* London: Sage.

Hicks, M. (2017). *Programmed Inequality: How Britain Discarded Women Technologists and Lost Its Edge in Computing.* Cambridge, MA: The MIT Press.

Higgins, D. (2001). Intermedia. *Leonardo, 34*(1) 49–54 (Original work published 1966).

Hilbert, M. (2016). The bad news is that the digital access divide is here to stay: Domestically installed bandwidths among 172 countries for 1986–2014. *Telecommunications Policy, 40*(6), 567–581.

Hillebrand, F. (Ed.). (2002). *GSM and UMTS: The Creation of Global Mobile Communications.* Chichester, UK and New York: Wiley.

Hills, J., & Michalis, M. (2000). The Internet: A challenge to public service broadcasting? *International Communication Gazette, 62*(6), 477–493.

Hiltzik, M. (2000). *Dealers of Lightning. Xerox Parc and the Dawn of the Computer Age.* New York: HarperCollins.

Himanen, P. (2001). *The Hacker Ethic and the Spirit of the Information Age.* New York: Random House.

Hirsch, P.M. (1972). Processing fads and fashions: An organization-set analysis of cultural industry systems. *American Journal of Sociology, 77*(4), 639–659.

Hjorth, L. (2005). Locating Mobility: Practices of co-presence and the persistence of the postal metaphor in SMS/MMS mobile phone customization in Melbourne. *The Fibreculture Journal, 6.*

Hodges, A. (1983). *Alan Turing: The Enigma.* New York: Touchstone-book.

Horst H.A., & Miller, D. (2006). *The Cell Phone: An Anthropology of Communication.* Oxford and New York: Berg.

Hu, T.-H. (2015). *A Prehistory of the Cloud.* Cambridge, MA: The MIT Press.

Hughes, T.P. (2004). *Human-Built World: How to Think about Technology and Culture.* Chicago, IL: University of Chicago Press.

Huhtamo, E., & Parikka, J. (Eds.). (2011). *Media Archaeology: Approaches, Applications, and Implications.* Berkeley, CA: University of California Press.

Hyysalo, S., Jensen, T.E., & Oudshoorn, N. (Eds.). (2016). *The New Production of Users: Changing Innovation Collectives and Involvement Strategies.* London and New York: Routledge.

IDATE. (2017). *DigitalWorld Yearbook 2016.* Montpellier, France: Idate.

Ifrah, G. (2001). *The Universal History of Computing: From the Abacus to the Quantum Computer.* New York: John Wiley & Sons.

Immink, K.A. (1998). The compact disc story. *Journal of The Audio Engineering Society, 46*(5), 458–465.

Information Infrastructure Task Force. (1993, September 15). *National In-Formation Infrastructure Agenda for Action.* Washington, DC: National Telecommunications and Information Administration.

Innis, H.A. (1951). *The Bias of Communication*. Toronto, Canada: University of Toronto Press.

Japan Computer Usage Development Institute. (1972). *The Plan for an Information Society: A National Goal Towards Year 2000*. Tokyo, Japan: Japan Computer Usage Development Institute.

Jasanoff, S. (Ed.). (2004). *States of Knowledge: The Co-Production of Science and the Social Order*. London: Routledge.

Jauert, P. (2017). Introduction: Symposium on digital radio: Strategies and visions. *Journal of Radio & Audio Media, 24*(1), 3-6.

Jenkins, H. (1992). *Textual Poachers: Television Fans and Participatory Culture*. London: Routledge.

Jenkins, H. (1999). The Work of Theory in the Age of Digital Transformation. In T. Miller & R. Stam (Eds.), *A Companion to Film Theory* (pp. 234-261). Malden, MA: Blackwell.

Jenkins, H. (2006). *Convergence Culture: Where Old and New Media Collide*. New York: New York University Press.

Jenkins, H., & Ford, S. (2013). *Spreadable Media: Creating Value and Meaning in a Networked Culture*. New York: New York University Press.

Jin, D.Y. (2017). *Smartland Korea: Mobile Communication, Culture, and Society*. Ann Arbor, MI: University of Michigan Press.

John, N. (2017). The Emergence of The Internet Service Provider (ISP) Industry in Israel. In G. Goggin & M. McLelland (Eds.), *Routledge Companion to Global Internet Histories* (pp. 90-104). New York: Routledge.

John, R.R. (1994). American Historians and the Concept of the Communications Revolution. In L. Bud-Frierman (Ed.), *Information Acumen* (pp. 98-110). London: Routledge.

Johns, A. (2009). *Piracy: The Intellectual Property Wars from Gutenberg to Gates*. Chicago, IL: University of Chicago Press.

Johns, A. (2010). *Death of a Pirate: British Radio and the Making of the Information Age*. New York: Norton and Company.

Jordan, M.F. (2013). Obama's iPod: Popular music and the perils of postpolitical populism. *Popular Communication, 11*(2), 99-115.

Katz, J.E. (2006). *Magic in the Air: Mobile Communication and the Transformation of Social Life*. New Brunswick, NJ: Transaction Publishers.

Katz, J.E., & Aakhus, M.A. (Eds.). (2002). *Perpetual Contact: Mobile Communication, Private Talk, Public Performance*. Cambridge: Cambridge University Press.

Kaun, A., & Schwarzenegger, C. (2014). "No media, less life?" Online disconnection in mediatized worlds. *First Monday, 19*(11).

Kay, A., & Goldberg, A. (1977). Personal dynamic media. *Computer, 10*(3), 31-41.

Keen, A. (2007). *The Cult of The Amateur: How Today's Internet Is Killing Our Culture*. New York: Doubleday/Currency.

Kelty, C.M. (2008). *Two Bits: The Cultural Significance of Free Software*. Durham, NC: Duke University Press.

Kibora, L. (2009). Téléphonie mobile. L'appropriation du SMS par une société de l'oralité. In M. de Bruijn, F. Nyamnjoh & I. Brinkman (Eds.), *Mobile Phones: The News Talking Drums of Everyday Africa* (pp. 110-124). Bamenda, Cameroon: Langaa and Leiden, the Netherlands: African Studies Centre.

Kim, S.J. (2016). A repertoire approach to cross-platform media use behavior. *New Media & Society, 18*(3), 353-372.

Kirkpatrick, D. (2011). *The Facebook Effect: The Inside Story of the Company that Is Connecting the World*. New York: Simon and Schuster.

Kirriemuir, J. (2006). A history of digital games. In J. Rutter & J. Bryce (Eds.), *Understanding Digital Games* (pp. 21-35). London: Sage.

Knight, P.T. (2014). *The Internet in Brazil. Origins, Strategy, Development, and Governance*. Bloominghton, IL: AuthorHouse.

Kozak, N. (2015). "If you build it, they will come": Lusk, Wyoming, and the information highway imaginaire, 1989-1999. *Information & Culture, 50*(2), 237-256.

Kramer, R. (1993). The politics of information: A study of the French Minitel system. In J.R. Schement & B.D. Ruben (Eds.), *Between Communication and Information, vol. 4* (pp. 453-486). New Brunswick, NJ: Transaction Publishers.

Kuwahara, Y. (Ed.). (2014). *Korean Popular Culture in Global Context*. London: Palgrave.

Lally, E. (2002). *At Home with Computers*. Oxford: Berg.

Landow, G.P. (1991). *HyperText: The Convergence of Contemporary Critical Theory and Technology*. Baltimore, MD: Johns Hopkins University Press.

Lasen, A. (2005). History Repeating? A Comparison of the Launch and Uses of Fixed and Mobile Phones. In L. Hamill & A. Lasen (Eds.), *Mobile World. Past, Present and Future* (pp. 29-60). London: Springer.

Latour, B. (1987). *Science in Action: How to Follow Scientists and Engineers through Society*. Cambridge, MA: Harvard University Press.

Latour, B. (1993). *We have Never Been Modern*. New York: Harvester Wheatsheaf (Original French version 1991).

Latour, B. (2005). *Reassembling the Social*. Cambridge: Oxford University Press.

Law, J. (1987). Technology and heterogeneous engineering: The case of Portuguese expansion. In W.E. Bijker, T.P. Hughes & T. Pinch (Eds.), *The Social Construction of Technological Systems: New Directions in the Sociology and History of Technology* (pp. 111-134). Cambridge, MA: The MIT Press.

Lax, S., Ala-Fossi, M., Jauert, P., & Shaw, H. (2008). DAB: The future of radio? The development of digital radio in four European countries. *Media, Culture & Society, 30*(2), 151-166.

Lebert, M. (2009). *A Short History of Ebooks*. Toronto: University of Toronto.

Lee, C.S., & Kuwahara, Y. (2014). Gangnam Style as Format: When a Localized Korean Song Meets a Global Audience. In Y. Kuwahara (Ed.), *Korean Popular Culture in Global Context* (pp. 101-116). London: Palgrave.

Lembke, J. (2003). *Competition for Technological Leadership. EU Policy for High Technology*. Cheltenham, UK: Edward Elgar Publishing.

Lessig, L. (2004). *Free Culture. The Nature and Future of Creativity*. New York: Penguin Books.

Lévy, P. (1997). *Collective Intelligence: Mankind's Emerging World in Cyberspace*. Cambridge, MA: Perseus Publishing (Original French version 1994).

Levy, S. (1984). *Hackers: Heroes of the Computer Revolution*. New York: Doubleday.

Li, S.L., Lin, Y.-R., Hou-Ming Huang, A. (2017). A Brief History of Taiwanese Internet. The BBS Culture. In G. Goggin & M. McLelland (Eds.), *Routledge Companion to Global Internet Histories* (pp. 182-196). New York: Routledge.

Licklider, J.C., & Taylor, R.W. (1968). The computer as a communication device. *Science and Technology, 76*(2), 1-3.

Light, J.S. (1999). When computers were women. *Technology and Culture, 40*(3), 455-483.

Ling, R. (2004). *The Mobile Connection. The Cell Phone's Impact on Society*. San Francisco, CA: Morgan Kaufmann.

Ling, R. (2008). *New Tech, New Ties: How Mobile Communication is Reshaping Social Cohesion*. Cambridge, MA: The MIT Press.

Ling, R., & Horst, H.A. (2011). Mobile communication in the global south. *New Media & Society, 13*(3), 363-374.

Lipartito, K. (2003). Picturephone and the Information Age: The Social Meaning of Failure. *Technology and Culture, 44*(1), 50-81.

Lister, M. (Ed.). (1995). *The Photographic Image in Digital Culture*. London and New York: Routledge.

Lister, M. (2013). Introduction to the 2nd Edition. In M. Lister (Ed.), *The Photographic Image in Digital Culture* (pp. 1-21). London: Routledge.

Lister, M., Dovey, J., Giddings, S., Grant, I., & Kelly, K. (2009). *New Media: a Critical Introduction*. London: Routledge.

Liu, J. (2010). The tough reality of copyright piracy: A case study of the music industry in China. *Cardozo Arts & Entertainment Law Journal, 27*(3), 621-661.

Lucas, H.C., & Goh, J.M. (2009). Disruptive technology: How Kodak missed the digital photography revolution. *The Journal of Strategic Information Systems, 18*(1), 46-55.

Lyon, D. (1994). *The Electronic Eye: The Rise of Surveillance Society*. Cambridge: Polity Press and Oxford: Blackwell.

Lyon, D. (2015). *Surveillance after Snowden*. Cambridge: Polity Press

McKenzie, D., & Wajcman, J. (1986). *The Social Shaping of Technology*. Milton Keynes, UK: Open University Press.

McLuhan, H.M. (1962). *The Gutenberg Galaxy: The Making of Typographic Man*. Toronto, Canada: University of Toronto Press.

McLuhan, H.M. (2004). *Understanding Me: Lectures and Interviews*. Toronto, Canada: McLelland & Steward.

McQuillan, J. (1980). A retrospective on ARPANET electronic mail. *ACM SIGOA Newsletter Archive, 1*(1), 8-9.

Magaudda, P. (2011). When materiality 'bites back'. Digital music consumption practices in the age of dematerialization. *Journal of Consumer Culture, 11*(1), 15-36.

Magaudda, P. (2012). What Happens to Materiality in Digital Virtual Consumption? In M. Molesworth & J. Denegri-Knott (Eds.), *Digital Virtual Consumption* (pp. 111-126). London: Routledge.

Magaudda, P. (2015), Apple's iconicity: Digital society, consumer culture and the iconic power of technology. *Sociologica, (9)*1.

Malamud, C. (1997). *A World's Fair for the Global Village*. Cambridge, MA: The MIT Press.

Malinowski, B. (1948). Myth in Primitive Psychology. In B. Malinowski (Ed.), *Magic, Science and Religion and Other Essays* (pp. 72-120). Boston, MA: Beacon Press and Glencoe, IL: Free Press.

Manley, L., & Holley, R.P. (2012). History of the ebook: The changing face of books. *Technical Services Quarterly, 29*(4), 292-311.

Manovich, L. (1999). What is Digital Cinema? In P. Lunenfeld (Ed.), *The Digital Dialectic: New Essays on New Media* (pp. 173-192). Cambridge, MA: The MIT Press.

Manovich, L. (2001). *The Language of New Media*. Cambridge, MA: The MIT Press.

Mansell, R. (2012). *Imagining the Internet: Communication, Innovation, and Governance*. Oxford: Oxford University Press.

Mansell, R. (2014). Here Comes the Revolution: The European Digital Agenda. In K. Donders, C. Pauwels, & J. Loisen (Eds.), *The Palgrave Handbook of European Media Policy* (pp. 202-217). Houndmills, UK: Palgrave Macmillan.

Manuel, P. (2014). The regional North Indian popular music industry in 2014: From cassette culture to cyberculture. *Popular Music, 33*(3), 389-412.

Markoff, J. (2005). *What the Dormouse Said: How the Sixties Counterculture Shaped the Personal Computer Industry*. New York: Penguin.

Mariscal, J., & Bonina, C.M. (2008). Mobile Communication in Mexico: Policy and Popular Dimensions. In J. Katz (Ed.), *Handbook of Mobile Communication Studies* (pp. 65–78). Cambridge, MA: The MIT Press.

Marshall, L. (2005). *Bootlegging. Romanticism and Copyright in the Music Industry*. London: Sage.

Martin, E. (1992). *The Calculating Machines*. Cambridge, MA: The MIT Press (original German version 1925).

Marvin, C. (1988). *When Old Technologies Were New: Thinking about Electric Communications in the Late Nineteenth Century*. New York: Oxford University Press.

Matsuda, M. (2005). Discourses of Keitai in Japan. In M. Ito, D. Okabe, & M. Matsuda (Eds.), *Personal, Portable, Pedestrian: Mobile Phones in Japanese Life* (pp. 19–39). Cambridge, MA: The MIT Press.

Medina, E. (2011). *Cybernetic Revolutionaries: Technology and Politics in Allende's Chile*. Cambridge, MA: The MIT Press.

Menke, M., & Schwarzenegger, C. (2016). Media, Communication and Nostalgia. Finding a better tomorrow in the yesterday? *media&time, 4*, 2–5.

Meyrowitz, J. (1985). *No Sense of Place: The Impact of Electronic Media on Social Behavior*. Oxford: Oxford University Press.

Miège, B. (1989). *The Capitalization of Cultural Production*. New York: International General Editions.

Millard, A. (2005). *America on Record. A History of Recorded Sound*. Cambridge, MA: Cambridge University Press.

Minniti, S. (2016). Polaroid 2.0. Photo-objects and analogue instant photography in the digital age. *Tecnoscienza: Italian Journal of Science & Technology Studies, 7*(1), 17–44.

Mirrlees, T. (2013). *Global Entertainment Media, Between Cultural Imperialism and Cultural Globalization*. London: Routledge.

Mirzoeff, N. (2016). *How to See the World: An Introduction to Images, from Self-portraits to Selfies, Maps to Movies, and More*. New York: Basic Books.

Mitchell, W.J. (1992). *The Reconfigured Eye: Visual Truth in the Post-Photographic Era*. Cambridge, MA: The MIT Press.

Mittell, J. (2009). Sites of participation: Wiki fandom and the case of Lostpedia. *Transformative Works & Cultures, 3*.

Moe, H., & Van den Bulck, H. (Eds.). (2016). *Teletext in Europe From the Analog to the Digital Era*. Goteborg: Nordicom.

Montfort, N., & Bogost, I. (2009). *Racing the Beam: The Atari Video Computer System*. Cambridge, MA: The MIT Press.

Moody, G. (2001). *Rebel Code. Linux and the Open Source Revolution*. London: Basic Books.

Moor, J.H. (Ed.). (2003). *The Turing Test – the Elusive Standard of Artificial Intelligence*. Dordrecht: Springer.

Moores, S. (1993). *Interpreting Audiences: The Ethnography of Media Consumption*. London: Sage.

Morawczynski, O., & Pickens, M. (2009). *Poor People Using mobile financial services: Observations on customer usage and impact from M-PESA*. Retrieved from www.cgap.org/sites/default/files/CGAP-Brief-Poor-People-Using-Mobile-Financial-Services-Observations-on-Customer-Usage-and-Impact-from-M-PESA-Aug-2009.pdf.

Morley, D. (1999). The 'Nationwide' Audience: Structure and Decoding. In D. Morley & C. Brunsdon, *The Nationwide Television Studies,* London: Routledge (original work published 1980).

Morley, D. (2006). *Globalisation and Cultural Imperialism Reconsidered: Old Questions in New Guises.* In J. Curran & D. Morley (Eds.), *Media and Cultural Theory* (pp. 30-43). London: Routledge.

Morozov, E. (2011). *The Net Delusion: The Dark Side of Internet Freedom.* New York: Public Affairs.

Morris, J. (2011). Sounds in the cloud: Cloud computing and the digital music commodity. *First Monday, 16*(5).

Mosco, V. (1998). Myth-ing links: Power and community on the communication highway. *The Information Society, 14*(1), 57-62.

Mosco, V. (2004). *The Digital Sublime: Myth, Power, and Cyberspace.* Cambridge, MA: The MIT Press.

Mosco, V. (2009). *The Political Economy of Communication.* London: Sage.

Mounier-Kuhn, P.-E. (1994). French computer manufacturers and the component industry, 1952-1972. *History & Technology, 11*(2), 195-216.

Mumford, L. (1964). Authoritarian and democratic technics. *Technology & Culture, 5*(1), 1-8.

Mumford, L. (1970). *The Myth of the Machine.* New York: Harcourt Brace Jovanovich.

Murdoch, G., & Golding, P. (2005). Culture, Communications and Political Economy. In J. Curran & M. Gurevitch (Eds.), *Mass Media and Society–4th Edition* (pp. 60-83). London: Arnold.

Murray, J.B. (2001). *The Wireless Nation: The Frenzied Launch of the Cellular Revolution in America.* New York: Perseus Publishing.

Musiani, F., & Méadel, C. (2016). "Reclaiming the Internet" with distributed architectures: An introduction. *First Monday, 21*(12).

Musiani, F., & Schafer, V. (2011). Le modèle internet en question (années 1970-2010). *Flux, 3*(85-86), 62-71.

Napoli, P.M. (2010). *Audience Evolution: New Technologies and the Transformation of Media Audiences.* New York: Columbia University Press.

Natale, S. (2016). There are no old media. *Journal of Communication, 66*(4), 585-603.

Naughton, J. (1999). *A Brief History of the Future: The Origins of the Internet.* London: Weidenfeld & Nicolson.

Negro, G. (2017). *The Internet in China. From Infrastructure to a Nascent Civil Society.* New York: Palgrave Macmillan.

Negroponte, N. (1995). *Being Digital.* New York: Knopf.

Nelson, T.H. (1974). *Computer Lib: You Can and Must Understand Computers Now / Dream Machines: New Freedoms Through Computer Screens–A Minority Report.* Self-published.

Nerone, J. (2006). The future of communication history. *Critical Studies in Media Communication, 23*(3), 254-262.

Niemeyer, K. (Ed.). (2014). *Media and Nostalgia. Yearning for the Past, Present and Future.* London: Palgrave Macmillan.

Nolan, R. (2001). *Dot Vertigo: Doing Business in a Permeable World.* New York: John Wiley & Sons.

Norris, P. (2001). *Digital Divide: Civic Engagement, Information Poverty, and the Internet Worldwide.* Cambridge, MA: Cambridge University Press.

Nyce, J.M., & Kahn, P. (1991). *From Memex to Hypertext: Vannevar Bush and the Mind's Machine*. Boston, MA: Academic Press.

O'Malley, T. (2002). Media History and Media Studies: Aspects of the development of the study of media history in the UK 1945-2000. *Media History, 8*(2), 155-173.

O'Neill, B. (2009). DAB Eureka-147: A European vision for digital radio. *New Media & Society, 11*(1-2), 261-278.

O'Neill, B., Ala-Fossi, M., Jauert, P., Lax, S., Nyre, L., & Shaw, H. (2010). *Digital Radio in Europe. Technologies, Industries and Cultures*. Bristol, UK: Intellect.

O'Neill, R. (2016). *Digital Character Development: Theory and Practice*. Boca Raton, FL: CRC Press.

OECD. (2013). *OECD Communications Outlook 2013*. Paris: OECD Publishing.

OECD. (2015). *Digital Economy Outlook 2015*. Paris: OECD Publishing.

Oh, I. (2013). The globalization of K-pop: Korea's place in the global music industry. *Korea Observer, 44*(3), 389-409.

Ong, W.J. (1982). *Orality and Literacy: The Technologizing of the Word*. London: Routledge.

Ortoleva, P. (1995). *Mediastoria: Comunicazione e cambiamento sociale nel mondo contemporaneo*. Parma, Italy: Pratiche.

Oudshoorn, N., & Pinch, T. (Eds.). (2003). *How Users Matter. The Co-construction of Technologies and Users*. Cambridge, MA: The MIT Press.

Parikka, J. (2012). *What is Media Archaeology?* Cambridge: Polity Press.

Pariser, E. (2011). *The Filter Bubble: What the Internet is Hiding from You*. New York: Penguin Press.

Park, D.W., Jankowski, N.W., & Jones, S. (Eds.). (2001). *The Long History of New Media. Technology, Historiography and Contextualising Newness*. New York: Peter Lang.

Park, D.W., & Pooley, J. (Eds.). (2008). *The History of Media and Communication Research. Contested Memories*. New York: Peter Lang.

Parks, L., & Starosielski, N. (2015). *Signal Traffic: Critical Studies of Media Infrastructures*. Indiana, IL: University of Illinois Press.

Peil, C. (2011). *Mobilkommunikation in Japan: Zur kulturellen Infrastruktur der Handy-Aneignung*. Bielefeld: Transcript.

Pelkmans, J. (2001). The GSM standard: Explaining a success story. *Journal of European Public Policy, 8*(3), 432-453.

Pellegrino, G. (2005) Thickening the frame: cross-theoretical accounts of contexts inside and around technology. *Bulletin of Science, Technology & Society, 25*(1), 63-72.

Pereira, C. (2016). *Informatics Education in Europe: Institutions, Degrees, Students, Positions, Salaries. Key Data 2010-2015*, Zurich: Informatics Europe.

Peters, B. (2009). And lead us not into thinking the new is new: A bibliographic case for new media history. *New Media & Society, 11*(1/2), 13-30.

Peters, B. (2016a). Digital. In B. Peters (Ed.), *Digital Keywords: A Vocabulary of Information Society and Culture* (pp. 93-108). Princeton, NJ: Princeton University Press.

Peters, B. (2016b). *How Not to Network a Nation: The Uneasy History of the Soviet Internet*. Cambridge, MA: The MIT Press.

Peters, J.D. (2008). History as a Communication Problem. In B. Zelizer (Ed.), *Explorations in Communication and History* (pp. 19-34). London: Sage.

Peters, J.D. (2015). *The Marvelous Clouds: Toward a Philosophy of Elemental Media*. Chicago, IL: University of Chicago Press.

Peukert, C., Claussen, J., & Kretschmer, T. (2017). Piracy and box office movie revenues: Evidence from Megaupload. *International Journal of Industrial Organization, 52*, 188-215.

Pinch, T., & Bijker, W.E. (1987). The Social Construction of Facts and Artifacts: Or How the Sociology of Science and the Sociology of Technology Might Benefit Each Other. In W.E. Bijker, T.P. Hughes & T. Pinch (Eds.), *The Social Construction of Technological Systems: New directions in the Sociology and History of Technology* (pp. 17-50). Cambridge, MA: The MIT Press.

Pinch, T., & Trocco, F. (2002). *Analog Days: The Invention and Impact of the Moog Synthesizer*. Cambridge, MA: Harvard University Press.

Plantin, J.-C., Lagoze, C., Edwards, P.N., & Sandvig, C. (2018). Infrastructure studies meet platform studies in the age of Google and Facebook. *New Media & Society, 20*(1), 293-310.

PMA. (2005). *Photo Industry 2005: Review and Forecast*. Jackson, MI: PMA.

Poster, M. (1995). *The Second Media Age*. Cambridge: Polity Press.

Poster, M. (2007). Manifesto for a History of the Media. In K. Jenkins, S. Morgan, & A. Munslow (Eds.), *Manifestos for History* (pp. 39-49). New York and Abingdon, UK: Routledge.

Priest, E. (2014). Copyright extremophiles: Do creative industries thrive or just survive in China's high piracy environment? *Harvard Journal of Law & Technology, 27*(2), 467-541.

Pugh, E.W. (1995). *Building IBM: Shaping an Industry and Its Technology*. Cambridge, MA: The MIT Press.

Pype, K. (2016). "[Not] talking like a Motorola": Mobile phone practices and politics of masking and unmasking in postcolonial Kinshasa. *Journal of the Royal Anthropological Institute, 22*(3), 633-652.

Rabinovich, Z.L. (2011). The Work of Sergey Alekseevich Lebedev in Kiev and Its Subsequent Influence on Further Scientific Progress There. In J. Impagliazzo & E. Proydakov (Eds.), *Perspectives on Soviet and Russian Computing* (pp. 1-5). Dordrecht: Springer.

Rafael, V.L. (2003). The cell phone and the crowd: Messianic politics in the contemporary Philippines. *Public Culture, 15*(3), 399-425.

Ragnedda, M., & Glenn, W.M. (2013). *The Digital Divide: The Internet and Social Inequality in International Perspective*. Abingdon, UK: Routledge.

Ren, X. (2016). Copyright, media and modernization in China: A historical review, 1890-2015. *Interactions: Studies in Communication & Culture, 7*(3), 311-326.

Rheingold, H. (1993). *The Virtual Community: Homesteading on the Electronic Frontier*. Reading, MA: Addison-Wesley Pub. Co.

Richeri, G. (1995). Le 'autostrade dell'informazione'. Modelli e problemi. *Problemi dell'Informazione, 1*, 25-38.

Ricker Schulte, S. (2013). *Cached: Decoding the Internet in global popular culture*. New York: New York University Press.

Ritchin, F. (2009). *After Photography*. New York: W.W. Norton.

Rodowick, D.N. (2007). *The Virtual Life of Film*. Cambridge, MA: Harvard University Press.

Rojas, R. (2000). The Architecture of Konrad Zuse's Early Computing Machines. In R. Rojas & U. Hashagen (Eds.), *The First Computers: History and Architectures* (pp. 237-261). Cambridge, MA: The MIT Press.

Roscoe, T. (1999). The construction of the World Wide Web audience. *Media Culture & Society, 21*(5), 673-684.

Rosenzweig, R. (1998). Wizards, bureaucrats, warriors, and hackers: Writing the history of the internet. *The American Historical Review, 103*(5), 1530-1552.

Rudin, R. (2006). The development of DAB digital radio in the UK. The battle for control of a new technology in an old medium. *Convergence, 12*(2), 163-178.

Russell, A.L. (2014). *Open Standards and the Digital Age: History, Ideology, and Networks.* Cambridge, MA: Cambridge University Press.

Russell, A.L., & Schafer, V. (2014). In the shadow of ARPANET and Internet: Louis Pouzin and the Cyclades network in the 1970s. *Technology and Culture, 55*(4), 880-907.

Ryan, J. (2010). *A History of the Internet and the Digital Future.* London: Reaktion Books.

Said, E. (1978). *Orientalism.* New York: Vintage.

Saltz, J. (2014, February 3). Art at arm's length: A history of the selfie. *Vulture*, January, 26. Retrieved from www.vulture.com/2014/01/history-of-the-selfie.html.

Sanger, L. (2005). The Early History of Nupedia and Wikipedia: A Memoir. In C. DiBona, D. Cooper, & M. Stone (Eds.), *Open Sources 2.0: The Continuing Evolution.* Sebastopol, CA: O'Reilly.

Sarpong, D., Dong, S., & Appiah, G. (2016). "Vinyl never say die": The re-incarnation, adoption and diffusion of retro-technologies. *Technological Forecasting and Social Change*, 103, 109-118.

Sawhney, H., & Lee, S. (2005). Arenas of innovation: Understanding new configurational potentialities of communication technologies. *Media, Culture & Society, 27*(3), 391-414.

Scannell, P. (1989). Public Service Broadcasting: History of a Concept. In A. Goodwin & G. Whannel (Eds.), *Understanding Television* (pp. 11-29). London: Routledge.

Schafer, V., & Thierry, B.G. (2012). *Le Minitel: l'enfance Numérique de la France.* Paris: Nuvis.

Schudson, M. (2011). *The Sociology of News.* New York: Norton & Company.

Scott, L.M. (1991). 'For the Rest of Us': A reader-oriented interpretation of Apple's '1984' commercial. *Journal of Popular Culture, 25*(1) 67-81.

Shahin, J. (2006), A European history of the Internet. *Science and Public Policy, 33*(9), 681-693.

Shome, R., & Hegde, R.S. (2002). Postcolonial approaches to communication theory: Chartering the terrain, engaging the intersections. *Communication Theory, 12*(3), 249-270.

Shoup, R. (2001). SuperPaint: An early frame buffer graphics system. *Annals of the History of Computing Archive, 23*(2), 32-37.

Sigurdson, J. (2001). *Wap off–Origin, Failure and Future.* The Stockholm School of Economics, Working Paper No. 135. Retrieved from www2.hhs.se/eijswp/135.pdf.

Siles, I. (2011). From online filter to web format: Articulating materiality and meaning in the early history of blogs. *Social Studies of Science, 41*(5), 737-758.

Silverstone, R., & Hirsh, E. (Eds.). (1992). *Consuming Technologies: Media and Information in Domestic Spaces.* London: Routledge.

Simonson, P.,& Park, D.W. (Eds.). (2016). *The International History of Communication Study.* New York: Routledge.

Singel, R. (2009, May 3). Video killed the video store. *The Wired.*

Smith, M.D., & Telang, R. (2012, August 19). Assessing the Academic Literature Regarding the Impact of Media Piracy on Sales. *SSRN*. Retrieved from https://ssrn.com/abstract=2132153 or http://dx.doi.org/10.2139/ssrn.2132153.

Söderberg, J. (2015). *Hacking Capitalism: The Free and Open Source Software Movement.* London: Routledge.

Spiegel, L. (2001). Portable TV: Studies in Domestic Travel Space. In L. Spiegel (Ed.), *Welcome to the Dreamhouse: Popular Media in Postwar Suburbs* (pp. 60-106). Durham, NC: Duke University Press.

Srivastava, L. (2008). The Mobile Makes Its Mark. In J. Katz (Ed.), *Handbook of Mobile Communication Studies* (pp. 15-27). Cambridge, MA: The MIT Press.

Starosielski, N. (2015). *The Undersea Network*. Durham, NC: Duke University Press.

Starr, P. (2004), *The Creation of the Media: Political Origins of Modern Communications*. New York: Basic Books.

Steinbock, D. (2001). *The Nokia Revolution: The Story of an Extraordinary Company that Transformed an Industry*. New York: AMACOM.

Sterne, J. (2012). *Mp3. The Meaning of a Format*. Durham, NC: Duke University Press.

Sterne, J. (2014). There is no music industry. *Media Industries, 1*(1).

Sterne, J. (2016). Analog. In B. Peters (Ed.), *Digital Keywords: A Vocabulary of Information Society and Culture* (pp. 31-44). Princeton, NJ: Princeton University Press.

Stevenson, M. (2016). Rethinking the participatory web: A history of HotWired's "new publishing paradigm," 1994-1997. *New Media & Society, 18*(7), 1331-1346.

Stöber, R. (2004). What media evolution is: A theoretical approach to the history of new media. *European Journal of Communication, 19*(4), 483-505.

Storsul, T., & Stuedahl, D. (Eds.). (2007). *Ambivalence Towards Convergence: Digitalization and Media Change*. Göteborg: Nordicom.

Strangelove, M. (2015). *Post-TV: Piracy, Cord-Cutting, and the Future of Television*. Toronto, Canada: University of Toronto Press.

Streeter, T. (2010). *The Net Effect: Romanticism, Capitalism, and the Internet*. New York: New York University Press.

Tai, Z. (2006). *The Internet in China: Cyberspace and Civil Society*. New York: Routledge.

Tall, S.M. (2003). *Les émigrés sénégalais face aux enjeux des nouvelles technologies de l'information et de la communication*. Technologie, entreprise et société Document du programme no. 7, May, Institut de recherche des Nations Unies pour le dèveloppement social.

Taneja, H., Webster, J.G., Malthouse, E.C., &. Ksiazek, T.B. (2012). Media consumption across platforms: Identifying user-defined repertoires. *New Media & Society, 14*(6), 951-968.

Targowski, A. (2016). *The History, Present State, and Future of Information Technology*. Santa Rosa: Informing Science Press.

Taylor, A.S., & Vincent, J. (2005). An SMS History. In L. Hamill & A. Lasen (Eds.), *Mobile World. Past, Present and Future* (pp. 75-91). London: Springer.

Thomas, D. (2002). *Hacker Culture*. Minneapolis, MN: University of Minnesota Press.

Thomas, D. (2016). Digitally weary users switch to 'dumb' phones. *Financial Times*, February 22.

Thompson, J.B. (1995). *The Media and Modernity. A Social Theory of the Media*. Stanford, CA: Stanford University Press.

Thorburn, D., & Jenkins, H. (Eds.). (2003). *Rethinking Media Change: The Aesthetics of Transition*. Cambridge, MA: The MIT Press.

Thussu, D.K. (2015). Digital BRICS: Building a NWICO 2.0? In K. Nordenstreng & D.K. Thussu (Eds.), *Mapping BRICS Media* (pp. 242-263). New York: Routledge.

Tischleder, B.B., & Wasserman, S. (2015). *Cultures of Obsolescence. History, Materiality, and the Digital Age*. London: Palgrave.

Terranova, T. (2000). Free Labor: Producing Culture for the Digital Economy. *Social Text, 18*(2), 33-58.

Townes, M.D. (2012). The spread of TCP/IP: How the Internet became the Internet. *Millennium: Journal of International Studies, 41*(1), 43-64.

Turing, A. (2004). Can Digital Computers Think? In J.B. Copeland (Ed.), *The Essential Turing: Seminal Writings in Computing, Logic, Philosophy, Artificial Intelligence, and Artificial Life* (pp. 483-486). Oxford: Oxford University Press.

Turkle, S. (1995). *Life on the screen: Identity in the age of the Internet*. New York: Simon & Schuster.

Turner, F. (2006). *From Counterculture to Cyberculture: Stewart Brand, the Whole Earth Network, and the Rise of Digital Utopianism*. Chicago, IL: University of Chicago Press.

UNESCO. (2013). *Emerging Markets and the Digitalization of the Film Industry*. Information Paper, No. 14. Montreal, Canada: Unesco-UIS.

UNESCO, EY and CISAC. (2015). *Cultural Times. The first Global Map of Cultural and Creative Industries*. Retrieved from www.ey.com/Publication/vwLUAssets/ey-cultural-times-2015/$FILE/ey-cultural-times-2015.pdf.

Uricchio, W. (2004). Re-discovering the Challenge of Textual Instability: New Media's Lessons for Old Media Historians. In J. Fullerton (Ed.), *Screen Culture: History and Textuality* (pp. 161-168). Eastleigh, UK: John Libbey Publishing.

Uricchio, W. (2009). The Future of a Medium Once Known as Television. In P. Snikkars & P. Vonderau (Eds.), *The YouTube Reader* (pp. 24-39). London: Wallflower Press.

van Dijk, J. (2005). *The Deepening Divide: Inequality in the Information Society*. Thousand Oaks, CA: Sage.

van Dijk, J. (2008). Digital Photography: Communication, identity, memory. *Visual Communication, 7*(1), 57-76.

Van Rees, K., & Van Eijck, K. (2003). Media repertoires of selective audiences: The impact of status, gender, and age on media use. *Poetics, 31*(5-6), 465-490.

Vial, S. (2013). *L'être e l'écran. Comment le numérique change la perception*. Paris: Presses Universitaires de France.

Vise, D.A., & Malseed, M. (2005). *The Google Story*. New York: Delacorte Press.

Wajcman, J., & Jones, P.K. (2012). Border communication: Media sociology and STS. *Media, Culture & Society, 34*(6), 673-690.

Wallace, J., & Erickson, J. (1992). *Hard Drive: Bill Gates and the Making of the Microsoft Empire*. New York: Harper Collins.

WAN-IFRA (2017). *World Press Trends*, Paris: WAN-IFRA.

Warschauer, M. (2003). *Technology and Social Inclusion: Rethinking the Digital Divide*. Cambridge, MA: The MIT Press.

Wei, L. (2014, December 15) "Cyber Sovereignty Must Rule Global Internet". *The Huffington Post*, USA . Retrieved from www.huffingtonpost.com/lu-wei/china-cyber-sovereignty_b_6324060.html.

Weiser, M. (1991). The computer for the 21st century. *Scientific American, 265*(3), 94-104.

Wershler-Henry, J. (2005). *The Iron Whim: A Fragmented History of Typewriting*. Ithaca, NY: Cornell University Press.

Wiener, N. (1948). *Cybernetics, or control and communication in the animal and the machine*. Cambridge, MA: The MIT Press.

Wikström, P. (2013). *The Music Industry: Music in the Cloud* (2nd edition). Cambridge: Polity.

Willett, R. (2009). In the Frame: Mapping Camcorder Cultures. In D. Buckingham & R. Willett (Eds.), *Video Cultures. Media Technology and Everyday Creativity* (pp. 1-22). Houndmills, UK and New York: Palgrave Macmillan.

Williams, R. (1974). *Television: Technology and Cultural Form.* London: Fontana.

Williams, S. (2002). *Free as in Freedom: Richard Stallman's Crusade for Free Software.* Sebastopol, CA: O'Reilly Media.

Winsek, D. (2016). Reconstructing the political economy of communication for the digital media age. *The Political Economy of Communication 4*(2), 73-114.

Winston, B. (1998). *Media Technology and Society. A History: From the Telegraph to the Internet.* London and New York: Routledge.

Wolf, M.J.P. (2015). *Video Games Around the World.* Cambridge, MA: The MIT Press.

Wozniak, S., & Smiths, G. (2006). *iWoz. How I Invented the Personal Computer and Had Fun Along the Way.* New York: Norton Company.

Yang, G. (2009). *The Power of the Internet in China: Citizen Activism Online.* New York: Columbia University Press.

Yang, G. (2012). A Chinese Internet? History, practice, and globalization. *Chinese Journal of Communication, 5*(1), 49-54.

Ytreberg, E. (2002). Continuity in environments: The evolution of basic practices and dilemmas in Nordic television scheduling. *European Journal of Communication, 17*(3), 283-304.

Zachary, P.G. (1994). *Show Stopper! The Breakneck Race to Create Windows NT and the Next Generation at Microsoft.* New York: The Free Press.

Zorn, W. (2007). How China was connected to the international computer networks. *The Amateur Computerist, 15*(2), 36-49.

Index

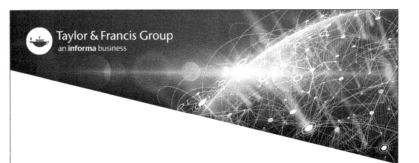

For Product Safety Concerns and Information please contact our EU
representative GPSR@taylorandfrancis.com
Taylor & Francis Verlag GmbH, Kaufingerstraße 24, 80331 München, Germany

www.ingramcontent.com/pod-product-compliance
Lightning Source LLC
Chambersburg PA
CBHW070937050326
40689CB00014B/3242